Dr Patricia Carrington is a clinical psychologist, researcher and psychotherapist specializing in the use of stress management techniques. She was a Lecturer in the Department of Psychology at Princeton University for eleven years and is presently Associate Clinical Professor of Psychiatry at UMDNJ-Robert Wood Johnson Medical School in New Jersey, where she instructs medical students in how to relate to patients in a manner that honors their dignity as human beings.

Dr Carrington has long been involved with meditation both personally, as a regular meditator, and professionally. She uses meditation with many of her patients and has been conducting research in this area since the early 1970s. She has published more than thirty papers on the subject in professional journals and is internationally recognized as the leading authority on the clinical use of meditation.

Her own widely acclaimed, medically approved method of meditation, known as Clinically Standardized Meditation (CSM), is presently being used by numerous organizations throughout the world and by individuals from all walks of life who want to reduce stress and enhance their quality of life. As Administrative Consultant to the Employee Health Maintenance Program at the New York Telephone Company, she assisted this company's medical department to institute one of the largest, most successful stress management programs ever undertaken by a major corporation – close on 5,000 employees of that company have learned her CSM method of meditation.

Dr Carrington's first book, *Freedom in Meditation*, the earlier version of this one, has been recognized as a classic in the field of meditation literature. Her book *Releasing* (1984) which presents an innovative stress management technique, has also received widespread critical acclaim.

At present Dr Carrington divides her professional time between work with patients, teaching, research and writing. At home she finds time to enjoy a quiet Japanese garden which she describes as ideal for leisurely reading and gardening, designing of art posters and interludes of peaceful meditation.

Also available by Dr Patricia Carrington

Learn to Meditate Kit
(workbook with audiocassettes)

The Book of
MEDITATION

THE COMPLETE GUIDE TO
MODERN MEDITATION

Patricia Carrington PhD

ELEMENT
Shaftesbury, Dorset • Boston, Massachusetts
Melbourne, Victoria

First published as *Freedom in Meditation* in 1975 by Pace Educational Systems

This new, revised edition first published in Great Britain in 1998 by
Element Books Limited
Shaftesbury, Dorset SP7 8BP

Published in the USA in 1998 by
Element Books, Inc.
160 North Washington Street
Boston, MA 02114

Published in Australia in 1998 by
Element Books and distributed
by Penguin Books Australia Ltd
487 Maroondah Highway, Ringwood,
Victoria 3134

Cover design by Slatter-Anderson
Page design by Roger Lightfoot
Phototypeset by Intype London Ltd
Printed and bound in Great Britain by
Creative Print and Design Wales, Ebbw Vale

British Library Cataloguing in Publication
data available

Library of Congress Cataloging in Publication
data available

ISBN 1 86204 236 5

Permission to quote from the following sources is gratefully acknowledged: From M.
Csikzentmihalyi, *Beyond Boredom and Anxiety*, San Francisco: Jossey-Bass, Inc, 1975,
copyright ©Jossey-Bass, Inc. From 'Meditation as an Adjunct to Psychotherapy' by
Patricia Carrington PhD and Harmon S. Ephron MD from S. Arieti and G.
Chtzanowski, *New Dimensions in Psychiatry*, New York: John Wiley & Sons, 1975,
copyright ©by John Wiley & Sons, Inc.

To the memory of my husband, Harmon, whose deep sensitivity to meditation, and wide grasp of its possibilities made a vital contribution to this book.

SOME WORDS OF THANKS

A book dealing with a skill such as meditation grows through the mingling of many people's observations, thoughts and experiences. It takes shape through their challenges and achieves final form with their criticism. It's impossible to identify all the people who have helped with this book but here are a few who have contributed enormously.

- My late husband Dr Harmon S. Ephron's sensitivity to human values and his broad philosophical perspective on meditation shaped much of my thinking about the field. In many ways this is his book as well as mine.

- My understanding of meditation grew immensely through the work of my students at Princeton University and in various other universities where graduate students conducted innovative research on this subject. Their enthusiasm and determination were contagious. Many of the conclusions expressed in this book emerged from our joint efforts.

- In the course of preparing the book I discovered that I needed to explore the ancient traditions of meditation as well as the modern ones because these venerable sources contained much wisdom that is of use to us today. The information about Indian traditional thought, particularly that on Yogic customs and the meaning of the mantra – much of it unavailable in written form – was largely obtained from interviews with Sri Shyam Bhatnagar, Honorary Professor of Chakric Studies at the University of Lugano, Switzerland, and a master of sound and mantra. His deep knowledge of the spiritual life of India, coupled with his extensive experience of teaching meditation at an advanced level, made an important contribution to this book. The manuscript for the mantra chapter was also critically read by Raja Mrigendra Singh, Adjunct Professor of Philosophy at City College of New York, and Dr Ishwar Harris, Professor of Oriental Religion at Rutgers University; their helpful comments are incorporated in that chapter.

- In completing the major revisions which the present version of the book represents, I was fortunate to have the editorial assistance of Richard Berg, a colleague in England who is a BAC (British Association for Counselling) accredited counselor. Richard generously shared with me his knowledge of the mental health field in the United Kingdom and the growing place of meditation in that field. He also supplied much valuable information from his personal experience of using meditation with patients. Beyond that, he is a fine writer who cast a keen eye over my finished work, relentlessly demanding the best from the book and myself.

To all these people I give my deepest thanks

CONTENTS

PART 2 **Managing Meditation**

PART 4 **Conclusions**

AUTHOR'S NOTE

To avoid gender preference throughout this book I use the pronouns 'she' or 'he' alternately when referring to an unidentified person.

Part 1

SCIENCE EXPLORES MEDITATION

Chapter 1

THE START OF THE JOURNEY

In the early 1970s I was teaching at Princeton University when a 'relaxation practice' known as meditation came to my attention. Claims were being made that meditation could reduce stress, and I was interested in this possibility, but at that time I knew almost nothing about the practice. I had an idea, though, that this ancient method for turning our attention within might have something special to offer us in this fast-paced modern world.

The reports coming in showed that meditation could reduce anxiety remarkably and that it was useful for many stress-related illnesses. It was said to be effective for sleep problems, to lower irritability, and to be of assistance to athletes who sought to improve their hand–eye coordination and to students who wished to increase their concentration – among other things. These were claims that certainly warranted my attention.

In my profession as a psychologist I am involved in helping people to deal with emotional problems and stress, and any new techniques for improving my work always arouse my interest. The reports coming in dealt with some new, simplified forms of meditation. Did this mean that meditation was no longer the exclusive domain of the spiritual masters and their followers? Might my patients benefit from learning this method? And what about me – could meditation be beneficial to me personally, and in my work?

These questions were put on hold as such questions often are because I was busy with other matters. Then one day I received a phone call from my brother who was living in London at the time. He is a screen writer, and was completing a writing assignment on location in England under extreme time pressure when his doctor discovered that for the first time his blood pressure had risen above the normal range. At that point Bob decided on his own initiative to learn a modern form of meditation that was becoming increasingly popular at the time: Transcendental Meditation (known as 'TM' for short). He told me on the phone that he was finding meditation surprisingly effective. After he had been meditating for only two weeks, a follow-up visit to his doctor revealed that his blood pressure had now come down to well within the normal range, and his physician had said, 'Continue whatever you're doing. It's working!'

Bob was also noticing other benefits from meditation – a general sense of well-being and confidence about the deadlines that faced him and a relaxed energy. He phoned me to recommend that I too learn meditation. 'As a therapist you just have to look into it,' he said.

His recommendation interested me because it confirmed what I had suspected: that meditation was something I could no longer ignore. Perhaps it could supply an ingredient lacking in our hectic, fast-paced society – a sense of genuine inner peace? I hoped that it might do so.

I Learn to Meditate

To discover what meditation was I decided to try it on myself first – something I regularly do when investigating any new technique I may want to recommend to my patients. I had absolutely no idea, however, what a profound impact it would have on my life.

In the 1970s the form of meditation most widely available to the public was Transcendental Meditation, the type my brother had learned. Since it was being taught in many locations in the United States it was easy to sign up for a course. Right after the phone call from my brother I made plans to attend an introductory TM lecture and prepared myself, not without some reservations, for the experience. I must admit that I felt considerably more comfortable after attending that lecture and seeing the scientific data which were presented. It reassured me to know that responsible research was being conducted on this method and that the results were positive.

I decided to go ahead with instruction in the TM technique and discovered that it isn't possible to really know what meditation is until one experiences it. I did of course know what the *word* meant. Meditation, I knew, is a simple mental technique that is typically practiced seated, and in a quiet environment. The object of the meditator's attention can be either a mentally repeated sound known as a 'mantra', one's own breathing, or some other appropriate center of attention: sometimes a visual image or candle flame is used to focus upon. I also knew that when I learned the TM technique a mantra would be assigned to me by my TM teacher and that this particular form of meditation used certain rituals which would be unfamiliar to me. I had no more information than that.

The first day I received my instruction I was quite unprepared for the ease with which I took to the practice and the gentle, profound peace which suffused my whole being as I meditated for the first time. I didn't want to stop meditating that first day, I wanted to go on and on. I was immensely affected on a level I could not comprehend but which I was experiencing with my whole being.

During the weeks that followed I carefully documented my reactions to meditation in my journal and was fascinated to see some unexpected changes take place. My startle response, the tendency to jump when confronted by sudden loud noises or unexpected occurrences, began to reduce markedly. After two weeks of meditating it was gone unless there was an exceptionally strong stimulus such as the backfiring of a car.

I also found myself reacting entirely differently to frustrating everyday circumstances which before would have distressed me. I would now 'roll with the punch' when they occurred, no longer experiencing the same sense of urgency about these matters. It was clear that this was a result of meditation because it continued only as long as I meditated daily – this welcome new experience gradually faded away when I purposely *stopped* meditating for two weeks (the researcher in me had to 'prove' the value of this unexpected gift).

However, I did have one reaction that was disconcerting. I had learned meditation right before the end of the academic year, at a time when I had eighty final exam papers to correct for the Princeton seniors who had taken my class on 'The Humanistic Management of Stress'. Grading was to be completed within four days so that the students' final marks could be turned in on time for them to graduate. I had become so relaxed and laid back from my new meditation practice, however, that I found myself undertaking the grading task in a disconcertingly slow and dreamy manner, and I realized that at the rate I was going I would not get the marks in on time.

I quickly phoned my TM checker (the person assigned to advise new meditators like myself) and explained to him that my meditation practice was seriously impeding my work. He told me that my excessive over-relaxation was only temporary, a form of 'unstressing' (throwing off stress) which is often seen in new meditators, and that I was to continue meditating exactly as I had been. Within a week or so, he assured me, this unwanted reaction would go away.

This might have been useful advice if I had had the time to follow it, but the students' marks had to be turned in immediately and I couldn't wait. I realized that the only way I could handle the situation was to stop meditating entirely for several days. This I did, on my own initiative and with some trepidation. When the grading was completed, I resumed my practice of meditation, and just as predicted, within about a week the slow, dreamy state left me and I found myself relaxed yet super-alert at the same time.

While all was now well with my meditation practice, this event taught me something that was to become important later on when I myself began to teach meditation. I learned that under certain conditions it's essential to modify standard instructions (in this case the instruction had been to meditate twenty minutes twice a day) to enable meditators to handle their practice in a manner that would not disrupt their life. In the modern form of meditation that I was later to develop, Clinically Standardized Meditation, or 'CSM' for short – I will tell you about this in the next chapter for it has an interesting story – I would emphasize individual adjustment of the technique to suit the life-style and special circumstances of the meditator. I am strongly in favor of this more flexible approach and it has worked out remarkably well.

My Husband Joins the 'Club'

After I had been meditating for several months, my husband Harmon told me he was noticing a new calm with which I was supposedly responding to his suggestions – and even to his disagreements! I was a bit taken aback by his comments – I hadn't thought of myself as *not* being calm. I was soon to realize, however, that many meditators report this same experience. A family member will often notice changes in a new meditator that the meditator himself is not yet aware of.

After three months of carefully observing the effects that meditation had on me, Harmon finally agreed to learn it himself. Before this he had objected to the TM organization's require-ment that he bring several fresh flowers, three fresh fruits and a white handkerchief to his initiation session, and that he remove his shoes before entering the meditation room. He felt that as a physician and a professor this was inappropriate for him, and it had completely deterred him from learning the method up until that time.

Even after he had made plans to learn, Harmon grumbled about these requirements until the last moment and told me that he wouldn't go to the session unless I carried the fresh fruit, flowers and handkerchief to the door of the meditation room *for* him! Fortunately for him I agreed because I was so eager that he learn, but I often wonder what would have hap-pened if I had not cooperated with his request. He might have continued to be unable to accept these simple requirements because they did not fit his self-image – and he would have missed one of the most compelling experiences of his life.

Once again I learned an important lesson. When I was later developing my CSM system of meditation, I was careful to keep the teaching of it respectful of the special, deeply peaceful nature of meditation, while at the same time ensuring that the method did not contain a ritual that might conflict with *anyone's* belief system. I believe rituals can be beautiful and meaningful for those who voluntarily subscribe to them, and I personally responded excellently to the initiation ritual of TM. There are, however, certain people who, like my husband, can't reconcile a ritual of this sort with a scientific attitude, and there are others who have religious convictions that may conflict with particular meditation ceremonies. I therefore decided to present those who were to learn my CSM training with a neutral yet compelling form of meditation which would be entirely compatible with anyone's personal beliefs. I have never regretted this decision. It has made a highly effective form of modern meditation available to a number of people who might otherwise have been unable to learn the method.

When Harmon finally learned to meditate he took to it like a duck to water and became a staunch advocate of meditation. With myself as co-author he eventually wrote a number of papers for professional journals describing the benefits of meditation for patients in psychotherapy, and giving a theoretical rationale for its use in psychoanalysis – these were ground-breaking concepts at the time we wrote about them.

As for the benefits that he experienced, they were quite different from mine. At the time he learned meditation, he had been putting off writing an article he had promised to a journal, for over six months – he simply couldn't make himself get down to writing it. After he had been meditating for only three days he sat down easily, pen in hand, and in one sitting turned out a forty-page paper for the journal in question. The words just flowed onto the paper, seemingly effortlessly, and they required almost no revision. He attributed this triumph directly to the exceptionally free flow of thoughts which he was experiencing during his meditation sessions.

From that day on I began noticing beneficial changes in Harmon's personality of which he himself was not aware. Meditation brought a softening in his approach to other people. He had a brilliant and powerful mind and this change gave just the perfect touch to his personality, increasing its impact perceptibly.

The Birth of Clinically Standardized Meditation

The next step was to recommend meditation to our patients and to start supervising their use of it. We commenced by referring them to local TM centers. We did this cautiously since we didn't know what the effects would be, even though we ourselves were benefiting from meditation, and we kept careful records of patients' reactions. We discovered that meditation could be a remarkable help to psychotherapy, and on the basis of our clinical observations we subsequently published a number of papers on the use of meditation as an adjunct to psychotherapy.

Our first period of involvement in meditation was then

followed by a more difficult stage. We were occasionally running into a problem using meditation with a patient in psychotherapy, or with a particular participant in one of my research studies. We even saw several patients become more anxious after learning meditation than before, a clearly undesirable effect. These problems could, however, almost always be corrected if the meditation procedure was carefully adjusted to suit the individual's needs. When, for example, we instructed the people involved to shorten their meditation sessions, or to use some other variation of the basic technique, the original benefits of meditation would almost always be restored, unwanted anxiety eliminated, and a positive result obtained.

To do this, however, required that we have clinical control over the meditation process, something that was not possible with our patients who had learned TM. The TM organization permits only trained TM teachers and checkers to regulate its trainees' meditation, and they must do so according to strict rules set down by TM's founder, Maharishi Mahesh Yogi. While this is understandable from the organization's point of view, it did not suit our clinical requirements, nor was it meeting my research needs at the University.

Much as we respected the TM training, and grateful as I was to TM for giving me my first authentic experience of meditation, I Iarmon and I decided that if we were going to use meditation in our professional work we would have to establish a way of teaching it that was more appropriate for our patients. Clinically Standardized Meditation (CSM) was born of necessity. But it soon grew into an exciting project.

We spent the next few years collecting information for this new meditation system and experimenting to find out how its instructions might be modified to suit differing circumstances. We also spent much time trying to understand the process of meditation in greater depth so that we could help people use it more effectively.

As I looked into meditation more closely, however, I was confronted by a baffling number of conflicting statements, opinions and directives from leading meditation teachers. Here are examples of some of the contradictions I came across, all of them from highly authoritative sources. Perhaps you too have heard similarly confusing directions from various meditation teachers:

- For meditation it is best to sit cross-legged either in full or half-lotus position.[1]

- You should sit upright when meditating, with your back against a straight-backed chair.[2]

- The easiest way to practice the meditative exercises is to relax on a couch or bed, lying on the back, legs slightly apart and relaxed.[3]

- You should meditate morning and evening but never late at night, unless you are planning to stay up all night.[4]

- You should meditate at the darkest hour of the night, midway between sunset and sunrise.[5]

- Never attempt to meditate when you feel any fever or have a cold or pain. Let them pass before you start.[6]

- If you are ill in bed you should meditate as much as is comfortable.[7]

- A trained instructor should select a specific mantra according to an exact procedure.[8]

- A mantra can just be any interesting, or not interesting, sound notation.[9]

- Meditating together, everyone sharing a single group mantra, can become a very high vehicle for group-consciousness modification.[10]

- If you tell your own mantra to anyone else it won't achieve the desired results with them and it might have a deterrent effect on that person.[11]

As I studied these and similar contradictory instructions many questions came to my mind. What was the reason for these conflicting instructions? Who was right? Why? These statements and others like them had been made by teachers of meditation who sincerely believed they were giving the correct advice. Most of the instructions were based on traditional practices, often ancient in origin. While innovations in teaching were certainly being made by creative teachers, I could find none that had been backed up by scientific evidence about which modifications work best or which are more suitable for

particular types of people. And I could find absolutely no meditation instructions that gave reliably documented research on
whether following one routine when practicing meditation is
any better than following another.

Because of the care with which they have been developed,
the traditional meditative practices supply much information to
anyone who takes up the practice of meditation, even in one of
its simplified Western forms. But which pieces of information
are soundly based and which are simply followed because of
custom or sometimes even because of superstition?

These questions were the starting-point for an investigation
that led me, on the one hand, to explore the fascinating field of
traditional Eastern meditation and, on the other, to sift through
the rapidly growing number of modern scientific studies on
meditation. I needed to separate the useful instructions about
meditation from the useless ones: the methods of handling
meditation that are appropriate for our modern world from
those that are suitable only for very small numbers of people
under very special conditions, or those which may not be useful
at all.

My first book, *Freedom in Meditation* (the precursor to the
present volume) was born from these explorations. To prepare
for it I examined a large body of research on meditation.
Hundreds of research studies had already been published on
this subject, but virtually all of them had been directed to discovering what the meditative state 'is' – that is, what its special
characteristics are, or how it affects people. I discussed much
of this interesting research in that book, and I report on more
recent studies in this revised version, but the research didn't
answer certain urgent practical questions, such as how difficulties arising from the practice of a form of modern meditation
can best be handled; how blocks to meditation can be overcome;
whether certain types of meditation suit certain types of people
better than they do others. All these and many other matters of
importance to the modern meditator have remained largely
unexplored territory as far as science is concerned.

Even today, research conducted by myself and my late
husband, Harmon S. Ephron, MD, and by some of my colleagues in the field of psychotherapy, represents virtually the
only attempt to investigate these aspects of meditation in a
systematic way. In discussing various ways of managing

meditation I therefore draw largely on our work. Together we have collected data from many sources: more than 600 meditating patients whom we have collectively treated in clinical practice; the thousands who have by now learned CSM and reported on their experiences with it; subjects who participated in research studies conducted by my students at Princeton University and by graduate students whom I have supervised in their research on meditation at other universities; surveys on meditation practices among campus meditators; and finally, the compelling experience of having myself been a regular meditator for more than twenty-five years, an experience shared by several other psychotherapists with whom I have been working closely in a joint exploration of the potential uses of meditation.

Putting all this data together, I have assembled a body of information which I hope will make meditation more satisfying and helpful to those who are considering learning it for the first time (or relearning it in a new form); to those who have learned a form of meditation but may be having difficulty with it; and to those who simply want to know more about the intriguing subject and practice of meditation.

The Family of Practices

To evaluate the contradictory instructions on meditation one must distinguish between its various forms. Under the word 'meditation' are grouped a large number of different techniques and intents.

First, there are the historic, centuries-old religious traditions of meditation: here the object is to enhance spiritual development, to change the entire life of a human being undergoing the experience, and to use meditation as a tool for deepening the range of the human spirit. For the purposes of this book, I call these traditional approaches 'spiritual meditation'.

There is also an essentially different form of meditation available today, that is, meditation as it is frequently practiced in the West. It has its roots in the great meditative traditions but is used to achieve somewhat more limited goals. This second form does not necessarily aim at changing life-style (although in some cases it may) nor is it intended as a profound spiritual experience (although sometimes it leads to one). Its basic intent is to affect those who practice it in a *practical* manner and to enrich the experience of the average person of today who continues to function within the confines of everyday reality as we know it. I call this second form of meditation 'practical meditation'. Under this name are included CSM, TM, and several other forms of meditation.

It is practical meditation which is the subject of this book. These chapters are intended, among other things, to guide you the reader through the maze of information which is now accumulating on different types of meditation. Since many new questions are being raised, we need to go further than a survey from one point of view. It may even be necessary to go beyond meditation itself to find some of the answers. There are fast-growing areas of science which hold important clues – some of the new research on biological rhythms, for instance, and unusual fields such as biometeorology. Many of these will be considered here in order to widen our understanding of meditation.

In searching for answers to some of the more puzzling aspects of meditation, it is also helpful to view it in a new light in relation to psychotherapy – not as a replacement for it but as a promising partner. I have had many opportunities in the intimate therapist–patient relationship to observe the effects of meditation on the deeper levels of human experience, and I will report on some case material which illustrates the effects of meditation on people's lives and emotions.

I have also included a section in this book teaching some methods of meditation for the benefit of readers interested in the subject. It is to be considered as an introduction to meditation for those who have never meditated, and as an invitation for those who are already meditating to experience techniques other than their own. With a first-hand knowledge of the approaches we will be talking about, the reader should be better able to follow the subsequent discussions. I have included several methods because my experience has led me to feel strongly that meditation should be carefully adjusted to the individual using it. There is no one 'right' method. There are just different methods. Each individual should find the technique that is congenial to their personality.*

---

* The companion to this volume, the *Learn to Meditate* Kit, provides a complete instruction system for those who wish to learn meditation through audiotapes (see back of book).

As our exploration of meditation and its effects unfolds, you should remember that meditation only came to the attention of serious researchers in the 1960s, so research in this field is still in its infancy. We have barely opened the door on the possibilities that meditation could bring in the future. For those who want to assess for themselves the value of the new research in this field as it unfolds, I will provide some pointers which may help to distinguish the genuine from the spurious, and straighten out some confusions.

I believe that we are on the threshold of a world in which meditation will become an accepted part of everyday life for many people who seek to step beyond the confines of our present stress-ridden and materialistic society. Who knows, as we enter the twenty-first century we may even find that meditation and its complementary practices help us create a more relaxed, peaceful world in which people will feel more mutually supported and affirmed in their life's journey. I certainly hold out that hope.

But for now we can get started by looking at what meditation *is*.

Chapter 2

THE AGELESS
PRACTICE

Meditation is one of the most ancient of human activities. Man is the animal who uses language, responds to beauty, laughs, sheds tears . . . and meditates. What is unique about the ritual of meditation is the prolongation of the event, and the capacity to induce it at will. The experience that underlies it, however – the meditative mood – is familiar to all of us:

- A mother holding her infant close is united with the child in a gentle rhythm as she rocks and sings to it.

- A traveler leaning against a tree listens to the sounds of the breeze rustling the treetops and barely senses his own breath: it is as though he had become the wind.

- An elderly Jew, draped in his impressively trimmed prayer shawl and cubes of black leather (tefillin) sways back and forth in the dawn light, monotonously repeating a simple prayer which brings him exaltation.

- A vacationer lies on the beach, giving herself over quietly to the sun and the air, engulfed by the lulling rhythms of the sea.

- A man hears organ tones cascading through a cathedral; as they vibrate through him, he is carried into a reverie where memories and images of childhood flood him. He has become a child again.

- A camper gazes into a lowering fire following the trail of the glowing ashes as they drift upward and fade into darkness; she feels as though she, too, were floating gently through space.

- A rock climber on a mountaintop breathes in the silence above the earth; he is shaken by its immensity and his mind becomes as still as the snows in the mountain passes.

Except perhaps for the old man at prayer, these people experience meditative moods which they have not purposely induced. Their moods are spontaneous. They are welcomed as moments of unusual aliveness and include some of the profound states which Abraham Maslow[1] has referred to as 'peak experiences'. Are they different from the moments of inner stillness intentionally evoked by the ritual of meditation? An excerpt from the meditation journal of a friend talks about this:

> Tonight at 8:45 p.m. I sat on the porch and watched the last twilight darken into night, I think I've learned to cheat on my meditation teacher's prohibition against extra sessions. I would let a thought come popping into my mind and then gently replace it with some element of sensory perception – the dark line of treetops against the sky, the rushing of the overfed brook hurtling to the sea, the air against my face, the feel of my body against the chair, the smell of woods and growing things. . . . It was very soothing and peaceful.[2]

The writer clearly sees his experience when sitting for formal meditation and his experience with an informal 'meditative mood' as being so alike that during the latter it seemed as though he were cheating on his formal meditations. Actually such moods are like true meditation in many ways and one could even argue that they *are* meditations. Perhaps meditation as a discipline is no more than this spontaneous process developed into a formal practice.

Despite the fact that the meditative mood frequently occurs naturally, people throughout the ages have nevertheless developed hundreds of ingenious methods for intentionally evoking it, methods which have been carefully cultivated and handed down over the generations. Perhaps spontaneous meditative moods occur less often than is desirable. Perhaps they are less intense than human beings want or need them to be. In modern industrial society, based on machine-like efficiency rather than on natural rhythms, meditative moods may so seldom occur spontaneously that formal types of meditation are particularly necessary. What are some of these methods that man has worked out for evoking and holding onto this fragile mood?

The Techniques

There are literally hundreds of practices which can be listed under the heading of 'meditation'. All these have in common the ability to bring about a special kind of free-floating attention where rational thought is bypassed and words are of far less importance than in everyday life. It is characteristic of this state that when in it, the person is completely absorbed by his particular object of meditation. If something else comes to mind, it will usually drift in with a sort of vague, faraway quality, then drift out again.

The devices used to bring about this state are as diverse as gazing quietly at a candle flame; attending to the mental repetition of a sound (mantra); following one's own breathing; concentrating on the imagined sound of rainfall; chanting out loud a ritual word or phrase; attending to body sensations; concentrating on an unanswerable riddle (koan); passively witnessing the flow of thoughts through one's mind; or whirling in a stereotyped dance. Whatever, the aim is the same: to alter the way the meditator experiences her own existence.

All these techniques close out the distractions of the outer world in much the same way as an isolation chamber. In a sensory-deprivation experiment the subject is removed from incoming sense impressions by being placed in a soundproofed room, by wearing goggles to eliminate patterned vision, or by undergoing other sense-reducing manipulations.[3] In meditation, the meditator removes his attention from distracting sense impressions and thoughts by creating an inner 'isolation chamber' of his own making. It is when the outer world is removed that meditation can take effect and the individual is said to become 'centered'.

In the meditative traditions the words 'centered' and 'centering' refer to the restoration of an inner balance accomplished through the use of devices which serve to focus the mind. This process is seen as acting like a psychological gyroscope which stabilizes mind and body and neutralizes the tendency to pull away from the center of one's being.

Despite the fact that attention is directed toward a meditational 'object', however, each technique copes with a basic property of meditation which can best be described as a counter-tendency, a need to *pull away* from the object of focus. Even the calm and centered mind is not entirely still. Periodically it reaches for renewed contact with the environment, either through sense impressions or thoughts, and each meditational system has its own way of dealing with this 'outward stroke' of meditation.

Some systems are not permissive, or may even be coercive with respect to the handling of 'distractions of the mind' during meditation. A *non-permissive* form of meditation will demand strict concentration on the meditational object. Practitioners will be directed to pinpoint their attention, to banish intruding thoughts from their mind by an act of will, and to return immediately and forcefully to the object of focus whenever they find their attention has wandered. This approach is seen in extreme form in instructions given to a meditator in a fifth-century Buddhist treatise dealing with thoughts that may intrude into the meditation:

> ... with teeth clenched and tongue pressed against the gums, he should by means of sheer mental effort hold back, crush and burn out the [offending] thought; in doing so, these evil and unwholesome ideas, bound up with greed, hate or delusion, will be forsaken, then thought will become inwardly calm, composed and concentrated.[4]

In contrast, many meditative systems use varying degrees of permissiveness toward intruding thoughts. In these more permissive techniques, the meditator is instructed to return gently and without effort to the object of focus.

Although there are no experimental findings dealing with the effects on the meditator of permissive versus non-permissive forms of meditation, it may well make a difference whether the meditator practices one approach or the other. The effects may even be different if he mistakenly interprets his form of meditation as being non-permissive when it is not. Most techniques for meditation require that the meditator make no conscious effort, but 'let things happen' rather than make them happen. Often, however, the average person automatically injects coercion into a meditative practice unless carefully trained to do otherwise. The result is roughly the same as it would be if a stern teacher were standing close by and commanding one to 'shape up' the whole time one meditates.

A non-permissive approach to meditation (self-produced or

produced by instructions from someone else) can increase guilt in the meditator as she begins to blame herself for not meditating 'correctly', or for the kinds of intruding thoughts she is having. A permissive approach, on the other hand, because it encourages an accepting attitude toward the thoughts or feelings which may inadvertently arise during meditation, may help the meditator to handle previously unacceptable feelings which she might have been hiding or 'repressing'. It may also help release emotional tensions, because these have an opportunity to play themselves out in fantasy in this more permissive state.

Right now I can only speculate about the effects on the meditator of different kinds of meditation instruction. There is no experimental evidence which sheds light on the subject. As the study of meditation proceeds, no doubt this will be looked into and a good deal more will be known.

Meditation Versus Centering

In the great meditative traditions of both East and West, meditation is looked upon as a spiritual exercise, a means of attaining a special kind of awareness which many consider to be the highest state of consciousness of which human beings are capable. This advanced state can only be arrived at, however, as part of a total way of life. An ascetic life, special physical exercises, diet and social arrangements, together with long hours of meditation each day, are the typical procedures followed. Even then it may take a lifetime (some people believe it takes many lifetimes) to arrive at or even approximate this desired state.

The average Westerner, however, approaches meditation, for the most part, on a practical level. Ordinarily he does not consider it a deep spiritual commitment, if he thinks of it as being spiritual at all. Most often it is learned to make life easier or more pleasant.

At first glance these different uses of meditation might seem merely a matter of degree – the mystic might be thought to be more intensely involved with meditation and the average person less so. This is so, but there is a more fundamental difference. The typical modem meditator, not being tied to any particular belief system, can use self-discretion in her approach to practical meditation and can experiment with it. Such a person is free to use meditation effectively outside of the context of the traditional systems, and can, if need be, combine it effectively with other methods of self-improvement or with medical or psychological treatments.

The person seriously seeking spiritual growth, on the other hand, will sooner or later need to embrace a discipline. He must learn the delicate nuances of the technique assigned by his teacher so as to be able to apply it accurately and exactly. For this a highly experienced teacher is needed to guide the aspirant along the path of inner development; a teacher who knows exactly how and when to alter the meditative technique to produce further spiritual growth in the pupil. Warming-up exercises such as the silent repetition of a mantra or concentration on one's breathing (or any one of a number of others) may be prescribed for such a pupil, but these are not considered 'meditation'. They are *devices* used to center the individual in preparation for the deep state of communion or oneness which is true meditation. The Hindu spiritual leader Bhagwan Shree Rajneesh has pointed out that 'meditation has two steps: first the active, which is not meditation at all; second, that which is really meditation [and is completely non-active . . . just passive awareness] . . .'[5]

Because of a limitation of vocabulary, the West refers to the simple psychological centering devices, the preliminary steps, as 'meditation'. We thereby give the same name to the techniques used to produce meditation as we do to the end-state itself. According to the great meditative traditions, however, the centering techniques are *not* meditation. They are simply a means toward this state. They are preliminary devices which are more or less interchangeable. The advanced practitioner will eventually discard all of them when she can achieve meditation directly.

The vocabulary of a society reflects its preoccupations. We devise numerous words for technological processes which are exact and informative but we have only one word for 'mind'. Other societies, such as that of India, have many different words for 'mind' according to its many functions as conceived by ancient beliefs. As Western scientists continue to investigate the various meditative states and the devices used to reach them, we too may create words to distinguish these states from each other and to identify different classes of centering devices.

In writing this book, I did not want to create a new word to refer to these simple centering devices – I felt that would confuse matters – but it is these devices which I will talk about. Since most people think of them as 'meditation', that is the word I will use. When I speak of meditation, therefore (unless I specify otherwise), I will be referring to the centering techniques that constitute what I call 'practical meditation'. What I say about their use may or may not apply, in a given instance, to the rigorous disciplined forms of *true* meditation which are used as a road to spiritual growth.

Despite my attempt to be clear about this, however, it will be obvious to anyone who has ever meditated, by whatever technique, that there is no hard and fast line between the simple centering exercises and the deep meditative states. One can commence by naively using the simplest of centering devices (for example, mentally repeating a mantra with eyes closed) and end up having a profound mystical experience that changes one's entire view of life. Or one can set out diligently to achieve deep spiritual awareness through meditation and wind up with a pleasant, relaxing centering experience and nothing more.

The boundaries, in other words, are permeable. Inner experience extends where it will. It resists control and refuses to be confined to categories. We cannot legislate the inmost segments of our lives. In discussing people's centering experiences we will therefore inevitably find ourselves touching on the deeper implications of meditation as well.

I cannot of course discuss *all* the types of practical meditation available in the West today. New ones are cropping up all the time and many are as yet untested. Some of these forms of meditation may fade before they have ever been studied. What will be considered are the *standardized* forms, because they are the ones most apt to become part of the new scientific body of knowledge on meditation. I will start with the best-known of them all, Transcendental Meditation.

Transcendental Meditation (TM)

Transcendental Meditation is a standardized form of mantra meditation adapted for Western use from ancient Indian techniques.⁶ The student instructed in TM is assigned a Sanskrit word (mantra) said to possess soothing properties, which he is asked to repeat silently for twenty minutes, sitting quietly in a chair with eyes closed. This is done twice daily. When the meditator finds that his attention has wandered, he is to make no effort to return deliberately to his mantra, but to resume its repetition in a passive manner by 'favoring' the mantra over other thoughts.

The TM instructors give considerable reassurance to practitioners with regard to the nature of thoughts which arise during meditation, and the meditator is taught to look upon the spontaneous emergence of thoughts, feelings, images or bodily sensations during meditation as evidence of a process said to have therapeutic properties, called 'normalizing'. By means of normalizing, residual tensions produced by previous traumatic or stressful events in a person's life are said to be released spontaneously.

TM is readily available in the West and there are TM centers in and around most of the major cities of the United States and Europe. The technique itself is easy to learn. It is mastered in four lessons taught over a period of four days and does not require adoption of any particular life-style for ordinary meditators (although it may for TM teachers), nor does it use special postures or methods of breathing.

TM's founder, Maharishi Mahesh Yogi, performed an historic service in bringing a simple, widely usable form of meditation to the West for the first time. With the spread of the TM organization and the extensive publicity which has resulted, countless people have become familiar with the concept of meditation who would never have heard of it otherwise, and a sizable number of people have learned it.

The Maharishi's form of meditation possesses certain features which may cause difficulty for some people, however. The TM method is based on the Hindu cosmology, a metaphysical system of ancient and honorable vintage which may nevertheless be difficult for some Westerners to accept, even in its simplified forms. In Chapter 1 I described my husband's personal reaction to one aspect of TM: the poetic *puja* (Hindu devotional ceremony) by which the learner is initiated into TM conflicted strongly with his scientific bent of mind. By contrast, for me the *puja* was a very meaningful experience. People differ markedly in this respect.

Regardless of the diversity of individual reactions, however, certain aspects of the TM training present clear disadvantages for some forms of research. If, for example, a subject is responding well to TM, it is difficult to tell whether this is because the technique is effective in and of itself or whether it is because the person is receiving emotional support from participating in a group of other meditators with a compatible point of view. Or is it because the person has had her expectations raised by a TM teacher's earnest belief that this technique is a panacea? This could result in the creation of so-called 'demand characteristics' – the effect of an experimenter's *expectations* on the outcome of a study. Experimenters may want to see a certain result so much (or be so certain that they will see that result) that they inadvertently influence the behavior of subjects in the experiment. This can occur in a number of ways, from non-verbal signals the experimenter sends out, to words he may use when addressing the subjects. Such demand characteristics must always be guarded against in research for they can easily occur in *any* experiment.

TM studies comprise the largest single body of evidence with respect to the value of modern meditation and many of them have been excellently conducted. As an example of the *difficulties* which some researchers face, the TM organization steadfastly refuses to reveal the secret mantras which they assign to their trainees because to do so would violate their belief system and the directives of TM's founder, Maharishi Mahesh Yogi. This makes certain kinds of research on the method difficult because the investigator does not know all the variables she is dealing with. Generally speaking, it is considered contrary to scientific protocol to withhold information which may have a bearing on a problem under investigation, and in this case it prevents the experimenter from comparing the effectiveness of one specific mantra with another, one method of assigning the mantra with another, or exploring other crucial questions concerned with the effects of differing sounds upon personality.

In addition, for ideological reasons, the TM organization has not sanctioned research comparing TM with any other technique of meditation, although it has often allowed it to be compared to *relaxation* techniques. When I enquired of TM's World Plan Organization in Los Angeles about the reasons for this, I was informed that the directive is based on Maharishi Mahesh Yogi's conviction that other forms of meditation can damage their practitioners if practiced regularly. To understand the Maharishi's strong stand on this matter one must realize that those who subscribe to traditional schools of meditation often firmly believe that their *own* form of meditation is the only way to achieve enlightenment. Other forms may be seen as undesirable or even dangerous to those who practice them. Quite probably the Maharishi is following his own tradition's teachings when he cautions against meditation methods other than TM. The result, however, is that comparative studies, the lifeblood of scientific enquiry, cannot always be carried out with TM.

It was considerations such as these and others described in Chapter 1 that led me to create a standardized form of modern meditation which could more readily be used for my own and others' research purposes. It was also apparent that this form needed to be one which psychotherapists could teach their patients directly.

Clinically Standardized Meditation (CSM)

I developed my new form of meditation by selecting a classical type of mantra meditation, modifying it so that it became suitable for Western use, and creating a standardized set of instructions for teaching it.

The first group of people to use this method were Princeton University students who were attending a seminar I was teaching at the time. The students were enthusiastic about the technique, and on a series of personality tests administered before learning this meditation method, and again after they had practiced it for ten weeks, they showed changes similar to those reported by subjects who had been practising TM in a comparable study being conducted on the campus. Both groups of meditators showed clear-cut evidence of anxiety reduction over a ten-week period.

The new technique I had developed was then revised, elaborated and given the name Clinically Standardized Meditation (CSM) to indicate its research and clinical nature. A teaching manual was prepared, successful testing of the method was carried out, and since that time CSM has been taught to numerous psychotherapists throughout the world for use with their patients. Many organizations have also used it with their employees, and a large numbers of individuals have learned it either through recordings or by personal instruction.

CSM is closer in its structure to TM than to any other currently used form of meditation but differs from it in some important respects. Our trainees select their own mantra from a list of sixteen mantras presented to them, or if they wish to make up their own mantra they do this by following some simple rules.

My first task in developing CSM was to assemble a list of suitable mantras, resonant and soothing sounds which would be used as objects of concentration during the meditation process. Since I was devising a system to suit widely divergent groups of people, I did not select the sounds to be used by following religious or spiritual guidelines. In the great traditions, mantras have very specific meanings and are dispensed with much careful thought by teachers well versed in their use, but for our purposes, the sounds used merely needed to have especially soothing qualities.

I assembled 100 words from the Sanskrit, Hebrew and English languages which had particularly resonant sounds and (in English) calming connotations. I then presented this list to 150 college students and asked each of them to rate these sounds according to how 'soothing' they found them to be. The sixteen sounds rated as most soothing by the students became the list from which CSM trainees later selected their own special sounds. This way I was able to avoid assignment of a word or sound that might be unsuitable for a particular individual.

I have never regretted my decision to use this method of mantra selection. Not one of the thousands of people who have been trained in CSM has complained about having a wrong or unpleasant sound to repeat in their mind. If the first sound they selected was later felt to be unsuitable, the person was encouraged to select (or to create) another. This method has worked beautifully and is universally appreciated by those who learn CSM.

CSM is learned in one instruction session and is mastered in about a week's time, with only a few hours' practice necessary. Most people prefer to learn it by means of the *Learn to Meditate* audiotapes and workbook, but it is sometimes taught in person. Since the recorded training method has proven to be as effective as personal instruction, the choice depends on individual preference.*

The CSM instruction session, whether conveyed on tape or in person, does not involve any special ceremony but merely the use of a quiet room, some plants pleasantly arranged, and (if the person wishes it) incense and a candle placed on a small table. We then use a short, standardized, soothing means of transferring the mantra which the learner has personally selected. I developed a simple, non-cultic ritual for imparting the mantra because I found that the dignity and emphasis lent to the occasion by a ceremony, however informal, is an important part of the process. Meditation is, in a sense, a rebirth. It is a new beginning, a significant commitment to one's own growth. Since CSM instruction emphasizes the effortlessness of the meditation technique and its permissive nature, CSM lies, as does TM, at the permissive end of the scale relative to other meditation techniques which can require considerable concentration. The main advantages of CSM are its simplicity, its flexibility and its sensitivity to the individual needs of the people who learn it.

Benson's Method

Boston cardiologist Dr Herbert Benson's investigations of TM (carried out in collaboration with Dr R. Keith Wallace) are landmarks in meditation research,[7] the first laboratory proof that a form of practical meditation can lower metabolism in a significant manner. Although his original studies were based solely on TM, Benson later developed his own form of meditation, known formally as the Respiratory One Method (ROM), but more commonly referred to simply as 'Benson's technique' or the 'Relaxation Response'. He devised this method in order to check on whether other meditative techniques than TM could evoke the same generalized state of relaxation, a condition Benson calls the Relaxation Response.

He discovered they could. His method, a simple form of

---

* Those interested in the CSM tape-recorded instruction will find information at the back of the book.

breathing meditation where a person thinks the word 'one' (or any other sound she chooses) to herself on every out-breath, brought about in laboratory studies exactly the same physiological changes which had been noted during TM: decreased oxygen consumption; decreased carbon dioxide elimination; and decreased rate of breathing.[8] As a result, Benson concluded that 'any one of the age-old or newly derived techniques [for meditation] produces the same physiologic results regardless of the mental device used'.[9]

Benson has described his method as a 'non-cultic' meditative technique. It requires some initial relaxation of the body muscles from toes to head, a quiet environment, a mental device (attending to one's breathing) and a 'let it happen' or 'passive' attitude. Like CSM, it is a scientific form of meditation which can be studied openly in the laboratory without strings attached and used at a physician's discretion in any manner he feels is appropriate.

Is Benson's method interchangeable with TM, however? Are, as Benson contends, the two techniques merely different versions of one basic mental procedure capable of eliciting the Relaxation Response? Benson believes that the specific mental device used is of little importance, a mere matter of personal choice. I agree that the type of meditation used should be based on personal preference, but I feel we do not have enough experimental evidence as yet to conclude that all the practical meditative devices are interchangeable.

Benson's method differs from both TM and CSM, for example, in that it requires a greater degree of concentration. He gives his trainees the following instructions: 'When distracting thoughts occur, try to ignore them by not dwelling upon them and return to repeating "ONE" – this word is to coordinate with the out-breath.' He does not require his practitioners to force these thoughts out of their mind (as some non-permissive forms of meditation do), but simply calls for them to 'ignore them' and return their attention to their breathing and their mantra. This is somewhat different from the more permissive directions of CSM, which do not suggest that meditators ignore their thoughts but rather that they flow with them, simply keeping in mind the possibility of returning to the mantra periodically.

In contrast to Benson's method, both TM and CSM teach a more easy-going way of handling the special sound which the person repeats mentally. In these techniques the meditator is instructed to allow the mantra to proceed at its own pace, to get faster or slower, louder or softer, or even to disappear 'if it wants to.' This is different from trying to link the mantra with one's breathing, as in Benson's method. When we link the two in this fashion, the breathing controls the mantra. Benson's method therefore operates within tighter limits than TM or CSM – it is less of a free-floating, self-determined experience.

This is not to say that Benson's method is not useful, but simply that it is different from others, and the difference may be important. Some people may prefer Benson's method to TM or CSM because it is more structured and follows set rules. These may be people who like to have things spelled out for them and feel more comfortable with clear-cut regulations. On the other hand, a more creative, artistic or emotional type of person might find such rules stifling and prefer a freer, more open-ended form of meditation. By the same token, a more religious person or one who particularly enjoys rituals might prefer the traditional ceremony of initiation offered by TM to the strictly secular ceremony of CSM or to the more impersonal instructions of Benson's method. It may in fact turn out to be that the personality of the meditator is the most important factor of all when judging the 'merits' of any of these techniques.

To sum up the characteristics of Benson's method, his method demands more formal concentration than either TM or CSM, but for this very reason may be preferred by people who require more structure in their meditation. With Benson's permission, his method is included as an option in the CSM training for those who may need such structure.

Other Methods

TM, CSM and Benson's method are the main types of meditation we will be referring to in this book because they are standard-ized and form part of a growing body of scientific evidence. There are other useful meditation techniques, however.

A number of Westernized Zazen techniques have been studied in various experiments. These are usually forms of breathing meditation, but without the strict seating require-ments and other rigorous demands of true Zazen, a Japanese sect of Buddhism which requires long hours of dedicated meditation conducted in special postures; often exhausting to those unaccustomed to them. Most of these modern forms of breathing meditation have not been too carefully standardized but are nevertheless useful. They do require considerable concentration to master, however, which can prove a drawback for some people.

In recent years a Buddhist practice known as 'mindfulness meditation' has been used with increasing frequency in the United States and the United Kingdom. In this Buddhist-derived method practitioners develop the skill to observe clearly what is happening to themselves and their surroundings, moment to moment. In doing this they learn to distinguish their reactions to what they are experiencing – thoughts or feelings about it – from the raw sense impressions. People practicing mindfulness meditation become witnesses to the entire array of thoughts and feelings that pass through their mind. They are taught to note the contents of their mind without identifying with or reacting to any of it.

While this process can be extremely rewarding for those willing to undertake the discipline required, it demands considerable training to absorb the fundamentals and their applications to daily life, and is not for the faint of heart. In many ways, mindfulness meditation is more of a life-style than a technique. It is associated with values such as self-responsibility, self-observation, emphasis on non-striving, a non-judgmental stance toward present-moment experience, conscious exercise of kindness in support of one's own and others' effort, and adoption of a long-term perspective on one's own personal mindfulness practice.

Teachers of this method emphasize that mindfulness meditation is a way of being rather than a technique to be practiced to achieve immediate *ends*. In this respect it differs from the standardized meditation techniques described here which are less demanding and therefore applicable to many more people.

Research has shown that a stress-reduction program based on mindfulness meditation can be highly beneficial for many medical conditions as well as helping to improve the participants' sense of well-being.[10,11] Because only a certain type of person is drawn to this form of meditation, however, research findings concerning it cannot be applied widely to the public because many people may be unable or unwilling to submit to its requirements.

For this reason, although I include mindfulness meditation, especially simple Zazen practices, among the techniques of 'practical meditation' which we will be looking at in this book, it should be kept in mind that it is less applicable to the general population than some of the other techniques we will discuss. Research on this method is often quite innovative, however, and can provide some important insights into meditation. For those interested in learning about the mindfulness approach in some detail, I recommend Jon Kabat-Zinn's book, *Wherever You Go, There You Are* as an introduction to the subject.[12]

Where, then, do we stand with respect to the similarities and differences, the ease and difficulty of the various forms of practical meditation?

The answer seems to be that since our experimental evidence is still limited, each person will have to judge for himself how he responds to any particular technique. I teach a type of mantra meditation in this book which has much in common with both CSM and TM, and I teach Woolfolk's breathing meditation, which is much like Benson's technique. This way, if you like, you will be able to experience both mantra and breathing meditations, and see how each feels. Your opinion, based on first-hand experience, can then become a piece of scientific data which you can use while reading this book. You will, in effect, be conducting your own experiment on meditation.

Chapter 3

IS MEDITATION
UNIQUE?

People often ask me whether meditation is merely 'another relaxation technique' or simply a form of prayer, a type of self-hypnosis, or so similar to some other method of self-development as to be indistinguishable from it. Some teachers of meditation dismiss these questions lightly. This is not very helpful. Meditation, particularly in its practical forms, does have a number of points in common with some of the other methods used to promote personal growth and the line between them is not always easy to draw. We will look at a few of the related techniques to see what the similarities and differences between them and meditation may be.

Religious Meditation and Prayer

The formal discipline of meditation originated in religious practice and the use of meditation as a spiritual exercise still outstrips by far its use as a practical technique in most parts of the world. The Hindu and Buddhist religions and that of the Sufi sect among the Moslems have developed meditation into a fine art, but other religious traditions through the ages have also developed their own highly effective meditative practices.

Some forms of Christian meditation, particularly those practiced in monasteries, are true 'meditation' in the sense in which we are using that word in this book. Other Christian practices loosely termed 'meditation' are, however, actually forms of 'contemplation'. Rather than evoking the meditative mood, they create an atmosphere where thought is directed in a disciplined manner to a specific theological problem or religious event. This process often ends with an effort to apply the religious idea contemplated to one's own life.

Much more commonly used by the religious lay person than meditation (at least in the West) is simple prayer, and the relationship of prayer to meditation is an elusive one. While profound prayer probably cannot take place without entering what we have called the meditative mood, mechanical repetition of standard prayers in order to fulfill religious obligations does not require this special mood at all.

Prayer is nevertheless closely related to meditation in many ways. It is usually an inward, contemplative state, undertaken in quiet, often in solitude. As in meditation, so in prayer outward stimuli are reduced and a special kind of soothing, monotonous environment is created. The echoing intonation of ritual words and phrases chanted over and over again; reverberating music; candlelight; votive offerings; incense; the sound of bells; awe-inspiring architecture with symbolic decorations; a special posture held for a period of time; the closing or partial closing of the eyes – these are all traditional accompaniments of prayer intended to evoke a sense of reverence and union with the deity. Through them the meditative mood is evoked in a highly effective manner.

There are some important differences between meditation and prayer, however, even when meditation is used for spiritual purposes. Although prayer relies upon the meditative mood, it is none the less a *goal-directed* activity. In prayer, a person calls upon a deity in some manner. They give praise or offer thanks; seek forgiveness, consolation or assistance; or enter into some other relationship with the deity. This goal-directed form of praying, by far the most common type, is quite different from the non-striving, relatively *goal-less* absorption of meditation.

As we turn to other forms of prayer, however, the distinction between them and meditation is not so clear. Prayer can be used as a genuine form of meditation in the sense in which we have been using this term. Psychiatrist Edward Maupin has described silent, contemplative prayer as having been for a long time the West's only widely used, socially approved 'form of meditation'.[1] He suggests that with the lessening of prayer in the West in recent years, we have lost a quiet contact with inner experience that is essential for the nourishment of the human spirit.

In some instances prayer is intentionally structured in a form belonging strictly to the realm of meditation. In Western monasteries, repetition of words in praise of God has been widely used to evoke a special state in which the outer world is shut out and the person is transported into an exalted sense of closeness with God. The 'Prayer of the Heart' used by Russian monks and devout lay people in pre-revolutionary Russia is an example of this. This prayer was used to 'purify the intellect' by means of a passive attitude and the repetition, on each successive out-breath, of the phrase 'Lord Jesus Christ, have mercy on me'. By this means the mind was thought to become emptied of all thoughts, images and passions. In this instance, a Christian religious phrase was being used in the same manner as mantras are used in India. Authentic Sanskrit mantras are either the names of deities or religious phrases.

Used as a form of silent inner communion, or coupled with a mantra-like repetition of religious words, prayer can be seen to blend imperceptibly into meditation. Although we cannot equate prayer and meditation, we cannot fully separate them either. The two states are closely related, not only historically, but often in their spirit or purpose, and both practices are in some sense related to another familiar method which evokes the meditative mood – that of self-hypnosis.

Self-Hypnosis

I'm often asked whether meditation and hypnosis are not the 'same thing' because they both involve entering a 'trance state'. The word 'trance' often brings a negative image to mind. According to Webster's Dictionary, it implies an inability to function or being in a state of daze or stupor. It is also frequently thought of in the sense of the trances of deep hypnosis, where a person has only limited contact with her surroundings and may be quite unable, afterward, to recall what went on during the trance.

These are certain kinds of trance, to be sure, but in actual fact they are neither the only ones nor the most prevalent. Light trance states, which are familiar to everyone, do not ordinarily possess these alarming qualities. Dr Ronald Shor, a specialist in hypnosis, has pointed out that these light trances are actually daily, commonplace occurrences for all of us.[2] They involve sharp narrowing of our attention, which becomes focused on one or on a few objects or events or thoughts. Because of this narrowing of attention, our generalized reality-orientation – that is, our awareness of our surroundings and of our usual ways of thinking and perceiving – begins to fade, creating a 'trance' effect. Shor describes his own experience with such a spontaneous trance:

> I was reading a rather difficult scientific book which required complete absorption of thought to follow the argument. I had lost myself in it and was unaware of the passage of time or my surroundings. Then without warning, something was intruding upon me; a vague, nebulous feeling of change. It all took place in a split second and when it was over I discovered that my wife had entered the room and had addressed a remark to me. I was then able to call forth the remark itself which had somehow etched itself into my memory even though at the time it was spoken I was not aware of it.[3]

Obviously many other everyday occurrences involve entering a state of light trance, although we may not label the state we experience by that name. We all know, for example, how artists may be intensely absorbed in their work during its inspirational phase and become practically oblivious to their surroundings. The same absorption can occur when one is deeply involved in some majestic scene or in an engrossing game, or in viewing a work of art, listening to music, making love . . . or meditating. Does this mean that we should think of all these activities as being forms of self-hypnosis?

Although both meditation and self-hypnosis involve some degree of trance, there are also some important differences between them. One of the identifying characteristics of self-hypnosis is the increased receptiveness of subjects to self-administered suggestions about mental or physical behavior which they want to bring about. The hypnotized person acts (or thinks) in the way he believes the hypnotist or he himself is directing him to act.

Self-hypnosis is therefore *goal-directed*, and psychologist Robert White, discussing the theory of hypnotism, has suggested that goal-directed striving is one of the primary characteristics of all hypnotic states.[4]

This description of hypnosis is very different from most descriptions of meditation. In the great traditions, meditation is looked upon as a goal-less, non-striving state. Although in actual practice the meditator may make some effort during meditation (perhaps in an attempt to reach some spiritual goal), this is usually only a minor aspect of the experience and is often discouraged by meditation teachers. Self-suggestions such as telling oneself to relax during meditation, or the implied 'suggestion' involved in repeating a mantra which has become a signal to oneself to enter a state of deep relaxation, do of course play some role in the meditative experience. Certain forms of Yoga also require the meditator to employ some suggestions to help her reach Brahman, the highest state of consciousness, but these minor uses of suggestion can scarcely be compared to the central position given to suggestion in self-hypnosis. With respect to active striving toward a goal *during the process itself* (although not ultimately since meditators as well as hypnotic subjects typically have long-range goals) these two states seem very different.

Meditation and self-hypnosis do not necessarily show the same kinds of physiological change either. As we shall see in the next chapter, meditation typically brings about a lowering of metabolism, a deep quietening of mind and body. By contrast, some hypnotic states *raise* metabolism, as when an athlete uses self-hypnosis before a game to 'psych' himself up. Other hypnotic states bring about no physiological changes at all, including no changes in brain waves,[5] and a number of researchers have shown that hypnotized subjects usually have an activated brain-wave pattern, which is no different from ordinary wakefulness.[6] The only time hypnotized persons show wave patterns similar to those seen during meditation is when they are given specific suggestions to enter a meditation-like state. If they are *directed* to become deeply relaxed, they will usually obligingly do so, just as they will do many other things, including going to sleep, under hypnosis.*

The relationship between meditation and hypnosis is not entirely solved, however. It is possible that in the broadest sense of the term, meditation is a form of 'hypnosis', although it is certainly not the kind most of us in the West know. Western

---

* It is interesting to note that Zen monks are taught to suppress the hypnotic trance. The name they give to it is *sanran* (meaning 'confusion'), because they feel that it interferes with their practice of meditation.[7]

hypnosis is a highly motivated state where the subject plays a 'role', acting out certain prescribed actions or thoughts. Abraham Maslow,[8] who has called this Western form 'striving-hypnosis', points out that a much less familiar type, 'being-hypnosis', allows the subject to move away from role-playing and enter an intense absorption similar to that of 'peak experiences' or mystic states of contemplation. This being-hypnosis is used almost exclusively for certain spiritual disciplines such as Yoga or Zen. It is possible that it is a form of meditation, or vice versa.

Because striving-hypnosis and meditation, while not the same thing, do have some points in common, however, it is perhaps not surprising that one of the most prominent of all the modem relaxation techniques, autogenic training, had its origin in the study of hypnosis as practiced in the West.

Autogenic Training

J. H. Schultz, a Berlin psychiatrist, published the first accounts of a new form of deep relaxation in 1926. It combined Western methods of self-suggestion with some ancient Yoga techniques and he referred to it as 'autogenic', meaning, in essence, 'self-generated'. It was to become the world's most widely used and extensively researched method of relaxation training, with almost 3,000 research studies presently in print dealing with innumerable medical uses of autogenic training, as this technique came to be called.[9]

Schultz's method arose out of research on sleep and hypnosis. In Berlin around the turn of the century, the renowned brain physiologist Dr Oskar Vogt had observed that a number of patients who had undergone a series of hypnotic sessions under his guidance began, quite independently, to put themselves into a state very similar to hypnosis during the day when they were alone, and that these self-hypnotic exercises seemed to be having a remarkably recuperative effect upon them. Patients who had practiced the exercises several times a day were reporting marked improvement in their ability to manage stress; they were also experiencing less fatigue and tension, a clearing-up of numerous physical symptoms, and gains in overall efficiency.

Dr Schultz became intrigued by Vogt's findings. Exploring

this technique of self-hypnosis with his own patients, he soon discovered that when they practiced it regularly they almost invariably reported two things: a feeling of *heaviness* in their limbs and sometimes in the whole body, and agreeable feelings of *warmth*. Because of this, Schultz reasoned that people might be able to induce effects like that of self-hypnosis merely by thinking of 'heaviness' and 'warmth', without any formal hypnotic induction at all.

He discovered that they could. By simply concentrating on verbal phrases suggesting heaviness or warmth, his subjects were able to bring about a state which seemed to have remarkable healing properties. This discovery launched the large body of work on autogenic training which is still accumulating. Schultz was soon joined by another physician, psychophysiologist Dr Wolfgang Luthe, and together these men brought autogenic training to hospitals and health clinics throughout Europe and many parts of Asia, Australia and Canada. Only the United States remained conservatively unreceptive to this technique so widely acclaimed elsewhere. In recent years, however, autogenic training has begun to attract the interest of Americans, since it has been combined with biofeedback training, apparently effectively.

Autogenic training typically uses a series of graded exercises involving successive concentration on various bodily states. Such phrases as 'My right arm is heavy' (used for right-handed people) are first repeated for very short periods of time, then as the trainee becomes accomplished, more advanced phrases are added, dealing with warmth in the arms, legs, and body, or cooling of the forehead, and so on.

Certain trainees, who have been undergoing autogenic training for a year or more, are taught to concentrate on producing certain mental as well as physical states. These mental exercises are called autogenic 'meditations,' but are far more controlled than the usual forms of meditation. They involve exact instructions such as asking the trainee to visualize certain colors in a particular sequence, and are probably better described as a form of guided imagery rather than meditation.

Regular autogenic training (comprising the basic relaxation exercises) does have much in common with the meditative states, however. The exercises must take place in a quiet room with lighting reduced, clothes loose, the body relaxed, and the eyes closed. The trainee either lies down on her back, leans back in a chair, or sits on a stool in a 'rag-doll' posture.

The entire process is 'meditative' in the sense in which we have been using that term because to perform the exercise subjects must enter an almost dreamlike state known as 'passive concentration', where they do not force any effects but simply 'let them happen'. If the trainee does not use 'passive concentration', autogenic exercises will not be effective. Because of this, many of the observations made by those involved in autogenic training are directly applicable to the study of meditation. As we shall see later, this is an advantage for meditation research because tens of thousands of autogenic training records, giving step-by-step accounts of persons practicing this relaxation technique, have been collected over the past seventy years. This forms a staggering body of information telling us what happens when people place themselves in a state of deep relaxation. We shall take a look at some of this carefully recorded evidence when we come to consider tension-release during meditation.

Free Association

Psychiatrists often compare another technique to meditation – the method of 'free association' which is regularly used with patients in psychoanalysis. Like autogenic training, this technique also originated in the study of hypnosis.

In their joint work on the treatment of hysteria, published in 1895,[10] Drs Sigmund Freud and Josef Breuer reported what was to turn out to be the first step in a major breakthrough in the treatment of psychiatric disturbances. They had discovered that when certain types of patient were able to discharge repressed emotions under light hypnosis, their hysterical symptoms frequently disappeared quite suddenly. When working further with this technique, however, Freud soon found that it had certain drawbacks. Many patients were unreceptive to hypnosis and he began to sense that a method where the doctor had such overriding control of the patient was undesirable.

Freud felt that perhaps the same results could be brought about by simply having the patient consciously recall and express her thoughts and emotions without being put into a hypnotic trance. On trying out this alternative plan, Freud soon discovered that it worked, and the method of 'free association' was born.[11] In this procedure the patient was directed to relax on a couch and verbalize any thoughts which crossed her mind, no matter how trivial or embarrassing. Using this technique, Freud was able to obtain the same kinds of cure for hysterical neuroses that had been possible under hypnosis, and the new technique could be expanded for use with other types of patients as well. Later it was to become a cornerstone of the psychoanalytic method.

The atmosphere necessary for the free-associative state is similar in many ways to that needed for meditation. In order to bring about either of these states, external stimulation must first be reduced. The free-associating patient is placed in a quiet room (the analyst's office) with few distractions. He does not look directly at the analyst but allows his mind to wander freely while lying on a couch. Neither the free-associating patient nor the meditator is to judge the nature of the thoughts which occur during the session but to accept whatever enters their mind. In this way, in both situations, emotionally 'charged' material not ordinarily available to consciousness is encouraged to rise to the surface. This non-judgmental attitude toward 'distractions' or thoughts during meditation is particularly characteristic of the permissive forms of meditation.

There are some important differences between the two techniques, however. During free association patients are required to *verbalize* all their thoughts – putting them immediately into words. While this is useful for therapy, doing so automatically excludes all those aspects of experience which cannot be converted rapidly enough (if at all) into word-symbols. There are thus a host of images, sensations, and feelings available to the meditator which free-associating patients must ignore because they are continually translating their experience into language *while the experience is still going on.*

Another difference between the two techniques is that free association is used for pinpointing special trouble areas, while meditation seems to handle more general areas of tension. For this reason many non-verbal reactions – feelings which may have developed in early childhood before we had the use of words – appear to be reached by the meditative state and are often resolved during it. This may lead to a kind of healing that is not available to the typical patient in psychotherapy.

There is another difference. The psychoanalytic patient

free-associates with a clear *purpose* in mind – he is trying to reveal to the analyst certain concerns. The situation of the meditator is entirely different. During meditation the person has no immediate goal in mind. The thoughts which drift through his head need serve no purpose, and there is no attempt to contemplate their meaning. In this sense, free association might be compared to a type of work and meditation (at least practical meditation) to a type of play.

The final distinction between meditation and free association is that free-associating requires a relationship between two people, while meditation involves a lessening of all outward ties. The patient in therapy is never totally free from her need to please or defy the therapist – she is always in some manner concerned with what the therapist thinks. The meditator, however, is beholden to no one while on his 'inward journey'.

Despite these important differences between the two techniques, there are moments during free association when the meditative mood needs to be evoked for the process to be effective. This mood may be disrupted by the patient's effort to put her thinking into words, but it is still a necessary component in the psychoanalytic process. If the patient can slip into this meditative mood easily, progress in psychoanalysis will presumably be better. Freud observed that people differ sharply in their ability to free themselves from what can be called 'intentional' (directed) thinking and learn to free-associate. Their capacity to do this may be a function of the degree to which they feel comfortable entering the meditative mood, a reason why patients undergoing psychoanalysis may benefit from practicing meditation. We will discuss this possibility later on, when we take up the question of using meditation as an adjunct to psychotherapy.

Progressive Relaxation

Psychophysiology studies the relationship between physical or chemical factors and behavior. In the mid-1930s psychophysiologist Dr Edmund Jacobson developed a method for combating tension and anxiety which involved an interesting notion. He reasoned that since anxiety (as he had demonstrated in his laboratory) involves muscular tension, then turning the situation around and eliminating tension in the muscles should remove anxiety.[12]

To reduce muscular tension turned out to be not so easy, however. People who are chronically tense often have no awareness of the fact that they are tensing their muscles or in which part of the body they are doing so. Perhaps if they were to be made aware of the process of tensing various muscle groups they would gain control over the tensing-relaxing process? What Jacobson had hit upon was a rudimentary form of 'biofeedback', the process of becoming aware of bodily processes and bodily controls.

On the basis of his theory, Jacobson commenced to teach patients to 'feel the tension' in various muscle groups, one at a time. They were asked to tighten their muscles deliberately in each area of the body and were then directed to let the muscles relax suddenly and pay close attention to how this felt. Through this method Jacobson's patients were eventually able to eliminate almost all muscle contractions and experience a feeling of deep relaxation.

Jacobson's training, which he named 'progressive relaxation', was long and arduous. It required a total of fifty-six one-hour training sessions to learn his basic technique, and further sessions were often desirable. This made his method too cumbersome for most research purposes, although it was undeniably effective, as Jacobson was able to prove over a long series of careful laboratory studies.[13]

In order to overcome this time drawback, behavioral psychologist Dr Joseph Wolpe later modified Jacobson's technique. In the new version, tensing and relaxing of the muscles were done much more rapidly and the training course was reduced to a total of six twenty-minute sessions.[14] Like many other quick methods, this shortened version lost some of the strength of the original. Jacobson cautions against having the trainee tense and relax his muscles more than two or three times each hour, because this can result in too much effort being expended and might counteract relaxation. Wolpe and his followers ask their subjects to tense and relax their muscles repeatedly during each twenty-minute period. It is important to realize this, because Wolpe's modification of Jacobson's technique is the one widely used today. When we speak about a high drop-out rate from progressive relaxation, it will be well to remember that the

Wolpe modification calls for real effort. Not too many people may be up to expending that kind of effort twice a day.

Are there similarities between progressive relaxation and meditation? Aside from the fact that they both bring about relaxation, progressive relaxation also calls for the atmosphere which is by now familiar to us in all the relaxation techniques – the quiet room, dim lighting, a comfortable position, and an easy, receptive attitude. But despite these points in common, there are important differences between this form of relaxation and meditation.

Wolpe's therapists often use goal-directed suggestion and even hypnotic procedures to bring about awareness of bodily sensations when teaching progressive relaxation. Directions such as the following are typical: 'Completely and totally relax . . . just let your muscles go. . . . Enjoy the feeling of deep relaxation. . . . Relax more and more. . . . Focus your attention on how it feels to have your muscles completely and totally relaxed . . .'[15]

Such phrases, repeated over and over again to the trainee in a soothing voice, are often mentally rehearsed by trainees when they practice this technique at home. Subjects also typically repeat muscle-tensing and relaxing commands to themselves when practicing progressive relaxation. This makes the technique a much more active one than meditation, with the exception of certain inevitable moments (longer or shorter according to the specific directions) when the practitioner remains entirely still.

In a study at Princeton University we compared progressive relaxers with meditators and found out something interesting about these 'silent' periods which the progressive relaxers experienced. During the ten minutes that our subjects spent lying still and relaxed after completing their muscle-tensing, about 65 percent of them reported that during at least a portion of this time they usually experienced states of mind which were unfocused, floating, passive and filled with shifting imagery. It seems as though they may have been entering a meditative mood during these still moments, a point to remember when we look upon the two techniques as distinct and then wonder why sometimes they have quite similar effects.

Biofeedback

The most technologically sophisticated of the relaxation techniques was developed in the 1950s. It does not rely on a mental device for obtaining its effects but on an electronic one. Biofeedback can be applied to brain waves as well as to other physiological systems to produce a relaxed state. A subject who is hooked up to an electroencephalograph (EEG) machine need only attend to a signal which goes on when their brain is producing a strong burst of the desired type of brain wave and with this information can usually learn to produce the desired brain-wave pattern on command, often within fifteen sessions or less.

This kind of biofeedback has important implications for the study of states of consciousness. Brain rhythms are characterized by their frequency – so many cycles or peaks per second. The alpha rhythm, measured from the back of the head, is between eight and twelve cycles per second. The beta rhythm is faster, between 18 and 30 cycles per second. These two kinds of brain wave are of particular interest to scientists because they seem to reflect specific mental states.

Alpha waves typically accompany drowsy, relaxed states where the mind is drifting in a somewhat unfocused manner. Subjects in the laboratory variously describe the alpha state as 'relaxing', 'passive', 'anxious', 'letting go', 'submissive', 'high', 'pleasant', and so on. Although it is not experienced in the same way by everyone, it is often present in abundance in the brain wave tracings of experienced meditators during their meditation, and sometimes outside of it as well.[16]

Theta is the state people reach just before sleep and some research even suggests that it may be the time when creative people receive some of their important inspirations.[17] Like alpha, theta also appears in the brain-wave tracings of meditating persons, but usually only in very experienced meditators and following a previous period of alpha.[18]

What are the implications of these findings? Do they mean that a person can bypass meditation and achieve what has been jokingly referred to as 'instant *satori*' (enlightenment) simply by bringing about certain changes in their brain waves? At first this seemed as though it might be the case, and the public was eager to purchase the portable alpha biofeedback machines which began to come on the market. It was soon discovered, however, that alpha does not do all the things that had been promised. While meditation may produce alpha, going into alpha does not necessarily produce meditation. Apparently a meditative state is more than the mere sum of its accompanying brain waves!

According to Dr Gary Schwartz of the Department of Human Relations at Harvard,[19] one of the most important things to realize when trying to influence various bodily systems is that they typically operate in patterns, something which in the first flush of enthusiasm about biofeedback may not have been properly appreciated. To take a single aspect of the body's operation, such as heart rate or blood pressure or a particular brain-wave pattern, *out of context* and train it by itself to respond to a signal (as has usually been done in biofeedback) may be a 'second-rate' imitation of nature.

Schwartz found, for instance, that he could train a subject in his lab to reduce his blood pressure a few points in response to a signal sent to him whenever his blood pressure lowered itself even slightly, but if the subject was taught this and nothing else, his blood pressure would go down while his heart rate remained the same. Under natural conditions, however, we see lowered blood pressure *accompanied* by a slowed heart rate more than half the time.

Do these systems (heart rate and blood pressure) naturally link up because in a sense they 'prefer' to move together rather than singly? To find out, the Harvard researchers then rigged the biofeedback signal so that it sounded only when both blood pressure and heart rate were being lowered at the same time. When this was tried the results were clear: blood pressure fell more sharply when the subjects were responding to a blood pressure-plus-heart rate signal than when they were responding to a blood pressure-alone signal. The subjects were also able to learn more rapidly when their task was to move *both* blood pressure and heart rate in the same direction (whether this direction was up or down).

This and other research suggest that body systems operate more efficiently when acting in unison with one another than when acting alone. Since these systems are interrelated, a training procedure which gets to all of them at once and tries to move them as a whole, the way a chord is transposed in music to another octave, may be the most effective. Schwartz has gone so far as to suggest that perhaps the main importance of biofeedback will be its potential as a research tool rather than its use as a form of therapy. Biofeedback training can give us extremely important information about physiology which previously we have not been able to identify. When a change in the functioning of body systems is desired for health reasons, however, it may be easier to bring it about by methods which automatically stimulate a *cluster* of physiologic systems – the same systems that tend, in nature, to vary in a coordinated fashion. This is what seems to happen with methods such as meditation which automatically bring about full relaxation in many systems at the same time. It may be the harmony between a number of different bodily processes that is responsible for a state of maximum calm.

In light of this reasoning, it might be a wise strategy in the long run to find ways of understanding, using and encouraging the relaxation response of the human body *as it occurs in nature*, rather than imitating it by machines, and this can probably be done best by using the various mental techniques for relaxation. Among these techniques, meditation ranks high as an effective tool. For certain purposes, in fact, it may well be the most useful tool of all

Looking back at the various techniques for personal growth reviewed in this chapter, we can see that virtually all of them require special conditions such as lowering of external stimulation or the presence of monotonous stimulation. In addition, every one of them sometimes evokes a meditative mood – with the possible exception of self-hypnosis, which only does so if the specific directions which the person gives himself are to 'relax'.

Despite the fact that they often involve a meditative mood, however, none of the techniques seems to be the same as meditation. They do not set out purposely to create the non-striving, goal-less experience of meditation, and none seems to achieve it in quite the same manner. We might view meditation therefore as a method which is related to, but also different from, the other techniques for relaxation or personality growth.

Knowing what meditation is not, the door has now been

opened to proceed to the next puzzling question: why did science become interested in this state?

Chapter 4

THE SCIENTIST
TAKES NOTE

Seated in a chair in the Biomedical Electronics Laboratory of the famed Menninger Foundation in Topeka, Kansas, a forty-five-year-old Indian yogi, Swami Rama, intentionally 'put himself into' various states of consciousness, seemingly able to alter his brain waves at will. As he did this, an EEG machine received minute electrical messages from electrodes attached to various sites on his head and conveyed them to recording equipment in an adjacent room. A research team, headed by psychophysiologist Dr Elmer Green, then collected the mass of data which was later analyzed. The team was making a careful record of some of the unusual abilities which the Swami had learned during his long years of practicing meditation. This information was to be used to refine methods for teaching Westerners to alter their own states of consciousness at will, to achieve a sense of inner peace and tranquility, perhaps even to tap the source of their creativity.[1]

The Swami's behavior was striking, but this scene is all the more impressive if we realize that it was of historic importance. That experiment was conducted in 1970. Only a few years before an investigation of this sort would never have taken place. Meditation was then considered a subject unsuitable for serious scientific research, and was classified among the so-called 'occult' disciplines. These had been looked upon, at best, as appropriate subjects for students of anthropology or religion, certainly not of interest to experimental scientists. From the 1960s on, however, the picture changed. The interest of the scientific community in meditation was awakened and research on it had become respectable. What happened?

The first crack in the barrier which had prevented the

meditative disciplines from being considered as bona fide ways of altering mental states was the 'psychedelic revolution' of the 1960s. This era of experimentation with mind-altering drugs resulted in radical changes in the way altered states of consciousness were regarded in the West. These states of consciousness had held the attention of people in Eastern countries for thousands of years but ironically, as 'rational' Westerners, we seemed to require the specific introduction of drugs to blast through our defenses and make us notice these different ways of experiencing. Once aware, research could no longer ignore them.

As time went on, an increasingly significant number of people, including scientists, began to experiment with altered states of consciousness in themselves and for a short while there were laboratory experiments on the effects of the mind-altering drugs. Researchers set out to discover whether the major psychedelics such as LSD, psilocybin or mescaline could be used in the treatment of chronic alcoholics, criminal offenders or others who were difficult to treat by the usual therapeutic methods. Marijuana was also studied in the laboratory, since scientists wanted to know what its effects on health and personality were. Then, in 1966, almost as abruptly as it had begun, such experimentation virtually came to a halt in the United States as a result of new and stringent regulations by the government. Since then only a handful of researchers in special hospital settings have been permitted to conduct a small number of experiments in this area.[2]

After the government regulations took effect, some of the scientists who had been interested in exploring consciousness in the laboratory now turned their attention to finding drugless means for inducing these unusual states of consciousness. Foremost among these other methods were the various forms of meditation. A new group of researchers then joined the research teams when meditation became the subject of study, and when a more practical reason – the general public was taking meditation up at an historically unprecedented rate – became evident.

As the 1970s were ushered in, a growing number of people in the Western world had by now reported that the elusive, ill-defined process known as meditation seemed to 'work' for them. They said they felt more inwardly peaceful since they had been meditating and claimed to have less anxiety and to have developed fewer tension-related diseases. In a society known for its driving pace, where illnesses which are related to stress were rapidly increasing, this was a not insignificant achievement.

Other things were also happening to make meditation an acceptable subject for scientific investigation. We in the West had long held the belief that involuntary processes such as heart rate, blood pressure, body temperature, brain waves, and others, could not be altered by an act of will; they were said to be 'autonomic', outside of conscious control. In the mid-1960s and early 1970s, however, this entire view of mind-body relationships began to turn around as psychophysiologists showed through ingenious experiments that humans and animals alike can learn to control their autonomic functions, and that they will do so in an extremely accurate manner, provided they are given adequate feedback information about how well (or how poorly) they are doing at the time they are learning.

The first result was a host of scientific studies on biofeedback (see previous chapter). People were taught to alter their brain waves 'at will' with the aid of an EEG machine hooked to an electrical device which sounded a beep when they were producing the correct waves. Others learned to control their finger temperature, lower or raise their blood pressure, slow down or speed up their hearts, or perform a number of other feats, simply by being informed on how they were doing while they were doing it.

It is interesting that before the discovery of biofeedback, for nearly 200 years physicians serving with the British Army or Civil Service in India had been sending back reports on a few people whom they had studied there who seemed to be able to regulate their involuntary body processes, such as heart rate, body temperature or pain. The doctors claimed that these unusual individuals, called yogis, were able to do so because of their long practice in special Indian mental and physical techniques, yet we in the West did not pay much attention to these scattered reports. It seems that we first needed to develop the technology to measure this capacity. When we could deal with it through a machine, it became 'real'.

The new interest in biofeedback undoubtedly contributed to the rising interest in meditation. Biofeedback and meditative techniques have much in common: both are based on a delicately attuned awareness of inner states. In each of these techniques we deal with experiences occurring within the self which are sensed, but cannot be defined. With the advent of machines which could measure changes in subjective states, 'inner space' became respectable scientific territory.

Another trend lending unexpected support to the study of meditation was the increasing use of a form of behavior therapy known as 'systematic desensitization', which relies on the production of a deep state of relaxation for its effects. During this relaxed state, various stimuli which ordinarily produce anxiety for the patient are presented to him in small, measured amounts. If the technique works properly, the relaxation 'takes the charge off' the patient's fears.

From the 1970s on systematic desensitization became increasingly popular, and because it made use of a relaxation technique, the concept of relaxation was suddenly of much more interest to a great many psychologists.

Studying the Masters

The scientific investigation of meditation commenced appropriately enough with the study of traditional meditative techniques in natural settings. Since the original studies were done in the late 1950s and early 1960s, a little before the era when meditation began to be widely used in the West, the obvious sources of meditators at that time were trained yogis or Zen monks. A person who has devoted many years or a lifetime to mastering a technique can be expected to demonstrate it better than anyone else. By studying these people the researchers hoped to learn about 'pure' Zazen or 'pure' Yogic meditation.

These investigations were not easy to conduct. It was difficult to locate a sufficient number of adequately trained and dedicated monks who were willing to be hooked up to machines and it was awkward to transport complex recording instruments. In India, neurophysiologists Drs Bagchi and Wenger carted a portable EEG machine 4,000 miles across the country and were only able to locate thirteen subjects.[3] Surprisingly, such obstacles were eventually overcome, and the result was several interesting studies.

Because of the inherent difficulties in such research, some

investigators used very small numbers of subjects. For example, Drs Anand, Chhina and Singh, a team of Indian physiologists, studied only a single meditator sealed in an airtight box in their laboratory.[4] The subject, an experienced yogi, remained meditating inside this contained space for ten hours while the researchers periodically sampled the air in the box for its oxygen content. They wanted to find out how much oxygen the yogi could *do without* without experiencing the brain damage or eventual death that would normally occur under these circumstances. They were startled to find that over a ten-hour period this yogi practitioner consumed oxygen at a rate 30 percent below the amount considered necessary to sustain life, and that during one period (halfway through the experiment) he was consuming oxygen at a rate as low as 50 percent below the presumed minimum. However, he emerged from the experiment *perfectly healthy*. Obviously he had been in an unusual state.

In another study by Drs Bagchi and Wenger,[5] various physiological practices were monitored in forty-five subjects who assumed Yogic postures accompanied by meditation. The researchers found that these subjects' heart rates slowed down by 6–9 percent (although they never went below sixty-two beats per minute) during meditation and their respiration rates decreased by an average of 23 percent. In some instances, respiration dropped by 50–60 percent and occasionally became so shallow that it was unmeasurable. Other studies have shown yogis easily able to maintain themselves during meditation by breathing only once or twice a minute. At the same time, Bagchi and Wenger's subjects showed an increase in the electrical resistance of the skin, a measure generally considered to be an indication of lessening stress. Their brain waves also showed some unusual patterns which we will discuss later.

At around the same time that the research groups in India were conducting their field studies, a team of Japanese neurophysiologists were studying the brain waves of meditating Zen monks in a Zen monastery. They gathered material which later was to be used for the first experimental comparisons between two traditional schools of meditation, Zen and Yoga.

Both research teams were interested in the same thing: the response of trained meditators to distractions that might be expected to disturb a person in a normal state. We all experience immense amounts of stimulation all the time; if we were conscious of all of it we would never be able to focus our attention on any one thing. Fortunately we automatically 'tune out' sensations once we are fairly sure they do not require action. For example, we are not ordinarily aware of a clock ticking unless it is particularly loud and therefore threatening to our peace of mind. If we should become curious about whether the clock is still running, then the ticks are 'tuned in' and we hear them clearly. This entirely automatic process which ensures that familiar things will eventually not be responded to, is called 'habituation'. The investigators wanted to find out whether their meditating subjects would habituate to distractions presented to them while they were in meditation.

By recording the brain waves of four yogis, Anand, Chhina and Singh studied their alpha rhythm during a normal resting state and found it to be unusually high.[6] They also studied two of the yogis to see how their alpha pattern behaved when certain sounds and sense impressions were introduced during a stage of meditation called *samadhi*. This is a deep state of meditation specific to Yogic tradition: yogis claim that during it they are oblivious to both external and internal stimuli and their higher nervous system is in a state of ecstasy, or 'bliss'. Accordingly the researchers chose to introduce strong stimuli at regular intervals while the yogis were in samadhi – bright lights, loud banging noises, touching the subjects with a hot glass tube, and ringing a tuning fork close to their ears. Two yogis even requested that their hands be immersed in icy water just above freezing point. They claimed that when in samadhi they were oblivious to this ordinarily painful procedure.

When distracting stimuli are introduced during the alpha state, the alpha rhythm normally 'blocks' (temporarily disappears) and a more alert pattern takes its place. This is what happened with the yogis, but with an important difference – when the same stimulus was presented to them repeatedly they did not habituate to it. No matter how many times a distracting sound or other sense impression was introduced, each time the yogi would react by total alpha-blocking as though it were the first time he had heard it.

During samadhi, however, as opposed to the situation seen during alpha, there was a dramatic change in the yogis' reaction pattern. When they entered this profound state of meditation, the EEG machine showed persistent alpha waves with well-marked increases in amplitude. As the waves became deeper and more rhythmic, the experimenters introduced the various distractions one by one and kept repeating them, but none of these intense stimuli presented to the subjects at this time produced any blockage of the alpha rhythm whatsoever. It was as though the subjects were oblivious to sense impressions. Lights, sounds, burning rods, freezing temperatures – they simply did not respond. The two yogis who had asked that their hands be immersed in icy water showed no response to the presumed painful effects of the cold. Yet none of these subjects showed any evidence of sleep patterns during samadhi. Their brains were obviously alert.

When two Japanese neuropsychiatrists, Drs Kasamatsu and Hirai, studied meditating Zen monks, they asked essentially the same questions in their experiment.[7] Using a click as a distraction, they had their subjects meditate in a soundproof room while listening to a click repeated every fifteen seconds. A group of average Japanese subjects (who were not Zen monks) were first introduced to the experiment. As might be expected, these people showed the usual reaction to clicks. After the third or fourth click, the brain's response to the sounds became less intense until finally it had habituated completely. Now each time the click occurred, the brain gave no evidence of responding – the sound had been tuned out.

When meditating Zen monks were exposed to the same repetitive clicks they reacted differently. The Zen monks showed no habituation to the clicks during their entire meditation. They responded to the last click in the series just as strongly as if it had been the first click they had ever heard. While the yogis in samadhi seemed oblivious to any stimulation, the meditating monks seemed open to all sense impressions at this time. The same openness to stimulation continued when the Zen monks were not meditating. They responded to all sense impressions without habituation.

The comments by the monks on their subjective experiences when hearing the clicks were interesting. They reported that they had perceived each sound more clearly than they would have in their ordinary waking state but that even though it was remarkably clear, they were never disturbed by or involved with it in any way. One monk described his state of mind as being similar to noticing every person one sees on the street but not looking back with emotional curiosity at any of them.

While in these studies samadhi and the Zazen state seemed to have the opposite effects during meditation, the after-effects of both forms of meditation were similar. When not meditating, both yogis and Zen monks seemed unusually open to stimuli. Is this perhaps the physiological parallel of 'expanded awareness'?

Kasamatsu and Hirai had also asked Zen masters to evaluate the degree of proficiency of each one of the meditating Zen monks by indicating whether they considered them 'advanced' in their training or not. Without knowing how the masters had rated these subjects, the researchers then independently classified the monks according to how pronounced the brain-wave changes had been. They found a surprising correspondence between the two groups of ratings. The more years the monk had spent in Zen training, the more striking were his brain-wave changes during meditation and the more 'proficient' that monk had been judged to be by his Zen master. In this study, machine and master–teacher were in agreement.

While these first studies of Zen monks and yogis proved extremely interesting, they soon arrived at somewhat of a dead end. Investigators could not rely for subjects on a few practitioners scattered around the world, some of whom might have taken twenty years or more to master the art of meditation. A simple Westernized form of meditation was necessary before wide-scale studies could be undertaken.

That form was first found in TM. While, as we have seen, TM was not ideal for certain research purposes, it definitely lent itself more easily to wide-scale systematic study than any previous form of meditation and made possible the launching of a new era of investigation which gathered momentum in the late 1960s. For the first time, meditation came to the laboratory, instead of the laboratory having to travel to it.

TM was useful because it was taught in a standardized manner which ensured that wherever it was taught and whoever the particular teacher might be, the method was the same and groups of subjects could accurately be compared with one another. People practicing TM were also widely available. As a result of these advantages, experimental studies of TM initially led the field by a wide margin and are still proliferating, thanks both to the zeal of the TM organization and to the interest of the scientific community in the study of relaxation techniques. Information on these TM studies is widely available and so we will review them only briefly here, but I will refer to some other important TM studies at various points as we go along.

The Modern Research

Now we come to the laboratory experiments and the systematic studies on meditation. If I were to report on all the research which has been published in this area over the last quarter-century this volume would become many volumes. Hundreds of research studies have been done on meditation, many of them impressive. Here I will just summarize the research. If you happen to find experimental studies or facts and figures uninteresting, you can easily skip the rest of this chapter and go directly to Chapter 6. There you will learn about the important phenomenon of tension-release in meditation, a subject which is directly relevant to your meditation practice.

Studies on the Physiology of Meditation

Some researchers consider meditation a unique physiological state, different from both sleep and ordinary wakefulness, although sharing some attributes of each.[8] Their studies suggest that during meditation the body enters a profound state of relaxation which resembles in certain respects the deepest stages of sleep, while the mind remains alert and wakeful. Some research, however, suggests that meditation may actually be an artificially prolonged pre-sleep (hypnagogic) state.[9] If so, this is different from the pre-sleep states that we ordinarily experience and may offer unique advantages in terms of re-energizing the organism.

The first studies on the physiology of meditation showed that the heart rate tended to slow down slightly during meditation, just as it does during the quiet phases of sleep, but that this physiological quieting down was achieved much more rapidly in meditation.[10] Oxygen consumption (the amount of oxygen the body uses regardless of speed of breathing) was also sharply lowered during meditation. Oxygen consumption is at its highest during intense physical effort such as running or jumping and at its lowest during sleep, when activity is at an absolute minimum. For the sleeping person, however, it takes a number of hours before oxygen consumption settles down to its lowest level. After four or five hours it is about ten to twenty percent lower than during wakefulness. In meditation, a similar reduction in oxygen consumption can occur within a matter of minutes after the subject enters meditation, and this drop usually lasts for the duration of the meditation session.

In addition to consuming less oxygen in a natural and healthy manner, subjects also tend to breathe more slowly when meditating.[11] On occasion a meditator has been reported to breathe at about half the rate shown when simply resting with eyes closed, and one researcher has reported that a single meditating subject's breathing slowed down so much that only about four breaths per minute were recorded (a rate comparable to that observed in certain meditating yogis and Zen monks).[12]

Brain Waves During Meditation

The findings from different laboratories seem to agree that when meditating, subjects tend to show a predominance of alpha waves.[13] These waves are particularly prominent during meditation in the frontal and central regions of the brain. It is as though the motor were idling as the brain drifts along in a peaceful, rhythmic fashion. These trains of alpha waves are sometimes followed by bursts of theta waves.[14] The Zen monks mentioned previously showed an ability to remain in 'theta' for extended periods of time without going to sleep at all – something of a feat – and meditators have also occasionally shown theta waves without any deterioration into a sleeping pattern.

Increasingly, however, we are getting reports that the brain waves during meditation are remarkably similar to those in states of drowsiness. The mind seems to hover between sleep and wakefulness during meditation and it is not unusual for actual sleep to occur at this time.[15] A group of TM teachers studied at the Stanford Research Institute, for example, showed definite sleep patterns during TM, although these apparent 'cat-naps' did not result in full descent into 'deep' sleep.[16] While subjects in other studies occasionally have entered deep sleep during meditation, we most frequently see brief periods of light sleep alternating with a drowsy but awake state.

In observing meditators, I have noticed that these brief naps that may occur during meditation seem to have a special subjective quality. People often report them as not feeling like sleep. They seem to have a more beneficial and alerting effect than a regular nap. Meditation has certain special properties which set it apart from ordinary drowsiness. We do not ordinarily sustain a delicate balance between sleeping and waking for long periods of time, but tend either to wake up fully or fall asleep. Yet a capacity for hovering between these two states of consciousness for an indefinite period seems to be a distinguishing characteristic of meditation. Perhaps this is the source of much of its value for human beings. We will consider this possibility when we look at the ways in which meditation acts to restore a natural balance.

The most interesting aspect of the meditator's brain activity, however, may not be one specific brain wave or pattern of waves which is identified with meditation, but the unusual evenness and rhythmicity of whichever wave form is occurring – the tendency for all areas of the brain to harmonize and pulsate together. Neurologist J. P. Banquet investigated this possibility in a novel fashion. He studied meditators who had buttons near their fingertips which they could push to record different 'stages' of meditation.[17] A different push-button signal was designated for each of five types of meditative experience. These were: body sensations; involuntary movements; visual imagery; 'deep meditation'; and an objectless mental state which some teachers of meditation have referred to as 'pure awareness'. During the course of the study, four advanced meditators pushed the button to show that they were either in 'deep meditation' or 'pure awareness'. Looking over their EEG records later, Banquet found that at the exact moments they had sent these signals, an unusual pattern was occurring in their brain-wave tracings. The alpha wave patterns shifted at these moments to fast beta waves (a wave form typical of active, awake states), but the beta that these subjects showed was different from the usual waking type – it was entirely 'in phase' in each lead wire attached to the scalp. That is, the recordings from a number of different areas of the brain were synchronized. Ordinarily waves are of random length, uneven and unpredictable.

Banquet called this occurrence 'hypersynchrony' and

concluded that it is the outstanding EEG characteristic of meditation. Not only did alpha waves tend to spread synchronously from the back to the front of the brain during meditation, but after subjects had been in meditation for a few minutes, the separate hemispheres of their brain also tended to come 'into phase' with one another. The random and chaotic brain waves of ordinary waking consciousness seemed to be replaced by coordinated rhythmic patterns.

At the Hartford Institute of Living, a team of researchers also found essentially the same thing in their EEG studies of meditators,[18] and neurophysiologist Dr Leonide Goldstein of the New Jersey College of Medicine and Dentistry reported having observed synchronous beta wave activity lasting for eighty seconds occurring in one subject immediately following the ending of a Yoga chant intended to induce deep meditation.[19]

GSR During Meditation

The galvanic skin response (GSR) is widely used as a measure of stress. It is recorded by placing electrodes on the skin surface and then attempting to conduct a mild electric current across the skin. If the person is in a calm state, the skin tends to resist electric current. In the presence of anxiety or stress, this 'skin resistance' takes a precipitous drop and an electric current flows easily on the skin. This is the measurement used in the well-known 'lie detector' test, supposedly to indicate if a particular question has made a person feel anxious.

In quiet states such as sleep, skin resistance typically rises. Not surprisingly, therefore, it sometimes rises during meditation too. When it does, the rise is much faster than in sleep. One researcher, Dr R. Keith Wallace, reported that within minutes of starting meditation, his subjects' skin resistance increased on average by 160 percent.[20] Later studies[21] failed to attain any such dramatic rise in skin resistance during meditation, but all have reported a rise of at least thirty–fourty percent.

Does regular meditation change the way a person handles stress? Psychologist David Orme-Johnson, then at the University of Texas in El Paso, reasoned that meditators should in general be calmer than non-meditators and therefore able to recover more quickly from disturbances. To test this possibility, he assembled a group of experienced meditators and a group of non-meditators. He then presented each group with intermittent noise which was about as loud as a pneumatic hammer drilling a pavement.[22]

As he presented each new burst of noise, he tested the subjects' skin resistance to find out how long it would take them to habituate to the sound so that they would no longer react with a startled drop in GSR (a stress response). His results showed that the meditators stopped reacting to the loud sound after about eleven repetitions of it, and the non-meditators kept right on reacting the same way for thirty or forty repetitions.

In another study the same research team investigated 'spontaneous GSRs' in meditators and non-meditators.[23] These are fluctuations in skin resistance which occur without any apparent reason. The average person seems to fire little 'alarm signals' (GSRs) at intervals, as though alerting themselves to possible danger even when there is none. In general, the more anxious people are, the more of these subliminal 'alerting' GSRs they produce. Again, meditators seemed less anxious than non-meditators. The non-meditators produced about three times as many of these spontaneous GSRs when simply sitting resting as did their seemingly calmer meditating friends.

The next step was to allow the non-meditators (the ones who had shown three times as many GSRs as the meditators) to be instructed in meditation. Within two weeks of learning meditation, this group's spontaneous GSRs were looked at again. This time they had less than half as many spontaneous GSRs as they had before, and their scores were in fact almost as low as those of long-term meditators, an example of the surprising rapidity with which meditation can affect the central nervous system.

In another study, psychologists Daniel Goleman and Gary Schwartz studied the ability of subjects (who were given a chance to meditate beforehand) to cope with a stress-producing film and compared their reactions to the film with those of subjects who simply relaxed (without meditation) for twenty minutes beforehand.[24] The experimenters found that the subjects who meditated just before seeing the film showed a greater alerting response to the announcement that the film was going to be shown. Their hearts beat faster, their GSRs showed a more exaggerated alarm response, and yet these same subjects also recovered much more rapidly from the stress during and after the showing of the film than did those who did not meditate beforehand. This suggested to the experimenters that meditation may bring about greater alertness to possible danger (on the whole, a desirable survival maneuver) while at the same time people who have meditated recently are more able to calm down rapidly once they perceive that the danger does not apply to themselves. This research is in agreement with findings on the greater 'recoverability' of meditators under stress conditions.

Other changes occur during meditation too. Blood lactate levels may drop sharply at this time,[25] and according to certain research studies (though not to others) this may indicate a reduction in anxiety.[26] Blood flow also tends to increase in forearms and forehead as meditation proceeds, allowing blood vessels to dilate and circulation to operate more easily.[27] While no consistent changes in blood pressure have been identified *during* meditation, long-term studies have shown that some hypertensive patients have been able to reduce their blood pressures significantly over time after commencing meditation.[28]

To sum up the physiological research on meditation, a great many different studies suggest that meditation is a low-stress state. Obviously, not all meditators find meditation restful on all occasions, but the averages are impressive, and the beneficial effects are apparently not confined to any one form of meditation. Dr Herbert Benson, for example, was able to repeat his original TM physiological studies using his own method of meditation and obtained an equally impressive slowing down of body metabolism. As a result, he concluded that he was measuring a fundamental response which was not exclusive to any particular meditation technique.[29]

Psychological Effects

It is usually easier to measure physiological changes than to study psychological ones. Psychological tests are often not as exact as physiological measurements and are not as well accepted as evidence of genuine change. In addition, many psychological tests fail to measure the changes which may be most important when studying meditation, such as the subjective feelings of well-being. Despite this, some tests are simple enough to use right on the spot and in this way investigators have been able to measure some psychological changes which occur immediately after meditation.

After lounging or taking a brief nap we are not usually at our best on tasks which require speed or concentration. After *meditating*, however, subjects in some experiments have done better on tests requiring manual skill and the ability to observe accurately than they did after a period of simple rest.[30] They could move faster and more nimbly and their scores were significantly higher than they had been before meditating.

Meditators have also been studied to find out how well they could identify subtle differences in the length of tones sounded just after they had finished relaxing with eyes closed and again just after they had meditated. One group of subjects showed a keener ability to discriminate pitch and loudness of tone following a twenty-minute session of meditating than after twenty minutes of resting.[31]

In another interesting study, meditators were monitored physiologically to find out if they were really in a state of deep relaxation during their meditation.[32] It turned out that some were and some were not. It was those meditators who had been more deeply relaxed who could afterward discriminate more accurately between different degrees of visual brightness and who had significantly faster reaction times. The meditators who did not fully relax did not do so well. It seems then that the degree of relaxation one reaches during a particular meditation session may have an effect on the immediate benefits that come after the meditation.

Some long-term psychological changes may also take place with meditation. The most commonly seen one is a reduction in anxiety. There is virtual agreement among researchers that by whatever test used, meditation reduces anxiety in many who practice it.[33] What has *not* been proven is that meditation has a clear advantage over other relaxation techniques in achieving this. When groups practicing other techniques such as progressive relaxation or alpha biofeedback have been studied, reduction in anxiety has also been found. It seems that if deep relaxation can be achieved, by whatever means, anxiety is very likely to be reduced.

There is one important practical difference between meditation and those other techniques, however. Only relatively few of the meditators in the experimental studies just described (about 20–30 percent on average) quit before these studies were over, while the percentage of people who stopped using the other techniques was so great that it often brought the research to a halt. Several investigators[34] have reported that anywhere from 70 to 100 percent of the persons practicing either progressive relaxation or alpha biofeedback stopped these practices before the research studies were completed, complaining that their techniques were 'tiresome' or 'boring'. The response to meditation was usually quite different. In general, subjects tended to look forward to meditation as a positive part of their day. It was, in effect, its own reward. This is an important practical difference. If people do not enjoy performing a certain technique, they will probably not continue with it long enough to get lasting benefits from it. Many people do enjoy meditating. This seems to give it a clear lead, for practical purposes, over many other relaxation methods.

As for the effects of meditation on habitual behavior, a number of questionnaire surveys have suggested that the regular practice of meditation has what might be called an 'anti-addictive' effect. Possibly it reduces the abuse of drugs such as marijuana, LSD, barbiturates, amphetamines, alcohol and cigarettes. We will consider some of the studies that suggest this later on.

A host of other psychological studies also indicate that such diverse activities as memorizing lists,[35] solving arithmetic problems,[36] and thinking creatively[37] may improve with meditation. In addition, practicing meditation is reported to have improved academic performance in college students,[38] increased job performance and job satisfaction among workers over an eleven-month period,[39] and increased a sense of having control over one's own life.[40]

These are only some of the research reports which have been used to support claims of meditation's benefits. The list also encompasses more lofty aspects of personality such as self-regard, spontaneity, capacity for intimate contact and self-actualization,[41] and includes studies on the effects of meditation in prisons[42] and on patients in drug rehabilitation programs.[43]

An important value of meditation is turning out to be its use along with standard medical treatment for a variety of medical conditions. Studies have shown meditation practice to be associated with decreased blood pressure in hypertensive patients;[44]

reduced heart irregularities in patients with ischaemic heart disease;[45] improved heart functioning in patients with coronary artery disease[46] and in those with angina pectoris;[47] reduction in blood-sugar levels in patients with Type II diabetes;[48] reduction in cholesterol levels in those with high cholesterol readings;[49] reduced frequency of seizures in epileptic patients;[50] reduced severity and frequency of tension headaches in headache-prone individuals;[51] improvement in symptoms of psoriasis,[52] and lessening of pain in fibromyalgia,[53] among others.

The use of meditation has also been shown to facilitate opening of airway passages in bronchial asthma patients;[54] to improve sleep patterns in those with insomnia;[55] to reduce coronary-prone behavior patterns,[56] and to improve the emotional state of psychiatric patients in hospitals and in the community.[57] In dentistry, the use of meditation has been associated with reduced salivary bacteria (useful in treating dental caries)[58] and possibly with decreased gum inflammation as well.[59]

Meditation looks impressive indeed from these reports, but this does not mean that all studies done on this method will be equally reliable. In any area of research it is important to be aware of the pitfalls into which even fine researchers may sometimes stumble. Knowing about these difficulties, you will be better able to judge for yourself the value of future research as it appears. The next chapter will show you how.

Chapter 5

THE OTHER SIDE OF RESEARCH

When a new area in science begins to be studied intensively enough for some of its original findings to be questioned, this is a signal that it's being taken seriously by experimenters. Contradictions in the research pave the way for a deeper under-standing of the processes being looked at. There has, however, been surprisingly little contradictory evidence in the meditation field although researchers have been studying it for more than twenty-five years. The recent research on meditation has served largely to confirm and extend the earlier findings. We have learned of more uses for the technique and become more certain of previously identified uses, but the basic research findings remain the same – meditation is an extremely useful tool and no one is disputing this.

To help you learn how to evaluate future research, here are some interesting problems people run across in exploring medi-tation.

Wallace's Work Seen Differently

In the course of their research at the Department of Anaesthesi-ology of the Royal College of Surgeons in London, Drs John Bushman and Peter Fenwick[1] set out to explore the dramatic drops in oxygen consumption and carbon dioxide output during meditation originally reported by Wallace and Benson. Wallace, for example, found a drop in oxygen consumption during meditation of between 16 and 18 percent when medi-tation was compared to the resting states which came before and after it.[2] A contrast is, however, always relative – the results found depend on what is being contrasted. If, for instance, we were to compare the level of oxygen consumption of a woman running at top speed with her level while sitting in a chair engaging only in occasional minor movements, we would find that her oxygen consumption had dropped. The statement 'Sitting in a chair lowers oxygen consumption' could then be made, but only relative to these *particular conditions*. If we were to measure her level of oxygen consumption when lying down quietly, we would find an even greater reduction in oxygen consumption, and if she were to sit up again and perhaps move occasionally, then 'sitting in a chair' could now be said to have *raised* her oxygen consumption.

The British research team was concerned with this problem. Could some of the dramatic physiological changes that Wallace and Benson had noticed in meditating persons have been due to a failure to take this contrast factor into account? To find out, these investigators carefully recorded all effortful behavior, as well as all changes in oxygen consumption and carbon dioxide output, made by a group of TM meditators during their period of pre-meditation resting in the laboratory, and then during and after their sessions of meditating.

What they discovered was that any movement made by the subjects during their pre-meditation resting period raised oxygen consumption. If the subjects merely lifted a leg, for example, their oxygen consumption might be raised by as much as 50 percent, and even minor things such as being spoken to or closing their eyes could cause a rise in the pre-meditation figures. When they measured the degree of tension or relaxation in their subjects during the pre-meditation period, they also found out something else. Those subjects who were tense before meditation showed large drops in oxygen consumption during their subsequent meditation sessions, while those who were relaxed beforehand showed only small drops.

The polygraph records of those people who were relaxed beforehand were revealing. Even before their meditation sessions commenced, their carbon dioxide output would begin to drop steadily. During meditation the drop simply continued, and after meditation it went up again because of body movement. This suggested to the experimenters that if they could find a group of meditators who were relaxed enough before meditation, these people might not show any drops at all in metabolic rate while meditating.

Such a group was found. It consisted of experienced TM meditators who came to the laboratory just after rising in the morning, and before having eaten. When they were studied, it turned out that these people were already so relaxed that they could not produce any further metabolic changes at all, even during meditation. This strengthened Bushman and Fenwick's opinion that many of the reported drops in metabolism during meditation in the past may have been due to a contrast effect.

By the time their experiment ended, the research team reported having found an overall drop in oxygen consumption during meditation in their regular subjects of about 7 percent, less than half the size of the drop reported by Wallace. They attributed this difference in their findings to the fact that they had taken particular care not to disturb their subjects before and after meditation, making sure that they remained completely still during all three experimental conditions.

It is important to understand the implications of such a 'failure to replicate'. This new research does not mean that meditation is not deeply relaxing – the subjects were extremely relaxed during their meditation. Nor does it mean that the earlier studies were not well conducted. Failures to replicate are a universal occurrence in research and are welcomed as an opportunity to learn more about the subject being studied. In this case, the British experiment means that future experimenters investigating changes in metabolism during meditation will now need to prove that the effects they obtain are not simply the result of muscle movement preceding meditation versus muscle stillness during it, but are due to some unique quality of the meditative state itself. Approaching the task from this standpoint should produce more precise information about meditation.

There is the possibility that formal meditation is only one of a larger group of physiological and mental states, all of which share at times what I have called the meditative mood. Perhaps whenever this meditative mood is present, even if the state in progress is not termed 'meditation', the physiology may be affected in a manner that causes a lowering of metabolism. Some further evidence from the Royal College of Surgeons suggests this possibility.

When Drs Bushman and Fenwick piped soothing music to their subjects over earphones, the drop in oxygen consumption while listening to the music was found to be as great as it had been during meditation. Music of course can induce the dreamy reverie state which I have classified as a meditative mood. Could this be the reason why the drop in oxygen consumption with music was equal to that during formal meditation? It may be that the meditative mood runs like a connecting thread through all the relaxation techniques, a potential which all of them can offer. If the mood is evoked by the technique, then metabolic changes may follow; if it is not, they may not occur. It is possible that future researchers may find it is more important to study the meditative mood.

Basic Designs

Now let's look at some meditation research from the standpoint of how well it was designed. A poorly designed study is like a house constructed from inadequate blueprints. No matter how much care goes into the actual construction of such a house, or how fine the materials used, it may collapse. If you are curious about research on meditation you may want to read the following account in order to obtain a perspective from which to judge the reports. If you don't care about the pros and cons of experimental design or the problems involved in meditation research, you can skip to the next chapter. Doing so won't interrupt the continuity of this book.

We'll commence by considering the easiest type of meditation study to conduct – a comparison between meditators and non-meditators.

This approach is a straightforward one. When meditators are compared with non-meditators, if the meditators do better on certain tasks, it can be all too easily assumed that this is because they meditate regularly while the other people do not, and the results are therefore reported as showing the benefits of meditation.

In science, however, we have to beware of hidden factors. There is a problem with these meditators versus non-meditators comparisons; namely, that people who undertake to learn meditation may have *always* been different from those who do not undertake to learn it.

Unfortunately, research thus far has been able to shed very little light on the special characteristics of people who decide to learn meditation versus those who do not, but we do have some indirect evidence. In a large-scale study of the effects of TM on the use of non-prescription drugs, Dr Mohammad Shafii of the University of Louisville School of Medicine asked meditators and non-meditators to indicate on an anonymous questionnaire how often they had used marijuana during a period of time *before* the meditating group had learned TM.[3] The reports of the meditators showed that they had been regularly using *twice* as much marijuana as the non-meditators before they started TM. Was this because the people who were later to become meditators were a less conventional group, more willing to experiment with drugs? Or was it because they were a more anxious group who had a greater need for marijuana or other outside aids to relax them? While we do not know the answers to these questions, what we can learn from this experiment is that these two groups – the meditators and the non-meditators – must have been composed of somewhat different kinds of people *to begin with*.

A study conducted at Princeton University also sheds some light on this question. Researcher Susan Shackman compared college students who had chosen to learn TM right away with another group who said they were willing to postpone learning it and agreed to study a simple relaxation technique in the meantime.[4] On personality tests administered to these subjects before they learned their respective techniques, Shackman found that both groups scored about the same with respect to the amount of anxiety they showed. On a test for self-image, however, the subjects who had chosen to learn TM without delay had significantly higher 'disparity' scores – that is, there was a greater contradiction between the way they presently saw themselves and the way they would, ideally, have liked to be. Discrepancy of this sort often means discontentment with the way one is.

The about-to-learn-meditation group also differed from the non-meditators in one other respect. On the California Personality Inventory (a well-known test of personality) the prospective meditators scored significantly *lower* on Dominance, Capacity for Status, Sociability, Self-Acceptance and Sense of Well-Being. This suggests they may have been more insecure people than those who were willing to postpone learning meditation. If they were, perhaps some of the glowing reports we hear from meditators arise from the fact that in general they tend to be more troubled than those who do not learn meditation, and therefore have more room for improvement in their emotional state. More stable people might not show as much improvement with meditation and perhaps are less likely to learn it in the first place. We might have arrived at this same conclusion through a common observation – people usually do not go out of their way to learn something for which they do not feel a particular need.

If meditators and non-meditators are basically different kinds of people, then how do we know whether any differences reported between these two groups in those studies which simply compare meditators with non-meditators are the results of *meditation*? The answer is we don't. We may very well be comparing fundamentally different personalities. Nevertheless, *some* of the differences found may be genuinely due to meditation and nothing else. The trouble with the research that relies on the meditator versus non-meditator comparison is that it doesn't give us any way of telling which findings are true results of meditation and which are not.

A second type of research compares regular meditators with people about to learn meditation ('beginning meditators'). Here both groups have signed up to learn meditation, the only difference between them being that subjects in one group have been randomly assigned to a meditation group and are practicing their technique, while the other group has been randomly assigned to a waiting list and will learn meditation sometime in the *future*.* For this reason we can be certain that in these studies we are dealing with people who are more or less the same in one important respect – they are equally attracted to learning meditation.** This makes this type of design preferable to the meditators versus non-meditators one. In looking over

---

* In Shackman's Princeton study her subjects were not randomly assigned to the meditation or relaxation groups – for practical reasons they had to be allowed to choose their group. This represents an unavoidable weakness in the study, but was the source of interesting information about the differences between subjects who chose meditation immediately and those who could wait.

** The same advantage is seen in those studies that compare regular meditators with *irregular* meditators. Here both groups are already meditating, making a comparison between them well-matched.

the research reports on meditation, all other things being equal, the latter type of study can be taken more seriously.

Whenever two separate human beings are compared with each other, however, it is somewhat like comparing an apple with an orange. People differ from each other in many ways and we can never be certain just what all these ways are in any particular instance. A method which compares two groups of subjects can therefore never be as exact as one which compares each subject with his or his *own self* under varying conditions.

Another type of meditation research compares regular meditators with *themselves* – before learning to meditate and again after some time has lapsed, making this a 'before and after' or 'longitudinal' design. This is in many ways an ideal method for studying meditation. For practical reasons, however, it is often not possible. It takes a great deal of time, effort and money to follow subjects over a period of months, and even more if the study extends for years, and it is discouraging to have subjects drop out of such an experiment in ever-increasing numbers, so that the study may yield only meager data in the end. Despite these difficulties, however, an encouraging number of studies have been reported using the longitudinal design.

Yet another way of comparing subjects to their own selves is a 'before and after' study which is completed in a *single* experimental session. This is easier and obviously less expensive than the longitudinal approach. By this method, a subject is tested before he meditates, again right after the session, and perhaps during the session as well. When it is appropriate to the particular problem being studied, this is a highly desirable way of going about research. Everything takes place in the laboratory and is under the experimenter's control. It is the design which has been used for most of the physiological studies and for the psychological ones which deal with performance on simple tasks such as visual or auditory discrimination, reaction time, memory, and the like.

In many studies also, measurements taken before and after meditating are compared with measurements taken before and after the same subject rests quietly with eyes closed. This is done to check on whether or not any changes which may have occurred after meditation are really due to the meditation itself, rather than being simply a result of the subject having taken it easy for a few minutes. Like so many other strategies, however, this one has a subtle catch to it.

Meditators usually consider meditation to be particularly beneficial and are much less likely to think of a simple rest period as being able to do them much good. Because of this difference in attitude toward the two states, an 'expectancy effect' may be created. This effect can be especially strong if the meditators have been taught to view meditation as possessing benefits no other state can possibly offer.

Expectations are potent forces. If we expect that a particular doctor will be able to cure us of an ailment while another will be unable to, we are more likely to recover quickly under the first doctor's care. If we believe that medicine X is a wonder drug and that medicine Y is a sugar pill (placebo), then medicine X may cure us of our ailment (even if it is really only a sugar pill), while medicine Y may have little effect on us.

If subjects consider a period of meditation more beneficial than a period of rest, how can we be sure that the different effects we see when we compare these two conditions may not merely be due to the convictions the meditating subjects had that one condition would be better for them than the other? In scientific language, how can we be sure this is not a placebo effect?

We cannot, and for this reason we need to recognize that expectation effects may be present. If we cannot eliminate them (and we never can completely), then they must be taken into account. Are there some other expectations that affect the results of meditation research?

Tracking Down the 'Placebo'

In a typical TM training course, new meditators receive two introductory and three teaching lectures during which a vast array of exciting promises and scientific facts 'proving' the beneficial effect of meditation are paraded before them. By the time the meditators are left on their own, they are deeply embedded in a belief system about the benefits TM brings. Of course, other forms of meditation have their indoctrinations too. The power of religious or quasi-religious ceremonies, incense, and the like is considerable wherever it is encountered. Any trained meditator is therefore expecting certain results and perhaps because of this is more likely to find them.

There is no easy answer to the problem of the placebo effect in research because the placebo is an elusive quarry. Often the more we pursue it, the more it seems to evade us. In trying to reduce the expectation factor in our experiments we run the risk of creating some new problems for ourselves. This is because the *state* of meditation and the techniques or exercises used to bring this state about are quite separate things. A person can do any meditation exercise according to instructions, but if the fragile meditative mood is not evoked by the exercise, then she will *not have been meditating*. In order to reduce the influence of expectations, experimenters could strip the teaching of meditation down to its 'bare bones' and use nothing more than a curt set of directions such as 'Just shut your eyes and think the following word silently to yourself for twenty minutes'. What then would the subject be doing when thinking this word?

The person would certainly be performing a mental exercise, but this could not be said to be genuine 'meditation' unless she brought to the experience some *emotional* component of central importance. If the experience did not take on a special meaning for this new meditator, if it did not become part of an almost nostalgic closeness with her own self and feelings, it probably would not evoke the meditative mood. Perhaps the expectations and colorful 'build-ups' surrounding the learning of meditation are essential in establishing this singular mood. If so, then they may be a very real and central part of the experience, something we should leave intact when teaching meditation. If we eliminate suggestions which are conveyed through a simple ritual or an encouragingly respectful attitude toward the technique on the part of the teacher, we may congratulate ourselves on being 'scientific' and 'objective', but in the process we may have eliminated the process of meditation.

Meditation research seems then to tread a very fine line. We need to find a way of reducing all *unnecessary* expectations without going so far as to eliminate the touch of magic and dream, the hopeful mood, the sense of warm contact with the teacher that makes meditation what it is, which is something apparently quite different from mere physical relaxation.

The Search for the Opposite

An experiment conducted by psychologist Jonathan Smith brings up another question that troubles researchers in this field – what state is sufficiently *like* meditation for it to be reasonably contrasted with it while at the same time sufficiently *unlike* it for us to be sure this 'control' condition is not really just another kind of meditation?

Smith compared a form of mantra meditation similar to TM to a condition which he termed 'anti-meditation', a technique which was designed to be the 'near antithesis of meditation'.[5] Anti-meditation involved sitting with the eyes closed and actively generating as many positive thoughts as possible. If the subject felt that he was lapsing into a 'lazy trance state or daze' at any point, he was to snap himself out of it by blinking his eyes. Thinking was to be *deliberate* and to consist of a fantasy daydream, telling oneself a story, or 'listing' positive qualities of something.

This ingenious effort to find an adequate 'control' for meditation nevertheless created certain difficulties. While the anti-meditation technique which Smith devised may be the opposite of some forms of mantra meditation, it seems closely to resemble certain forms of *concentrative* meditation; as, for example, keeping the mind purposely occupied with positive thoughts, often of a religious nature, such as 'God is good, God is kind, God loves me', repeated over and over again. A peculiar fact about meditative techniques is that two different methods, seemingly opposite on the surface, can often bring about identical results. The ceaselessly whirling dervish and the motionless yogi both arrive at a state of objectless absorption. Perhaps Smith assigned not a meditation antithesis, but simply a different type of meditation, to his control subjects.

The condition most commonly compared with meditation is obtained by asking control subjects simply to rest with eyes closed on the assumption that they are doing something quite different from meditating by following these directions. That seems reasonable at first glance, but it is nevertheless merely an assumption. Different people with eyes closed may be in many different places mentally. Some may be occupying their minds figuring out the dinner menu or planning how they will ask their boss for a raise. Others may hover on the edge of sleep.

Still others may enter a meditative mood which is virtually indistinguishable from the state of mind of the meditator, even though they are not repeating a mantra or performing any other centering exercise and have never learned meditation. What the examiner *thinks* is a single condition – resting with eyes closed – may then be any one of a number of different conditions.

There is a way to deal with this problem: ask the subject what was going on in her mind. In a long-term experiment, this means having the subject fill out a daily checklist after each meditation session which is designed to find out if she was in fact in a meditative mood during 'simple rest'. If she is the kind of person who often slips into a meditative mood when shutting her eyes, we might expect that several months of sitting twice daily with eyes shut would affect her much the same way as meditation does a meditator. On the other hand, if closing the eyes does not tend to evoke a meditative mood in a person we might expect her not to change in the same way a regular meditator would over a corresponding period of time. The presence or absence of the meditative mood may be one explanation for what often seems to experimenters to be puzzling and even contradictory findings.

This problem might be summed up by recognizing that there are several assumptions underlying much of the research that has been done on meditation. We tend to assume (1) that because a meditator is sitting and repeating a mantra or using some other meditational device, he is necessarily 'meditating'; (2) that because a subject is sitting for twenty minutes with eyes closed, he is necessarily *not* meditating; and (3) that people who have never been *taught* to meditate ('non-meditators') do not meditate in their own way, perhaps often.

All three assumptions can be challenged. To test them it is necessary to record the *experiences* of the participants along with measurements of their psychological changes or performance. The measurement of both the experiential and the objective components of the meditation experience is crucial in clarifying the real meaning of meditation and is the only way to avoid being trapped by the labels we have attached to various states of consciousness.

How Dropouts Affect Meditation Research

Whenever an activity is undertaken by a large number of people on a regular basis, no matter how beneficial they find it to be, a sizable number will sooner or later abandon the practice. This is the case with regimens of daily exercise, dieting, mental practices for self-improvement, and even the taking of necessary medicines. People terminate self-administered programs for a number of different reasons, but the dropout rate is always a factor to contend with in any program which leaves people on their own to accomplish their own goals. Meditation is no exception. The majority of studies on meditators who use a number of different techniques, including TM, cite a dropout rate which hovers around the 50 percent mark.[6]

This is not surprising, nor is it a reflection on the intrinsic value of meditation. It is simply another factor to keep in mind when considering the validity of meditation research. If a long-term study is being conducted and a group of meditators have dropped out along the way, the final testing procedures will obviously include only those subjects who had the stamina, determination, motivation, or whatever else was necessary to keep them meditating, while those who may not have had these qualities were automatically excluded from the final results. Under such conditions we have no way of knowing how much the 'quitters' might have improved if they had continued to practice meditation for the same period of time as the 'persisters'. Perhaps the quitters dropped out precisely because they were *not* improving and became discouraged. If so, leaving them out of the final results will make the research on the effects of meditation look more positive than it should. All we can legitimately conclude from such studies is that *among those who stayed with meditation*, a certain improvement has occurred. This is an acceptable enough statement from a scientific point of view – the only trouble is, it is seldom made. Readers looking over meditation research almost always have to supply such qualifications for themselves. They should therefore be aware of this pitfall, keep an eye on the dropout rate in any particular experiment, and notice whether the researcher has taken this factor into account when interpreting the results.

Where We Stand

I have described some ways in which a person reading about the research in the field can judge for himself how likely it is that any particular study will stand up under challenge; that is, how well designed it is. But are such considerations useful in terms of the *practical* value which meditation has for the meditator?

Actually, they may not be. The newer, more challenging research has not reversed the basic finding that meditation relaxes people, reduces tension and may bring about a number of valuable side benefits. Because of this, the *reasons* why meditation is restful, or the knowledge that other states may also be relaxing or beneficial, may be beside the point for the person who finds meditation to be a particularly compatible and effective means for inducing tranquility in herself. With this perspective in mind, we will now turn to the experience of meditation itself.

Part 2

MANAGING MEDITATION

Chapter 6

LEARNING HOW TO MEDITATE

When I was asked to write a chapter teaching people how to meditate for my first book on meditation I did not immediately agree to do so. The success of meditation depends on the spirit of the practice which is usually subtly conveyed through the voice and manner of a teacher. To me, meditation is a gift which generations of people have handed down to one another, gently and with reverence. It is personal.

I was, however, willing to begin teaching my CSM method by means of *recordings* because I thought that a carefully prepared recording could create the meditative mood and reflect its deep peace. This proved to be the case. Those who used the CSM recordings were able to learn from them just as well as if I had taught them in person. I therefore concluded that recordings were the best way to introduce meditation in the absence of person-to-person instruction with a fine teacher.

Although the written word is still not a substitute for personal or recorded instruction, I have since overcome my reluctance to teach introductory forms of meditation in writing because I discovered, when I finally did so in my first book, that there are a few people who are so ready to learn meditation that they *can* learn it satisfactorily from a book and even develop a successful ongoing practice this way.

One value of teaching meditation in a book is that the reader has the opportunity to sample several types of meditation and compare them. This chapter shows you a representative technique from each of the main forms of practical meditation. You can experiment with each of them if you wish.

However, if by any chance you plan to use my *Learn to Meditate* recorded course (for details see the end of this book),

I strongly suggest that you skip over the instruction section of this chapter, perhaps returning to it later when you are an experienced meditator. There is an indefinable impact from your first meditation that should not be missed. It is the experience of moving into the unknown. Meditation is unknown territory until you experience its power first-hand, and so, if you intend to accompany me step by step on the recorded tapes, I suggest you wait for this experience and allow meditation to be somewhat of a surprise to you when you first learn it – as my first experience of meditation was for me.

If you are already a meditator, you may want to skip the technique shown here which most closely resembles your own and try the others to broaden your acquaintance with the field.

Although the meditation instructions given here do not constitute full training in meditation, you should be aware that a few individuals practicing well-known forms of meditation, even at the introductory level, have had sufficiently unsatisfactory experiences so that their own inner wisdom has prompted them to abandon meditation. In the absence of a personal meditation teacher or a complete course in the method, my recommendation is that if for any reason you find one of the techniques of meditation described here in any way unpleasant, you should quietly give yourself permission to set it aside. Perhaps at some future time you may feel it is desirable to give it another try, perhaps not. The wisdom of your inner self on these matters is remarkable and each person should respect their own deepest intuition as to whether this practice is suitable for them.

If you do decide to sample the meditation methods taught in this chapter, a useful procedure can be to learn one of the techniques presented here on each of four consecutive days. If you plan to meditate *regularly* with any one of them, be sure to read the comments later on in this chapter or listen to the *Learn to Meditate* recordings.

Preparation

For all four meditative techniques taught here, the same preparations apply:

1 Plan your meditation sessions so you will not be meditating

within an hour of eating a meal, and avoid stimulants such as coffee, tea or cola drinks for two hours beforehand. A small glass of orange juice, milk or *decaffeinated* tea or coffee can occasionally be taken before meditating. The meditative traditions insist that meditation is relatively ineffective (if not actually harmful) on a full stomach, and the reasons for not taking a stimulant are obvious – meditation is for calming down.

2 Choose a relatively quiet room in which to meditate where you can be alone, and silence the telephone. Meditation should be undertaken in a serious manner with few distractions. Explain to others that you are not to be interrupted. The only reason for interruption should be an urgent situation which demands your attention – even children, who can usually understand what napping means, can soon learn not to interfere with your meditation.

3 For your first time meditating, it is best to sit facing a green plant, flowers, or some other natural object where it is pleasant to rest your eyes. If you enjoy the smell of incense, lighting it can add to the meditative experience, but it is not necessary. If you do use it, avoid overly sweet or artificial perfumes; ideally it should be a natural, unobtrusive scent which gives you a sense of being close to nature.

4 Face away from any direct source of light. The room need not be dark, but it's more pleasant if the lighting is subdued.

5 Sit on a chair or on the floor, whichever you prefer, in an easy, comfortable position. If you are experienced in using the Lotus Position, that's fine, but it is not necessary for our purposes – a straight-backed chair will do just as well. It will help you to relax if you remove your shoes and loosen all tight clothing before commencing to meditate.

6 If during meditation you find yourself uncomfortable at any point you can always change your position slightly, stretch or yawn, or scratch an itch. The point of this type of meditation is to be comfortable. You are not learning the more rigorous forms of meditation such as a Zen monk or a yogi might practice, so you do not have to be concerned with learning to master distractions as they do. This is to be an easy, quiet time with yourself – that is all.

7 Follow the instructions given for the specific type of meditation you are using. If, despite all precautions, you are

interrupted during the meditation, remember one thing: to play for time. Try not to jump up out of meditation suddenly, anymore than you would jump up from a deep sleep if you could avoid it. Your body is likely to be as relaxed during meditation as during the deepest stages of sleep. If someone is knocking on the door or calling to you, answer only after a pause (if possible) and say you will be there in a minute or so. Move slowly, yawn, stretch – and then get up. If feasible, return to your meditation after the interruption to finish off the remainder of your meditation time.

8 The best way to time your meditation is by occasionally looking at your clock or watch through half-closed eyes, squinting so as not to unsettle yourself. While you may, if you wish, use a timer placed beneath a pillow to muffle its sound, many people find this too startling and peremptory. Sometimes you may need to take a minute or two longer for a particular meditation. The timer will not 'know' this, but you will.

9 After finishing meditation, remain seated with your eyes closed and allow your mind to return to everyday thoughts. After a couple of minutes of just sitting, open your eyes very slowly. You may want to rub your hands together gently and run them lightly over your cheeks in a face-washing motion, or to stretch. Then rise in a leisurely manner.

Attitude

The techniques described here are simple forms of meditation and you should not have difficulty with them, even if you are quite unfamiliar with meditation. Some of these techniques are relatively more concentrative than others, although for all of them you should adopt a gentle, non-forcing attitude. The main thing to remember is not to try to do any of these meditation exercises 'correctly', but to let each meditation do itself. Whether it turns out 'good' or 'bad' is not your concern. Just go along with the meditation; drift with it, and find out what happens.

In these forms of meditation you will not be focusing your mind or *forcing* it to stick to the point. Whenever thoughts enter your mind (and they will often do so because that too is part of the meditative process), simply treat them as you might clouds drifting across the sky on a summer's day. You don't try to push the clouds away. You don't hold onto them. You simply watch them come and go. When you realize that your mind is drifting far away and is caught up in thoughts, gently come back to your object of focus. No forcing – you do this pleasantly, the way you would come home again to greet a good friend. The extraneous thoughts which you had are a natural and useful part of the meditative process.

Keep in mind that you are not to try to make anything 'happen' during meditation. Trust the meditation to 'know' best. Some people have compared these forms of meditation to the experience of being in a rowboat without oars, gently drifting on a quiet stream. Let the stream take you where it will.

Now let's turn to the first form of meditation you will learn. We have already spoken about the use of mantras (special sounds) in TM and CSM. While some forms of mantra meditation call for considerable concentration, neither TM nor CSM does this, and the mantra meditation taught in this chapter does not do so either.

Mantra Meditation

Directions: Select one of the three mantras suggested in the following list, or, if you wish, substitute a word of your own choosing which has a pleasant ringing sound. If you decide to create your own special sound, be sure to avoid using any word which is emotionally 'loaded' such as names of people, or words that convey too intense or exciting an image. The word should ring through your mind and give you a feeling of tranquility. If it has a touch of unfamiliarity or mystery to it, this can help remove you from everyday thoughts and concerns.

If you decide to tell someone close to you the mantra you have chosen, be sure this person understands that regardless of his personal reactions to it, your mantra should be respected. Your mantra will come to have a special meaning for you and will soon be a signal to turn inward toward a peaceful state, so do not lessen these effects by using it lightly or casually.

When choosing your mantra, first repeat each of the sounds listed below to yourself (either mentally or out loud in a soft voice) and then select the one that seems the most pleasant and soothing, or make up one of your own. In these mantras, the letter a is usually pronounced 'ah', but do whatever pleases you.

*MANTRAS**
Ah-nam
Shi-rim
Ra-mah

Having selected your mantra, sit down comfortably. With eyes open and resting upon some pleasant object such as a plant, say the mantra out loud to yourself, repeating it slowly and rhythmically. Enjoy saying your mantra. Experiment with the sound. Play with it. Let it rock you gently with its rhythm. As you repeat it, say it softer and softer, until finally you let it become almost a whisper.

Now stop saying the mantra out loud, close your eyes, and simply listen to the mantra in your mind. Think it, but do not say it. Let your facial muscles relax, do not pronounce the word, just quietly 'hear' the mantra, as, for example 'Ah-nam . . . Ah-nam . . . Ah-nam . . .'

This is how you meditate, sitting peacefully, hearing the mantra in your mind, allowing it to change any way it wants – to get louder or softer, to disappear or return, to stretch out or speed up. Meditation is like drifting on a stream in a boat without oars – because you need no oars, you are not going anywhere.

Continue meditating for twenty minutes. When the time is up, sit quietly without meditating for at least two or three minutes more (or longer if you wish), then follow the instructions in Point 9 on page 82 for coming out of meditation.

Meditation on Breathing

There are a number of forms of meditation on breathing, all of which are variations of ancient techniques. Some of these methods make more demands on the meditator than others. The instructions given here are a modification of those developed by

---

* *Ahnam* means 'nameless' (literally 'without name') in Sanskrit. *Ra-mah* refers to the Hindu deity Rama, a legendary being who represents integrity and compassion: *Ra-mah* is a highly esteemed Sanskrit mantra. *Shi-rim* (Hebrew for 'songs') was chosen because many people find it soothing.

psychologist Dr Robert Woolfolk and his associates in a study of insomnia to be described later. These researchers found this kind of meditation to be effective in reducing the amount of time it took people with severe insomnia to fall asleep. As described here, it can be considered a permissive meditation technique.

Directions: Sit in a comfortable position and take a single slow deep breath, thinking to yourself the word 'in' as you breathe in, and the word 'out' as you breathe out. After taking this first deep breath, do not intentionally influence your breathing. Let your breathing go its own way, fast or slow, shallow or deep, whatever way it wishes. As it does so you will think to yourself 'in' on every in-breath and 'out' on every out-breath.

While doing this breathing meditation, you can extend the sound in your mind so that at all points during the meditation you are either thinking 'in... n... n... n...' or 'ouuuuuuuut... t... t' in long, easy sounds. If the word 'out' feels too abrupt because it ends in t and this is distracting (as it is for some people), substitute the syllable 'ah' for the word 'out', saying 'in' as you breathe in, and 'ah' as you breathe out.

Do this meditation naturally, with no concern about its correctness. If you skip an 'in' or 'out' because your mind has wandered (as it will), you can always pick up the words on the next breath whenever you are ready. If the words fade away and you are just sensing the breathing alone, that is fine. It simply means you are becoming quieted down. The words are really only there to help you focus your attention on your breath; often during the quieter phases of meditation they fade out if they are not needed. But don't expect them to disappear – simply let them go if they want to. When twenty minutes are up, come out of the meditation gradually according to the instructions in Point 9 on page 82.

Moving Meditation

Two types of moving meditation are described here. You can select the one you prefer after trying both, or you may want to make up one of your own according to the instructions given.

Method 1: Sit with a pillow on your lap so that your hands can rest comfortably on the pillow. Place your hands on the pillow, palms together, in a 'prayer-like' position with your fingers lightly touching.

Now gently open your palms *at the top* while still keeping their *lower* edges in contact against the pillow. And then once again close your palms fully so that all your fingers are touching lightly – you are back at the original position.

This meditation consists of opening and closing your palms over and over again, gently and easily. As you do this you can be looking at your hands or resting your eyes on some pleasant object in the vicinity, or you can close your eyes. Use as little energy as possible for this exercise and let your motions be easy and rhythmic.

Method 2: Sit comfortably with your eyes open or closed. Slowly and gently begin to bob your head very slightly. At the same time tap one foot lightly in time with the movement of your head. Keep all motions small, easy and comfortable. If you tire moving one foot, shift to the other, or allow your feet to remain still. Use little energy, let yourself flow with your own natural rhythms.

Visual Meditation

Directions: Select a pleasant natural object such as a plant, flower, piece of fruit, bit of driftwood, or a simple vase. Although a candle flame is sometimes used for visual meditation, it is not suggested here because its glare may cause eye strain if not properly used.

Place your chosen object on a table at or near eye level and at a distance of 2–4, feet from you. Adjust this distance according to the most comfortable focus for your own eyes and eliminate distracting objects in the immediate background.

Sit comfortably and allow your eyes to come to rest on the object, but make no effort to focus on it. Instead, allow the object to come into your vision, let it enter your awareness. Do not make any conscious attempt to think about it in any way – what it is, what it means, its name, the class of objects it belongs to – although if such thoughts come to your mind spontaneously, that is fine. Just look at your object innocently, as a child might.

Avoid staring at any time, for this can cause eye strain. During this meditation your eyes will spontaneously want to move about, to travel over the object. Allow them to do this. Do not stop your eye movements – this is part of 'seeing'.

Because most of us can only look at things with 'the eye of the beginner' for a few seconds at a time (unless highly trained), this meditation consists of a series of new beginnings. After allowing the object to remain in your field of vision for about seven to ten seconds (this interval may be longer or shorter according to your own inclinations), purposely shift your eyes to a more distant place in the room. At this time you can remove your mental attention from the object as well, and let it wander where it will.

Continue repeating this process, gazing away from the object for a few seconds (you will 'feel' the right length for this time interval), and then, when you are ready, bringing your eyes and your attention back to it easily. Each time simply allow yourself to become absorbed in the object once more (again for about seven to ten seconds) and then systematically remove your gaze once again. Continue in this way, looking at the object, looking away from it, and then returning to it refreshed, for five minutes (this is a shorter meditation than the other forms). At the end of five minutes close your eyes for a minute or so and sit quietly, then finish off as described in Point 9 on page 82.

Comments

While the instructions given here for these forms of meditation call for a permissive, non-forcing attitude, any of these same methods can be conducted in a more concentrated, disciplined manner and are frequently taught that way. For purposes of relaxation, however, I find the permissive approach to be more easily learned, more effective, and more apt to be faithfully practiced by the average Westerner. This does not mean that the more rigorous concentrative approaches are either wrong or harmful – merely that they are different. Usually these more difficult approaches are for advanced students who have acquired a considerable degree of self-discipline and who are working with a teacher to achieve goals such as a sense of oneness with all creation, a more ambitious undertaking than we are seeking here.

The mantra meditation given here is the most permissive of the four techniques since it requires an absolute minimum of effort on the part of the meditator. The meditation on breathing is similar to the Zazen techniques which are mentioned elsewhere in this book in that it is derived from them, but it differs in its degree of rigor. In classical Zazen meditation, meditators must sit in the lotus or half-Lotus Position in a carefully prescribed manner. They cannot move during the sitting, even if a fly should crawl over them, their legs become numb, or if they have a burning itch, and they must keep their eyes open throughout, resting on a spot about 2–4 feet in front of them. In some forms of Zazen, meditators follow their breathing by counting each out-breath from one to ten, at which point they commence over again with 'one', 'two', etc.

The moving meditation, suggested by a classical Indian form of meditation known as *mudra*, is a far less exacting technique than the stylized Indian one. Mudra meditation makes use of ritualized gestures which are structured in a certain way in order, it is said, to trap 'vital energies'. The repetitive movements I have described are not based on traditional Indian mudras, but are designed for the Westerner. With thousands of gurus training disciples in various forms of meditation, however, it is impossible to know whether any particular gesture has or has not been used for purposes of centering during spiritual training. Perhaps the moving meditations presented here have at times been used that way. They also seem to resemble some forms of prayer.

The visual meditation described here differs from *tratak* (Hindu meditation upon light), in one form of which the meditator is required to stare unblinkingly at a small flame until tears come into the eyes. Allowing the sight to come to you (rather than actively seeking to 'see') is a familiar part of many exercises designed to relax the eyes. The process of looking away from and then back at the object is a device created here to bring about a perpetual sense of 'freshness' of vision. I consider this 'returning' process to be basic to this particular form of meditation.

Meditating as a Regular Practice

If you want to continue using any of these four techniques as a regular form of meditation, this can be done effectively if the following points are kept in mind:

1 When you first start meditating it is important to schedule your meditation sessions into your life so as to make them a regular daily routine – occasional use of the technique, while pleasant, will not bring about any lasting benefits. You need to establish for yourself what I describe elsewhere in this book as the 'meditative mood'. It is best to meditate twice daily, but if this is difficult, you should try to do so at least once daily.

2 Your meditation should always be done in a reasonably quiet place without distractions. If someone else is present, he should be meditating. Non-meditating adults and children, or animals, should not be in the room. A 'signal' that you are meditating is a good idea: it can be put on the outside of your door to let family, friends or room-mates know that you are in a meditation session – other people often do not realize this.

3 Morning and late afternoon are very good times for meditating, but there are many other satisfactory times as well.

4 Always come out of meditation slowly, taking a full minute or more to surface gradually – this helps carry over the tranquility of meditation into your daily life.

5 If you plan to begin regular meditation with one of these techniques, it is wise to finish reading Part II of this book, 'Managing Meditation', before commencing. In this way you can become familiar with some of the difficulties that you may encounter and some possible solutions.

6 If, after commencing meditation, you experience any discomforts during or following it that do not seem merely temporary (see Chapter 6), immediately cut your meditation time to only ten, or even five, minutes per session and continue on that level (visual meditation should be cut to one or two minutes). Usually the problem clears up with this reduction in time. If meditation continues to present difficulty, give yourself permission to stop the practice of it, without feeling either distressed or guilty; or you may want at this point to seek advice from an experienced meditation teacher or consult the instructions in the *Learn to Meditate* course.

7 If you are undertaking meditation in the hope of alleviating a physical condition which may be related to stress or tension, you should inform your physician and remain

under his careful supervision. Do not neglect going for regular medical checkups just because meditation may seem to be making you 'feel better' – this can be both misleading and dangerous.

8 If you are presently undergoing any form of psychotherapy, you should first discuss plans to start meditation with your therapist and decide in consultation with her whether it seems wise for you to practice meditation on a regular basis at this time. Part III of this book, 'Meditation and Personal Growth', which deals with the use of meditation as as adjunct to psychotherapy, may be of use to you in making this decision.

9 If you elect to practice visual meditation on a regular basis, it should feel relaxing to your eyes afterward. If it does not, or if you feel any eye strain, cut the meditation time by half. If the eye strain persists, stop doing this form of meditation. On the other hand, if you find that your eyes feel relaxed and rested after five minutes of visual meditation, you can proceed cautiously to buildup your visual meditation time by adding two minutes per day to the original five minutes, and observing the effect on your eyes. If this form of meditation continues to be relaxing to your eyes, you may gradually increase the amount of time spent meditating with it until you are doing a full twenty minutes of visual meditation.

10 If you have not found any of the four forms of meditation described here to be effective or to your liking, but still feel you want to obtain the benefits of meditation, do not be discouraged. There are other fine forms of meditation, one of which might be right for you. It may also be that you are one of those people who respond excellently to a teacher but cannot learn a non-verbal technique from a book. Some people can begin learning piano from a book alone and do very well with it; others must learn by example. If you are the type of person who finds it hard to learn from written instructions, I would urge you first to seek out reliable personal instruction in meditation before assuming that the practice is not for you.

Others' Experiences

As long as we have been meditating, a number of colleagues and I have intermittently kept meditation journals. The participants in my stress management seminars at Princeton and my students at the medical school have documented their meditations in the same way. The journal entries show that each meditation session tends to be a new and different experience, just as each dream is unique. Each meditator also appears to have her own characteristic style of meditating. This style may change and develop over time, as the following entries in my own meditation journal indicate:

> When I first learned meditation, I would hear in my mind the two-syllable mantra as a distinct word, usually personified. At first it seemed to come from a graceful feminine presence, a mermaid who swam before me during my meditation, calling to me in some strange yet intensely meaningful language – the language was the sound of my mantra. Sometimes the image was a bird soaring in the sky, leading me forward with its beautiful cry.

After several weeks of meditating, I no longer saw these 'guiding images' except when under particular stress, and the mantra became more indistinct, less word-like. After nine months of meditation I wrote:

> Often my mantra is now present during a large portion of my meditative session as a faint but steady background beat continuing beneath my foreground thoughts and preoccupations. It goes its own way yet it harmonizes like the contrapuntal rhythms in Bach's music. When it finally 'takes over' at some point during the meditation, the mantra becomes no longer a word but now just a pulsating rhythm, like slow rolling waves on the shore. The first syllable is the receding of the water, the second syllable is the long roll of the sea washing over the beach.

In the various forms of mantra meditation, the mantra itself may be experienced with seemingly infinite variety. At different times it may be loud, soft, fast, slow, melodic, harsh, resonant, muffled, clear, barely discernible, or may be experienced in some other fashion. One meditator described a form of thought during meditation which he said was deeply absorbing – during it the mantra was absent for long periods of time. When he found himself engaging actively with such thought, however, rather than flowing with it, the mantra reappeared spontaneously and continued along with his thinking, seeming to lead him back into his quiet state.

At certain times, meditators may experience a string of memories drifting through their minds during meditation. Sometimes these are scenes of tranquil, nostalgic places from childhood, carrying with them a strong sense of pleasure. At other times disturbing images may arise. These usually tend to lose their painfulness as the meditation continues, changing under the soothing rhythm of the mantra or the peacefulness of one's own breath quietly attended to, or just dissolving in the stillness.

Memories that emerge during meditation are often sensed as unusually vivid; it may seem to the meditator as though she is reliving an experience rather than remembering it. Meditators can almost smell the scents, taste the food, feel the touch on their skin, see the remote details of the scene involved – details they may not have previously recalled since the original event. These kinds of reliving do not seem to be stories with plots and do not have the structure of dreams. They are vivid impressions.

Aside from the imagery which may occur during meditation, the entire meditative session may be experienced in a manner which can best be described by comparing it with familiar images. My husband variously referred to his more positive meditative states as being like sitting high up on a mountainside listening to the wind; being by a fireside sipping fragrant tea; or watching a baby nursing peacefully. Others report that meditation has evoked in them a feeling of pleasant days in a quiet meadow, a boat rocking lazily at anchor, or a shower of cherry blossoms drifting toward the earth. The similes are endless and highly individual, but they also have certain things in common. Most of them depict tranquil moods. Often water, mist and rhythmic motions feature prominently in them.

The mantra, or any other object of focus used for meditation, may play a significant orienting and synthesizing function during meditation. As one meditator put it: 'I searched for the mantra, and having found it felt "pulled together" (as being oriented by the North Star). I was coalesced.'

The experience of yielding to internal rhythms, of not 'trying', is also commonly reported: 'I am in a state of alertness, yet without grasping or making any effort to cope. I do not try to succeed nor can I fail. Distant feelings, images, uninvitedly float into my ken, but there is no effort to define what I hear, see, sense . . .'

Occasionally during meditation, a meditator will have a spontaneous insight which may bring about a change in his life. I find these insights to be essentially similar to the deeper insights which may occur during psychotherapy, but with one difference – the preliminary conscious work leading up to the therapeutic insight is not present during meditation. The meditative process can even foster insights in people who have no previous experience in searching for meanings or causes for things that happen in their lives.

One other aspect of the meditative experience should be mentioned here. A meditation session will often follow a certain progression. Starting with an active type of thought, it may move toward more quiet types of thinking, and sometimes this process leads to a state where no thinking at all seems to occur. In mantra meditation, the mantra may become increasingly soft and indistinct as the meditation session continues, until, no longer needed, it gives way to profound quiet. In breathing meditation, awareness of the breath may recede until it becomes almost imperceptible and silence is the all-encompassing experience.

According to meditative tradition, at this point the mind is not focused on either thought or image, but is fully aware, conscious. The mind is said to be alert without having any object of alertness. This experience of utterly still awareness is one of the goals of the more advanced spiritual disciplines, although it is not necessarily a goal of the practical forms of meditation. Known as 'transcending' in TM, this state is not by any means experienced by all meditators who practice the simple centering techniques, perhaps not by the majority of them. Many people, if they have experienced it at all, have not identified it as being any special state of consciousness.

While attaining such an 'objectless' state is not necessary in order for personality change to take place, for those who do experience it, it seems to be deeply meaningful. One investigator has described this fleeting state as follows:

When, in full wakefulness, all inner activity comes to a stop, all thinking, all fantasy, all feeling, all images – everything – even the urge to think or to feel or to act; when all of this stops, stops on its own, without suppression or repression, one thing remains: a vast, inner stillness – a clear peace, and the firm realization that this, at the very least, is how it feels to be, simply, alive.[1]

Aware of what meditation as *experience* can be, we will now turn to the question of its management in everyday life. Understanding certain practical aspects of meditation can make the difference between a successful practice of this technique and a frustrating one. The following chapters in this section will look at ways of handling meditation.

Chapter 7

THE CHALLENGE OF TENSION-RELEASE

One of the striking features of the meditative state is its tendency to go its own way – sometimes not at all in the direction the meditator consciously intends. A person may learn all the correct procedures, obey all the rules of a particular form of meditation, and still be unable either to produce an altered state of consciousness at will or to legislate its contents. The meditative mood *may* emerge – or other things may happen.

These other things – the surprising alternatives to the expected peaceful state – are probably the most frequent source of discouragement for new meditators. Temporary side-effects or discomforting sensations are a common result of deep relaxation. Usually disappearing spontaneously, often within a matter of minutes, these side-effects occasionally require alterations in the meditation routine before they disappear, and teachers of all the various relaxation techniques have had to find ways to help their students cope with them.

The relaxation process (particularly if a formerly tense person is the one who is relaxing) is not always an even or smooth one. What occurs is somewhat similar to what happens if we release a tightly wound metal spring abruptly. There may be sudden jumps, jolts or tremors as the spring uncoils, adjusting itself by stages to each new reduced state of tension. Most of us remember a time when we went to bed after a tension-filled day. As we began to relax in the pre-sleep state, we experienced a sudden involuntary jerk that awakened us fully again. In the deep relaxation techniques, similar temporary startles or other forms of discomfort may appear. Often these are so mild that we hardly notice them and they usually require no special attention. Occasionally they are prominent enough to attract our interest.

This unwinding phenomenon has been given various names. The TM organization calls it 'normalizing' and the teachers of autogenic training refer to relaxation side-effects as 'autogenic discharges'. Other relaxation techniques such as progressive relaxation or alpha biofeedback, while describing such effects in their training manuals, do not give the process a specific name. I prefer to use the term 'tension-release' as it is simple and descriptive of what actually happens.

Side-effects from tension-release are more apt to be noticed in the first ten minutes of any meditation session and after that to disappear gradually. It usually takes this much time for the body and mind to become thoroughly quietened down. An initial period of throwing off tension should be viewed as both natural and useful, *not* as a signal to reduce meditation time. Only if side-effects persist throughout the whole session and are distinctly *uncomfortable* to the meditator, should the suggested reductions in meditation time be made. By being persistent and simply returning to the object of focus, any period of brief discomfort can almost always be weathered pleasantly, tension dispersed, and deep relaxation obtained.

It is useful to know about the forms these side-effects can take, however. The single largest body of evidence dealing with them has been compiled by the autogenic training researchers. As indicated in Chapter 3, teachers of autogenic training have collected vast numbers of carefully recorded training accounts of people practicing their relaxation technique. These are of particular interest because this method also evokes the meditative mood. Since autogenic trainees are usually required to report each sensation that arises during their relaxation session to their trainer, when present, or to write them down immediately after their home practice, the reports contain information on many different types of reaction experienced during these training sessions. The mass of information which has been collected is invaluable in exploring the side-effects of relaxation.

Tension-Release Side-Effects

The list of tension-release side-effects compiled by the teachers of autogenic training coincides remarkably with those we see in meditators.[1] Although they are entirely normal occurrences, the person who experiences these effects can sometimes be upset by them if not warned ahead of time and may need advice on how to handle them.

The relaxing person may, for instance, feel unaccountably heavy in the relaxed state, as though 'sinking down through the floor', or may feel quite the opposite – weightless, as if 'floating away'. Such sensations may affect the whole body, or only one specific part, such as arms, legs or head. After the relaxation session is over, there is usually no carry-over of these effects into daily life.

During deep relaxation, sensations of intense heat, icy cold or a burning feeling sometimes occur. The deeply relaxing person may have a sudden itch that comes and goes. She may experience feelings of tingling or even a temporary numbness in some part of the body, or may feel pulsations coursing through the body or over the top of the head. Often these sensations are pleasant. Occasionally they are disturbing, as if an 'electric current' was running through the body, or as if there was 'a steel band around the head' or a sudden tightness in certain parts of the body. Relaxers sometimes even perspire profusely, shiver or find themselves trembling, or if tension-release is particularly intense, their hearts may pound or they may breathe rapidly. These reactions seem ultimately to be useful in 'unwinding,' because the result of such a seemingly difficult session is often deep relaxation afterward.

A person in a state of deep relaxation sometimes has other experiences as well. He may have the impression that he can almost 'smell' certain scents, as though he were 'in a barn and there is hay which smells good', or 'on a beach feeling the wind and breathing in the strong salty smell of the sea', or 'in grandmother's kitchen breathing the scent of freshly baked bread'. Smells – pleasant, unpleasant or neutral – can seem startlingly real at this time. In the same way, the relaxer may experience vivid sensations of taste, such as that of freshly ground pepper on the tongue, or of milk, or honey, or mustard, and the like.

The person's concept of his own body may also change during deep relaxation: his hands may feel as though they were 'as large as the room' or his head feel 'like a blown-up balloon'. He may even feel as though his legs, arms or head were separated from his body or that he had no body; or he may experience himself as incredibly 'tiny'. Such sensations are often pleasant. On the other hand, the relaxer sometimes has momentary discomforts such as pains that come and go, a headache, a stinging sensation in a toe or finger or elsewhere. His throat may suddenly feel sore and then clear up again within a matter of minutes. Saliva may pour so that he must continually swallow, his mouth may dry up, his nose run, or he may sneeze or cough. Some may sigh involuntarily or yawn repeatedly or make automatic sucking movements with their lips, or their stomach may growl unmercifully. In rare cases of extreme tension-release, individuals sometimes experience some nausea or have a strong urge to urinate.

The relaxing person may also notice small muscle twitches or jerks or involuntary movements, or 'see' all kinds of fascinating images – showers of sparks, spirals, whirls, geometric forms, textile-like patterns, vivid colors, bright lights.

He may also 'hear' inner 'sounds' such as a humming in his head or a rushing, whirring, or ringing. Often these sounds are experienced as rare and beautiful, as 'a thousand crickets chirping' or 'a tinkling chorus of tiny bells'. At other times it seems as though the body were tilted over at an extreme angle, falling over, or upside-down. Again, these experiences may be either pleasant or unpleasant according to whether or not the person is threatened by their unusual quality.

It is not exceptional for those in deep relaxation to experience intermittent waves of intense restlessness where they feel they 'simply can't stand it another second without getting up', or they may have strong emotional reactions or burst into laughter or tears. They may also feel intense rage or have pleasurable sexual sensations or even experience orgasm.

These are just some of the forms that tension-release during deep relaxation can take. Very few of these side-effects are experienced by any one person, however, and they are usually most noticeable for about two weeks after commencing meditation, after which they fade rapidly. Some people, in fact, experience such mild forms of tension-release, even at first, that they never notice this process. Each person's particular *pattern* of stress-release also varies. Some may experience certain specific side-effects over and over again in a number of meditations until these are eventually replaced by other characteristic effects (or none).

It should be emphasized that side-effects need not be present for a person to benefit from meditation, although they can be beneficial when they occur. A meditator should neither expect them nor be surprised if they do not appear. Usually they will take care of themselves. If not, then there are several effective ways to handle them which we will discuss later.

Relation of Tension-Release to Life History

Not only does every meditator have a characteristic pattern of tension-release, but the particular pattern experienced may be meaningful in terms of the person's unique life history. Autogenic training specialists have reported some striking parallels between patients' past experiences and the tension-release patterns they characteristically report.

They found that particularly intense side-effects were most apt to occur in very anxious people who had at one time or another in their lives experienced severe accidents. Their pattern of tension-release was related to the site of the injury and often involved the sensations that were originally associated with the accident.

A young man of twenty-four who had come for autogenic treatment because of anxiety reactions and some troubling depression is reported to have suddenly burst out laughing during his relaxation session. Later he told his therapist that he had been experiencing a feeling as though a stick were being pushed into his left upper abdomen just below the ribs and that his eyelids had been very tense, as though held together. At the same time he had had a feeling as though his heart was beating more strongly. Interestingly enough, this young man felt quite comfortable after the relaxation session was over, a response which is not unusual following intense tension-release. When he discussed these side-effects with his therapist, he then recalled three minor hockey accidents in which he had been involved between the ages of thirteen and eighteen. During one collision a hockey stick had been pushed into his upper abdomen and he had lost his breath and almost fainted.

This patient's tension-release paralleled the feelings and

experiences he had during his accidents. Not only did he repeatedly feel the stick pushed into his abdomen below his ribs
during relaxation, but his eyelids had also been pressed
together, possibly in response to the shock of the accident which
was being 're-run' during the relaxation session. This particular
side-effect is reported to have recurred a number of times during
this patient's autogenic training sessions, as though a trauma
had to work off its effect by being repeated.[2]

Other traumatic situations as well may be reflected in specific
tension-release patterns. Women with a history of abortion
carried out under particularly unfavorable circumstances, or
who had had a traumatic delivery, showed disagreeable kinds
of stress-release involving their abdominal region and their
lower back when they relaxed in autogenic training.[3] These side-
effects diminished and often ceased later on, again as though the
physical traumas had been 'worked out' of their systems in
the deep relaxation of the autogenic state.*

Another group which showed tension-release patterns related
to previous trauma were schizophrenic patients who had
received long series of electroshock treatments. These patients
reported many more side-effects which involved a *loss of balance*
(floating, sinking, etc.) when in autogenic relaxation than did
schizophrenic patients who had *never* had shock treatments.[4]

Another area of trouble which may reflect itself in specific
side-effects is sexual deprivation. In a study conducted by autogenic training researchers, sexually deprived people were
compared with people who had fairly normal sex lives and
'satisfying affectionate relationships with persons of the
opposite sex'.[5] The sexually deprived people showed a great
many more side-effects of *all* kinds than did the non-deprived
people.* They also had more sexually oriented visual experi-

---

* No comparable studies of tension-release patterns during the various forms
of practical meditation have as yet been done, so it is uncertain whether such
specific reactions as these would be seen during meditation. A colleague of
mine reports that a patient of his who at age twelve had been confined to bed
for a year as a result of severe skull injury, experienced no unpleasant side-
effects during TM. Further research in this field is needed.
* This is not always the case with meditators. A colleague reports that a
patient of his, virtually celibate during all of his adult life due to severe
anxiety about any sexual contacts, has shown *no* unpleasant side-effects from
CSM.

ences and thoughts. The sensations and movements during relaxation which happened to involve thighs, lower abdomen and genitals were almost six times as frequent in this deprivation group as in people who were not sexually deprived.

What was striking about these studies was the way in which the stress-release process seemed to 'select' patterns of expression which related directly to deep conflicts and unconscious concerns in these persons. This sort of occurrence is not confined to autogenic training. It can happen during meditation in the same way, although such dramatic types of tension-release are usually seen in persons with either traumatic backgrounds or long-standing emotional problems.

The Management of Tension-Release

Fortunately, enough is now known from our practical work with meditation to enable us to begin to offer considerable guidance to meditators who are experiencing temporary discomforts. The first step in the management of tension-release is to become aware of the 'initial adjustment period', an interim period which lasts for roughly the first two to three weeks after beginning meditation. Its exact duration depends on the personality of the meditator and the life-pressure she has recently had to face.

Too rapid unwinding can take place in certain people when they first learn to meditate because the changeover from a consistently tense state to a relaxed state is too sudden to be assimilated. The switch to a more peaceful state can be a mixed blessing if the contrast brings with it a discomforting release of tension. In such instances, temporary side-effects may spill over and affect the daily life of the meditator, and signs of tension-release, perhaps tears or feelings of anger, may occur *between* meditation sessions. When this happens it is an indication that some backlog of tension and emotional stress is being released before a better emotional balance is achieved through meditation. Almost always these somewhat inconvenient side-effects disappear when meditation becomes established.

A problem that occasionally arises during the adjustment period is that if a person is very tired, having been deprived of sleep or rest for a considerable length of time before learning to meditate, or if he has been overworked or especially tense, the chances are that commencing meditation may lead to a temporary state where he starts 'making up for lost time'. At this point, the need to rest may be so strong that the person finds himself becoming inefficient. Usually the condition clears up on its own after a few weeks without the meditator having to do anything about it, but sometimes it may require adjustment of meditation time or even temporary suspension of meditation. In Chapter 1, where I describe my experiences on first learning to meditate, I discuss an example of this from my own life.

Practically speaking, the best way to handle extra-rapid stress-release is to reduce radically the amount of meditation time and do so *without delay*. Whenever we have made such a time adjustment with a trainee, almost without exception it has proved to be helpful. Meditating for shortened periods of time under such conditions, or perhaps only once a day, usually changes meditation back into a thoroughly satisfactory experience.

Reducing Meditation Time

In teaching CSM we frequently reduce a trainee's meditation time from twenty minutes to ten minutes and sometimes to five minutes or less when this is necessary. We even reduce the time after the very first session if the person has experienced some severe discomfort during meditation. This reduction is undertaken as quickly as possible without waiting to see if the strong side-effects go away on their own. If a person who is experiencing unpleasant tension-release is allowed to go on too long, she will often quit meditation and refuse to go back to it later on. This situation can almost invariably be avoided if the adjustment is made rapidly. Such a person will then be able to reinstate longer meditation times later on, increasing the time little by little, until she discovers a time period which is satisfactory for her permanent meditation schedule.

If we need to assign a meditation time under five minutes, we sometimes suggest that the person practice these shortened meditation periods more frequently, perhaps five or six times a day, although it is unusual to have to reduce the time by this much. Most people show only mild, easily manageable tension-release effects, even when commencing meditation.

Fortunately most of us have a built-in safety mechanism. Most people do not continue to do things that are causing them discomfort or that may threaten their emotional adjustment. This tendency usually acts as a brake to prevent more serious difficulties arising from tension-release. Occasionally a person will fail to listen to the wisdom of his own inner self and remain rigidly with a fifteen- or twenty-minute twice-daily schedule in the face of mounting side-effects which are not responding to this regime. This can cause a number of complications which we will presently consider. It is precisely at this point that a meditator should feel free to skip meditations if this feels right, cut back to once a day or once every other day, or temporarily stop meditating altogether – whichever maneuver corrects the situation. Each meditator must learn to listen to his own inner wisdom as to what duration is best for him under such circumstances.

Some of the useful effects of cutting down meditation time are illustrated by a friend of mine, an extremely competent administrator handling a position of considerable responsibility, to whom I had taught CSM. She experienced a very fulfilling first meditation, but within two days she was complaining that her meditations were leaving her 'too vulnerable'. On one occasion when she was interrupted by the sound of the telephone, she was so startled that she found herself nauseous and trembling afterward and telephoned me to ask what to do. I suggested that she return to her room, be sure to silence the phone this time, and continue meditating for another fifteen minutes. This was to help her 'take the charge off' the disturbing interruptions, and in fact it did so. Her anxiety and nausea disappeared and she once more felt tranquil.

Two days later, however, she reported that meditation was now causing her to lose efficiency in a distressing manner. While she felt comfortable and unusually rested during the day, she was making 'lazy errors' in her work, something uncharacteristic of her. She found herself taking twice as long to accomplish certain administrative tasks which would ordinarily be simple for her to do.

When we talked this over, we both had the impression that while letting up a bit from her regular pace might be a good idea for her in the long run, during the initial 'adjustment period' it seemed to be taking too extreme a form. Since she felt it was genuinely interfering with her work, she had begun to resist doing her meditations. I suggested that she cut her meditation time down to ten minutes twice daily. When she did this, her inefficiency cleared up. She was no longer slowed down to a point where she could not work and she continued to derive relaxation from meditation.

This anecdote points up the fact that it is important for anyone practicing the simple Westernized forms of meditation to realize that no time interval is necessarily 'correct' for these techniques. Twenty-minute sessions, for example, are simply one possibility. In the recorded training of CSM we begin with only ten minutes of meditating and have the person gradually increase their meditation time over the next few weeks until they reach twenty minutes. This has proven to be a very safe and satisfactory procedure for those learning the method at home without direct supervision.

Progressive Change

As time goes on and a person has been meditating for months or years, patterns of tension-release, if still evident, have usually undergone considerable change from the way they were initially. If they were prominent at first, they will probably have lessened, giving way to milder and more manageable side-effects, or to none.

Some of the observations that the autogenic training researchers have made on these types of change over time are interesting. They noticed that people who at first had many unpleasant feelings and images during their relaxation sessions reported that these side-effects were modified as the months or years passed. Eventually they had very few unpleasant experiences, or none at all, while healthy, positive images or feelings grew in frequency.

Although emotional experiences were more frequent in the earlier phases of relaxation, these became less with time. Disagreeable bodily symptoms during relaxation also lessened while good feelings of bodily well-being increased. 'Aggressive' and 'destructive' feelings during their sessions of autogenic training were very prominent in certain types of patient during the first few months of their relaxation sessions. These usually began to diminish with time, with the sessions eventually evoking largely positive feelings.

It is interesting that the autogenic researchers also observed a tendency for trainees to see dark, 'dangerous' or morbid colors during relaxation sessions at first, but after they had been regularly practicing relaxation, these tended to change to more agreeable, lighter shades of color. In general, people who had practiced autogenic training over a period of years showed a gradual lessening of all kinds of stress-release together with an increase in positive experiences during relaxation.

These changes are exactly the same as those we commonly see in meditators. During his meditations, one meditator used to see a series of faces which continuously dissolved into new and different faces with different expressions. In the first few weeks following his learning of meditation, the faces were threatening and disturbing. They were angry, florid, distorted with rage and almost inhuman – he described them as 'Satanic' in countenance. As he continued to meditate, however, over time the character of the faces began to change. Eventually, the florid coloring and Satanic look had disappeared and the 'pinched expressions' on the face and 'narrow, beady eyes' were gone. Now the faces had greater softness. They were lighter and more natural in color. The skin was smoother and was no longer wrinkled, and the frightening look had changed into a look of composure, peace and gentleness – a look that brought the meditator comfort. At the same time this man's family noticed that the uncontrolled outbursts of anger which he had always shown had disappeared. He had become much more easy-going, understanding and cooperative. His best qualities seemed to have come to the fore. He himself was able to recognize that the change in the faces must have reflected some deep inner change and release of tension in himself. Eventually, after he had been meditating for about two years, the faces rarely appeared anymore. Now he saw rural scenes, quiet cottages, fences, lawns and villages during meditation.

The Resolution of Tension-Release

If a person interrupts a meditation session prematurely because she suddenly feels restless (a rather common side-effect during meditation), this restlessness is often carried over into daily life instead of dissolving in the quiet of the meditative state. This can be disappointing if the person had hoped to come out of meditation quiet, calm and soothed.

In general, the best way to handle such an uncomfortable side-effect is to remain meditating, recognize that the effect is normal, and continue to bring your attention periodically back to the focus of meditation. Most often the side-effect disappears of its own accord when treated in this fashion.

Sometimes the meditator may find that he is still releasing tension when the time for meditation is up. When this happens there is often a feeling that the meditation session is 'incomplete' and that something is still unresolved. If the meditator then ends meditation abruptly, irritability and lingering tension of greater or lesser intensity may be experienced afterward. If the meditator strongly feels the need to remain longer to 'work' through some tension-release in meditation, then it is better to stay on with the meditation for another five or ten minutes until the process feels complete.

It seems that there are many ways in which the meditator signals to herself that disturbing or stressful material has been 'neutralized' and the meditation session is, in a sense, ready to terminate. Autogenic training researchers have noticed this phenomenon and studied it carefully.[6] Often the relaxed person will visualize a calm, peaceful atmosphere, perhaps a beautiful sunset or falling asleep in affectionate arms. If these follow a fairly disturbing session, they seem to indicate a resolution of the tension state.

Other terminating experiences take the form of spontaneous sleepiness, yawning, or a disappearance of all imagery. Or the person may find that an increasing number of positive thoughts and images are entering his mind, ones that are more peaceful, less active and less stress-related. At this time feelings of warmth may increase or the person may visualize light shades of uniform colors such as pale blue, turquoise, pale gray, silvery tones, or light yellow. He may even see a whiteness or a blankness or an empty space, and sometimes report a blinding white light, which resembles the enlightenment experiences reported by mystics.[7]

The fact that in numerous records of autogenic training, this sudden impression of blinding light was found to occur only after highly stressful material had been neutralized and 'handled' during the relaxation session suggests that it is a very positive sign indicating a peaceful inner resolution of disturbing material. Anyone experiencing the white light during meditation should probably be reassured by these observations and may want to notice for themselves whether the brilliant light did in fact signal the same sort of positive resolution. Some meditators also report that aqua or 'electric' blue light has these same implications for them. Whatever the specific manifestations, a feeling of completeness and a sense of relief are typical of the end of a period of stress-release.

Techniques for Handling Persistent Side-Effects

Very occasionally, side-effects from tension-release refuse to go away, but persist after the session. If this happens there are some effective techniques for dealing with it.

The first deals with physical side-effects. Let us say that stress-release takes the form of a physical symptom, perhaps a localized pain in the back of the head. If it is a pain that first appeared during meditation (an indication that it is probably due to tension-release) and refuses to leave by the end of the session, one strategy is to stop whatever meditative focus you ordinarily concentrate upon and turn your attention lightly onto the area of pain itself, absorbing yourself entirely in it. You are not trying to get rid of the pain or fighting against it in any way, but simply using it as a meditational focus, as you might use a mantra.

This way you will come to know the pain minutely and sensitively. You will 'fuse' with it, rather than opposing it as though it were an outside force, and by doing so will change the situation. As you come more into harmony with the pain, it may spontaneously dissolve without any effort on your part. Strange as it may seem, I have yet to see this device fail, and I recommend it for any persistent physical side-effect of meditation.

Emotional side-effects, such as uncontrollable crying, which continue after the session, may need to be handled differently. Usually such release phenomena have their own timetable. A 'crying jag', for example, may be beneficial if allowed to play itself out and will usually self-terminate.

If anxiety which is stirred up during meditation continues

afterward, an effective tactic is to take a few long, slow breaths, letting the air flow downward deeply into your lungs until it feels as though it has reached and permeated your entire abdomen. After this, very slowly exhale your breath until the last of the air seeps out. If you wish, you can even imagine that the air is flowing downward throughout your whole body as you breathe in, and that it is flowing out through the soles of your feet as you breathe out.

Deep-breathing exercises such as these, perhaps coupled with some simple physical exercises such as Yoga stretches, are usually effective in handling an upsurge of anxiety. It is also useful to talk over any uncomfortable thoughts or feelings which may have surfaced during meditation with a person you trust. The experience of sharing these discomforting sensations with another can sometimes lead to important insights and considerable relief.

If none of these tactics is effective, then you need a temporary rest from meditating and should suspend meditation for five days. This is an excellent strategy for helping stress-release to right itself. When this interval is up, return to meditating, slowly at first, perhaps starting with only five or ten minutes once a day and only gradually increasing meditation time as it feels comfortable to do so. Feel free to back off and shorten your meditation time again if necessary, or even to take another rest from it. Your own flexibility and good judgment should be the yardstick.

Temporary Setbacks

Something which causes difficulty in a small number of cases is the fact that certain symptoms which may have been present before learning to meditate may temporarily worsen after the person has learned to meditate. Usually these symptoms will then get better and disappear as the meditator continues with daily practice. Irritability, tension headaches, or other undesirable conditions related to stress, are occasionally symptomatic of this opposite or 'paradoxical' effect.

A striking instance of this occurred with a patient of mine whom I referred to a TM center for training in the days before I had developed CSM. The reason for the referral was that his severe tension headaches had not improved during psychotherapy. While he found meditation to be a very gratifying experience, during the first week after he began to meditate his headaches became worse than ever. They were more frequent than usual and would continue through his meditation sessions.

His meditation instructor explained to him that this was 'normalizing', to be expected, and that it would probably straighten out in the near future when some of the initial tension had been drained off. This is, in fact, what happened. The second week after learning to meditate, his tension headaches were much less frequent. By the third week they had lessened to a point where he had fewer headaches than before learning to meditate. After one month they had all but disappeared, and from then on, as long as he regularly maintained his meditation, he rarely experienced a tension headache.

In the example just given, the instructor's advice to stay with the meditation until the symptoms lessened was effective. Sometimes, however, this advice is inappropriate. Dr Leon Otis of the Stanford Research Institute tells of five subjects, three of whom were TM meditators, and two of whom had learned another form of mantra meditation in his laboratory, who, after commencing meditation, suffered a recurrence of serious psychosomatic symptoms which had previously been under control.[8] These included a bleeding ulcer (under control for the previous five years), a recurrence of depression requiring psychiatric care and medication, extreme agitation that resulted in the termination of employment, and other distressing symptoms.

Dr Arnold Lazarus also reports some incidents where learning TM precipitated psychiatric problems.[9] A thirty-four-year-old woman patient made a serious suicide attempt following a weekend training course in TM; several patients alleged that TM increased their feelings of depression; and some agitated individuals reported that meditating with TM tended to heighten their already existent tension and restlessness. Dr Robert Woolfolk also reports a case in which a schizophrenic breakdown seemed to have been precipitated by TM.[10] Lazarus concludes on the basis of evidence in the field of relaxation that relaxation training (including meditation) is not for everyone, but when properly applied to selected cases by informed practitioners, it can overcome many facets of stress, tension and anxiety. In my own psychotherapeutic work, I have seen several

TM meditators in whom tension-related physical symptoms or a latent emotional illness apparently became aggravated after commencing meditation. While these people are the extreme exceptions, they are a cause for concern.

It is interesting that this kind of symptom aggravation has been so well managed in autogenic training, a relaxation method which, in its more than fifty years of existence, has trained thousands of patients in hospitals and medical clinics, some of them people who were seriously ill and presumably vulnerable to the least disturbances in their delicate adjustment. I suspect the reason for this relaxation technique's excellent record is twofold:

1 Autogenic trainees are initially taught to do the exercises only for very brief periods of time. No more than thirty to sixty seconds are allowed for each Standard Training Exercise until the trainee becomes proficient in its use and until all side-effects of tension-release are brought under control.
2 Trained teachers work to adjust the technique carefully to suit each trainee's requirements.

CSM employs some of the same safeguards as autogenic training and it is interesting that among the thousands of people who have learned CSM to date, we have seen no symptom recurrences, emotional breakdowns, or other unfortunate occurrences following the learning of meditation. While there is always the possibility that something untoward might happen on some future occasion, I believe we have avoided such difficulties so far because, if anything, we err on the side of under-meditation. We immediately reduce meditation time at the first sign of an emerging difficulty, rather than risk any buildup of stress in a meditator. We also emphasize careful adjustment of the meditative technique to suit individual requirements.

While these may seem obvious precautions, they contrast with much of TM practice. TM teachers are reluctant to reduce meditation time (although they will sometimes do so) because they have strong feelings about the proper duration of meditation, the assumption being that TM by itself will automatically handle any problem if the person keeps meditating faithfully for fifteen to twenty minutes twice daily, and in fact this is usually what happens. In those occasional instances where this does not work, the TM teacher may then try to handle the problem of stress-release by instructing the meditator to practice Yoga breathing exercises or certain Yoga postures before meditation. This may be useful in some cases but not in all. If the TM teacher notices continued distress in the meditator which has not dissipated after some days or weeks of meditating-plus-exercise, he may then reduce meditation time to fifteen minutes, but will not lower it below ten minutes even if the side-effects are serious. At present writing, the TM organization also considers brief meditations of three to five minutes to be ineffective and, indeed, not 'meditation'. In addition they will not permit the trainee to change the mantra which has been assigned to her even if she reacts strongly against this sound.*

TM teachers' relative inflexibility in this regard may seem surprising to some people but can be understood if we consider that Maharishi Mahesh Yogi has strong convictions on these matters stemming from his traditional viewpoint and that his directives determine the TM teachers' advice.

Although tension-release is not a serious problem for most meditators, those who practice Westernized meditative techniques should recognize the importance of learning to regulate their own meditation practice if this becomes necessary. I have found on the basis of experience that most of the unfortunate complications reported by those practicing meditation need never occur if a radical adjustment downward in meditation time is undertaken promptly enough. As indicated, however, this should only be done if distinctly disagreeable side-effects continue unabated for one or more meditation sessions, and if returning to the mantra (or other meditational device) has proven not to be effective in dealing with them. Each person will judge this for himself by trusting in the wisdom of his own inner self to know what is correct for him in terms of how much meditation is beneficial. Handled with common sense, meditation can then become a highly useful means for self-development.

---

* We will discuss the problem of changing mantras when we come to consider the meaning of the mantra in Chapter 10.

Chapter 8

HOW TO USE MEDITATION UNDER STRESS

When meditation is practiced on a regular daily basis, this usually results in certain advantages for the meditator. Evidence suggests that it is the person who rarely misses having at least one full meditation per day who reaps the most benefits in the long run. But what about the short run? Can the selective use of meditation during times of momentary stress be useful?

Various schools of meditation differ on the answer to this question, but if we ask meditators themselves, we find that most of them have at one time or another tried meditating at some specific moment to overcome a particular difficulty, and they report that meditation is surprisingly effective for such purposes.

Since there have not been any systematic studies conducted on what we might call the 'strategic' use of meditation, we will consider reports from meditators who have invented their own ways of using meditation to help them through life crises, large and small. There are, by now, enough of these reports to give us useful information.

Mini-Meditations

Many meditators to whom I have taught CSM have reported that they effectively use very brief meditations at strategic points during the day. These meditative experiences may not be more than a minute or two in length and I have termed them 'mini-meditations'. One patient of mine who works under extreme pressure at her job says she repeats her mantra silently to herself for a minute or so during work whenever her job becomes particularly tense. This causes an 'immense calm' to descend over her and she then feels balanced.

I myself frequently use mini-meditations, and their use in the New York Telephone Company's extensive stress management program is described in detail in Chapter 18. Mini-meditations are part of the standard CSM instructions, and a significant portion of the *Learn to Meditate* recordings are devoted to their strategic use.

As an example of one time I used a mini-meditation to overcome stress, I recall being caught in a traffic jam in the Lincoln Tunnel outside New York City. I found myself becoming extremely tense because the tunnel was filled with highly irritating fumes and drivers were honking. As the moments ticked by, I became increasingly uneasy about whether the traffic jam would clear up or whether we were in for hours of waiting. To counteract my rising anxiety about this, I decided to do a mini-meditation. I did this by repeating my mantra and while thinking it I kept my eyes open, watching the other cars ahead of me. This seemed more reassuring than closing my eyes in the face of what I felt to be a situation where there might be danger. Within less than a minute this mini-meditation brought me a sense of calm and reassurance. I was now able to look at the whole problem with good-natured optimism, and to wait easily for the next fifteen minutes until the traffic began to move again.

Mini-meditations can also be useful to increase the effectiveness of one's regular meditations. A meditator who suffers from hypertension recently told me that his two scheduled meditations of the day, though very relaxing for him, had nevertheless been unable to hold in check an extreme buildup of tension during working hours. When faced with decisions at the office, he would feel his blood pressure rising to a high pitch and could do nothing about it. Eventually he discovered that this undesirable rise in tension could be reversed by taking time out to meditate for five minutes whenever he recognized that he was heading into trouble. These mini-meditations, scattered throughout his day, took the edge off his tension buildups and made a marked difference in his ability to handle the stress of work with a relaxed attitude. He describes this strategy as 'worth more than any tranquilizer I have ever known'. It might be valuable for any meditator suffering from high blood pressure to try this method. The *Learn to Meditate* Kit (see the back of the book for details) gives a complete program for combating high blood pressure which is based on the use of mini-meditations. By teaching people to use mini-meditations in addition to their regular meditation sessions, the effectiveness of meditation for combating hypertension can be substantially increased.

Meditations under highly stressful circumstances are usually mini-meditations. The nature of a threatening situation demands that we keep our attention focused on the external world, which means that deep and prolonged meditation is out of the question. This is also why many people will keep their eyes either fully or partially open during a mini-meditation. When we feel ourselves facing a threat of any kind, we instinctively glance around us and keep a sharp watch over our environment. Closing our eyes when we feel threatened may make us more anxious because it gives us a feeling of being unprotected and vulnerable.

Other relaxation techniques can also be used strategically. A young singer who had studied autogenic training is reported to have discovered by chance that during her relaxation exercises she could sing very fine, high notes which she had not been able to achieve otherwise. She decided to try inducing a state of relaxation during her singing practice, and found she could do so by repeating only one portion of her relaxation formula. Eventually this young woman was able to master alto passages when singing in actual stage performances by thinking this formula just before she commenced the aria.[1]

Relaxation literature also tells of an eleven-year-old boy, failing badly in his class work, who was encouraged to practice his autogenic relaxation exercises for several minutes between classes. Each time after he did so, he felt refreshed and it was easier for him to participate in class work during the following hour.[2]

In another instance, a golfer who had noticed after eight weeks of autogenic training that his swing had definitely improved, decided to try to increase his efficiency even more by repeating part of his relaxation formula to himself just before hitting the ball. When he did this the relaxation exercise dissolved disturbing tensions in his shoulders and added to the precision of his golf technique.[3]

Preparatory Meditation

Meditating when we are right in the midst of a stress situation is different from meditating ahead of time when a stressful situation is anticipated. When anticipating certain types of difficulty, a full deep meditation rather than a mini-meditation may be preferable – a full twenty minutes for meditators who are used to meditating for this amount of time.

A teenage patient of mine who was a regular CSM meditator was extremely nervous about her forthcoming performance in a school play. After talking it over with me, she decided to try meditating for a complete twenty-minute session about half an hour before the performance on each of the days she was to appear. When she did this, to her surprise she found it an extremely effective strategy. She felt calmer and less self-conscious on the stage after she had meditated beforehand.

At the American Conservatory Theater in San Francisco, meditation is regularly used as part of the training program and the company reports that the relationship between actors, and their overall performance, are improved when a cast meditates together before a play. In this connection, I remember how soothing it was for me to meditate just before a particular TV appearance. Both the director and the cameraman, as well as myself, were meditators, and we held a group meditation just before the TV cameras began to click. We all had the impression that it affected the show in a very positive manner.

Meditation and Exam Anxiety

An interesting use of preparatory meditation is for students who are preparing to take an examination. It is a very effective way to lessen exam anxiety, providing the meditator is familiar enough with his own reactions to be able to gauge how soon before the examination it is best for him to meditate. Getting to the examination room early and sitting quietly in the corner meditating may be an excellent way to enter an exam for certain students. These students will emerge from their meditation relaxed and with an improved perspective on the forthcoming test. For a person who tends to feel drowsy following meditation, however, meditating directly before an exam would be a poor idea since motivation to achieve could be lowered in this manner and so could alertness. She might also emerge from meditation lacking the degree of aggressiveness needed to tackle the examination successfully. For such people meditating about an hour before an exam, instead of in the examination room, would work much better.

I once conducted an experiment with students at Princeton who were facing their final examination. Many of them had indicated some anxiety about this exam since it constituted a large portion of their final grade. I decided to try to counteract their exam anxiety by leading the class in a mini-meditation (three minutes in length) just before I handed out the test booklets. I showed them a simple Zazen breathing method which I knew would be relatively easy for them to master even if they were not experienced meditators, and purposely kept the meditation time brief in order not to induce sleepiness or over-relaxation in the students.

Although the class was initially a bit startled at the announcement of the meditation (for which they had not been prepared) they entered readily into the spirit of it. In an anonymous questionnaire filled out after the exam, over 80 percent of the students reported that the meditation had been helpful in relaxing them during the examination, and the majority of these students said they would like to institute group meditations before other exams at the university. About 20 percent reported having felt annoyed at having to stop to meditate when they had been 'all psyched up' for the exam, but none reported that it had harmed their subsequent performance.

Pre-Surgical Meditation

An important potential use for strategic meditation is in preparing for surgery. Meditation has been used successfully to lower the anxiety experienced by patients preparing for cardiac surgery[4] and for ambulatory surgery.[5]

I have myself used mini-meditations prior to dental surgery and know several other people who have done so. The period of waiting in the office before being escorted to the dental chair affords a good opportunity to apply strategic mini-meditations unobtrusively. When I do this it calms me immensely and I am much better prepared for the dentistry. On one occasion I followed this preparatory meditation during the time the dentist was actually working on my teeth. Since this was a stressful situation, I kept my eyes open, and during the prolonged (hour-and-a-half) dental session, I allowed mini-meditations to come and go naturally. This was the most relaxing dental session I had ever experienced and it was surprisingly pain-free.

On other occasions I have not found it possible to meditate while in the dentist's chair and if I do not feel like meditating at such times, I never force it. I have not been able to identify the reason why mini-meditation sometimes comes naturally during the actual dentistry and at other times is unwanted by me. This may have something to do with the hour of the day, or perhaps it is due to some difference in my physical or emotional state at the time.

Meditation to Counteract Phobias

An interesting use of preparatory meditation has been reported by a behavioral psychologist, Leone Boudreau.[6] A college student who had come for treatment complained of a host of incapacitating fears. He feared enclosed places, elevators, 'being alone', and examinations. He was so frightened by these situations, in fact, that he had been attempting to avoid them at all costs since the age of thirteen. This of course hampered him considerably on many levels. In addition, the physical symptoms of anxiety which he experienced during his panic attacks contributed to a strong fear of becoming 'mentally ill'.

This student was first treated by 'systematic desensitization', the therapy in which the patient is instructed in methods of deep relaxation such as progressive (muscle) relaxation, or visualizing a calm, peaceful scene. The situations that he fears are then introduced to him, one by one (usually in verbal terms) in manageable steps. Only when he is finally able to remain calm and relaxed throughout the presentation of one step is he allowed to proceed to the next more anxiety-provoking visualization, until finally he can remain calm even when visualizing the most intense of images involving his most feared situation.

This method is frequently effective in reducing phobias which hang on even after the original emotional cause has been removed. In the case of this particular student, however, although both muscle relaxation and 'calm scenes' were used for systematic desensitization, the treatment had no effect on his particular phobias.

His therapist then introduced him to an even more stringent form of treatment called 'mass desensitization', where the patient is instructed to practice his desensitization sessions for three hours continuously on three consecutive days. Although sometimes this intensive approach works when a simple, milder method has failed, this student continued to show no improvement in his severe symptoms.

At this point the student happened to mention that he had once learned meditation and occasionally practiced it. Feeling that there was nothing to lose by trying an experiment, the therapist suggested that each day the student imagine vividly that he was in one of the situations that particularly frightened him. As soon as he had imagined his phobic scene clearly, he was to follow these imaginings immediately by one half-hour of meditation. He was also instructed that should he actually find himself in one of his fear-provoking situations, he was immediately to stop whatever he was doing and meditate for a half-hour.

The student cooperated with this plan and the results were surprising. Unlike the other techniques for desensitization, meditation was almost immediately effective. Shortly after he began to use meditation to deal with his fears the patient showed marked improvement. Within one month his need to avoid enclosed places, being alone, and elevators, had all but disappeared. What is more, since his tension level had decreased when he was in these situations, he now no longer experienced his abnormal physical sensations and this reassured him as to his physical and mental state.

This promising result suggests that meditation may be useful in treating phobias and other similar conditions.

Meditating Athletes

Probably the most widely publicized use of meditation for strategic purposes has been for athletics. A number of athletes report that they use meditation to prepare for athletic contests. It seems worth investigating what elements of meditation make it particularly useful for people engaged in sports.

Meditation, as we have seen, tends to reduce anxiety levels, making the meditator calmer, less worried and more quietly self-confident – obviously useful attributes for an athlete who is about to enter a contest. Relaxation and ease of mind can be helpful in almost any undertaking, but in sports it is important that the person not be so relaxed that he stops caring whether or not he wins the contest, a point which will be discussed later.

A student of mine at Princeton, Andy Rimol, became interested in this subject. Captain of the university's basketball team, he claimed that meditating had greatly improved his game. According to his report, after he started meditating with TM in his sophomore year, his stamina increased markedly and he was easily able to undertake extra sessions in basketball on the same day without feeling fatigue. He also reported that his coordination in the game improved.

Because he was so personally impressed by the effects of meditation on his athletic prowess, Rimol decided to conduct a research study in our laboratory to measure the perceptual-motor hand–eye coordination of meditators and non-meditators by comparing their performances. He also planned to compare two different groups of meditators, those who would be allowed to meditate just before the perceptual-motor task and those who would not.

Blasdall's Star Tracers

Before Rimol commenced his study, however, another researcher, Blasdall, had compared the performance of regular TM meditators with that of non-meditators on the Mirror Star Tracing Task, a rather difficult and sometimes quite frustrating puzzle-like test where the subject is handed a pencil and asked to trace a design of a star by looking at it in the mirror only.[7] This means, in effect, making your hand move backward, mirror-image fashion. Before being asked to perform this task, the meditators meditated for twenty minutes while the non-meditators simply rested for twenty minutes with their eyes closed. This way both groups were in a rested state when they undertook the Star Tracing Task. As the experimenter had predicted, the meditators performed significantly better in this task than the non-meditators.

Although this was certainly a promising start, Blasdall's study had left open certain questions. For example, how do we know that the meditators would not have done better than the non-meditators in the Star Tracing Task if they had just walked into the experimental laboratory 'cold', without being allowed to meditate first? In other words, maybe it is possible that people who have been meditating for a long time simply have better coordination – perhaps the immediate meditation before the task had absolutely nothing to do with Blasdall's results. Obviously this question is important when considering the value of a strategic use of meditation for athletics.

Rimol's Labyrinth Players

Rimol reasoned that meditation might have both long-term and immediate effects on perceptual-motor performances.[8] Based on his own experiences and those of other athletes whom he knew, he felt that regular meditation did improve coordination skills in general, but his own experience had taught him that meditating prior to an important basketball game also helped him do better in that specific game than if he had neglected to meditate beforehand. The challenge was to design an experiment which would test both these possibilities at once.

He chose three groups of male college students as the subjects in his experiment. The first two groups included students who had been practicing TM regularly for five months or more before the study started. The third group had never practiced TM or any other kind of meditation.

To measure the subjects' motor skills, Rimol chose to use a rather demanding game – the 'labyrinth game'. It consists of a movable board fastened in place in a box. Two controlling band dials on either side of the box can manipulate the board so it tilts forward, backward, or toward either side, and the player is allowed to use both bands at once to tilt the board. The board has a numbered path with sixty holes scattered along it, the goal of the game being to get a round metal ball from the start (hole one) to the finish (hole sixty). The score is the number by the hole where the ball finally falls in. What makes the game difficult is that even the smallest error results in the ball falling into one of the holes. Needless to say, all subjects were carefully screened beforehand to make sure they had never played this game before – practice gives a player a distinct advantage.

All Rimol's subjects were given a five-minute practice session and then were asked to try to make 'as high a score as possible'. After this, each group underwent a specific activity for twenty minutes. Half the meditators were asked to lie down on the couch and rest with their eyes closed but not to meditate, the other half were asked to sit and meditate. The non-meditators were also asked to lie on the couch and rest with their eyes closed for twenty minutes. After the twenty minutes were up, all subjects were given another formal 'test' in which they once again tried to do their best.

The first question which interested Rimol was whether or not meditators would do better than non-meditators in the pre-trial before any of the subjects had either rested or meditated. Would they show any long-term effects of meditation on their motor skills?

The results were clear-cut on this question. Right from the start, the meditators did score significantly higher on this unfamiliar perceptual-motor task than did the non-meditators. As a group they were superior in their coordination as measured by this particular task. The next question was whether meditators who had been allowed to meditate between the first and second tests would show more improvement from first to second than meditators who had not meditated between taking the two tests but had only rested, or than the non-meditating 'control' group. Again, the results were clear.

All three groups of subjects naturally improved somewhat on the second testing. This was to be expected since playing at any game for a while helps one improve through practice. The most interesting finding, however, was that the meditators who had meditated between the two tests did significantly better on the second test than either the meditators who had simply rested or the non-meditators. In fact, the meditators who had not been allowed to meditate between the two trials did not improve on their final test anymore than the non-meditators had. There appeared to be an immediate short-term effect of meditation on this perceptual-motor task. This suggested that the strategic use of meditation directly before the task in hand may be particularly important to persons engaged in special skills.

This idea does not, however, appear to be supported by a recent study of the effects of meditation on shooting performance.[9] While a group of elite shooters did significantly better in their overall performance in competition after they had received training in meditation, they did not improve further than this using special meditation sessions just before a shooting match. My recommendation, therefore, based on present evidence, is that you should experiment with your own performance on tasks requiring motor skills. If meditating just before these tasks improves your performance, then you may want to use meditation strategically for this purpose.

Unanswered Questions

Although meditation seems to affect perceptual and motor performance, there are some important things which we don't yet know about this process. How many weeks or months, for instance, must a person have been practicing meditation before its influence can be seen on his motor skills? Can someone who has been meditating for two weeks do as well in an athletic contest as someone who has been meditating for three months? Or as a person who has been meditating for a year?

We also don't know whether the immediate influence of a meditation session on motor performance depends upon the subject being an experienced meditator. Is it possible for a subject who has never meditated before in his life to get the same benefit out of a meditation experience if he is taught how to do it 'right on the spot,' as someone who is experienced at meditating and has been doing it for some time? My experience in teaching a class how to meditate just before their final exam suggests that prior knowledge of meditation may not be necessary to obtain good short-term results, and a study by psychologists Daniel Goleman and Gary Schwartz at Harvard showed that even novices who had learned to meditate for the first time that day in the lab were less anxious after a stress-inducing film and recovered more quickly from it than non-meditators, although they did not show as marked a recovery as did experienced meditators.[10]

One final question important for athletes who might want to learn meditation is: how long do the benefits of a meditation session last? In other words, if meditation improves motor skills and perception, how long does that improvement hold up? When does it begin to dwindle and taper off? In practical terms, how far ahead of a game should an athlete meditate to get the best results from his meditation?

Rimol thinks this varies with the individual. He personally found that if he meditated just before a game, he tended to feel so 'mellow' that he no longer cared much about defeating the other team; he just felt 'warm and friendly' toward them. For this reason, he made it a practice to meditate an hour and a half ahead of time when he planned to be in a game. This enabled him to increase his efficiency while at the same time letting a competitive state of mind build-up in him again. On the other hand, Bill Walton, former basketball star of the Portland Trail Blazers, found that he was more energetic and aggressive if he meditated immediately before the commencement of a game.

Obviously, such individual differences must be determined by trial and error and athletes discover for themselves just what timing they should follow for their strategic meditations if they are going to use this technique to obtain the best results.

These various strands of information suggest that the strategic use of meditation in the field of athletics is well worth investigating. Despite the need for more research, the results are sufficiently promising for individual athletes to feel secure in trying out for themselves the manner in which they may use meditation for this purpose. This advice applies in general to all the other strategic uses of meditation as well. Used with discretion and good common sense, the possibilities are wide for applying meditation to many specific situations in one's life.

Extra Meditation

Another important use of meditation does not depend upon mini-meditations or preparatory meditations, but relies upon increasing the number of meditations in any one day.

Meditations per day can be increased effectively under certain circumstances, provided the person proceeds with caution. The TM organization, for instance, advises TM initiates that they can meditate as often as they wish under two sets of circumstances – if they are sick or confined to bed or if the meditator is a pregnant woman. Clearly, they recognize the strategic value of extra meditation under particular circumstances. I would like, however, to expand on the list of situations for which it may be appropriate.

Meditating When Ill

Meditating as often as one wishes when ill can be very useful for certain persons. A friend of mine to whom I had taught CSM about a year previously had to have abdominal surgery. When she was lying in the hospital immediately following this surgery and under heavy medication for pain, she remembered being instructed that when ill, she could meditate as often as possible. Actually, she had not been meditating regularly before she went into hospital, but suddenly felt strongly that she wanted to do so, and proceeded to meditate about five or six times a day during her hospital stay.

The meditation had a 'startling' effect on her. A pain-killer was unnecessary after her first few post-operative hours and she required no sleeping medication while in hospital. Her doctor reported that her progress was so rapid that he wanted to know what special magic she had used to accomplish this. She told him that she had been meditating, and although initially skeptical, he finally commented that he was so impressed by the way she had responded to the surgery and particularly by her lack of need for sedative drugs that 'Whatever you're doing, it must be right.'

But what about the advice given to TMers that when sick they add extra meditations only if they are so ill that they cannot get out of bed? No doubt this advice serves the purpose of preventing over-meditation, but the distinction between being bedridden or not is to me an arbitrary one. The belief that extra meditations are indicated in one case and not in the other is certainly not supported by scientific research. I know of several instances where patients who were ill but not confined to bed added meditations to their day to cope with their illness and said that the results were excellent. A colleague tells me, for example, that extra meditation sessions helped him recover from a recent severe virus much more quickly than usual, although he never went to bed during the entire time.

Despite such glowing reports, people's impressions that meditation has helped them cope better with an illness are not scientific proof that meditation actually does help recovery. For this, a controlled study would have to be carried out with one group of persons having a known illness being referred for meditation training and another group of persons with the same illness not being trained to meditate. Records could then be kept as to which group recovered more rapidly. The only carefully controlled research in these areas to date has studied hypertensive and asthmatic patients. This will be discussed later, when we come to consider the relationship of meditation to stress-related illness.

A discussion of the strategic use of meditation when ill is not complete without making note of the fact that not everybody is able to meditate when ill. Certainly not all people can meditate during all types of illness. I have had several people report that when they had flu they were so weak that even though bedridden, they could not summon up the energy to meditate. If they tried to meditate it did not take, no matter how long they stayed with it. Eventually they had to abandon these attempts until they felt better. Interestingly, Yoga scriptures advise against meditating when one has fever, quite possibly a reflection of long experience with some of these difficulties.

The inability of some people to meditate when weak or feverish highlights the fact that although meditation is considered a relaxation technique, a person must possess a certain minimum amount of available energy to meditate. I have at times felt that I was, at a particular moment, too exhausted to meditate. I was so tired that the kind of alert–relaxed involvement that meditation requires was not possible. Rather than being comforting, it would become unpleasant and a strain at such a time.

As in so many other things concerning meditation, this is a highly individual matter. Some people report that meditation acts as a stimulant at times when they feel exhausted. I suspect that some of us may tend to use meditation as a calming agent while others may use it more as an energizer. This is not to say that we have a choice over the way we use meditation, but rather that our systems may have different requirements and thus make different use of this highly versatile technique.

Meditation During Prolonged Emotional Stress

Those of us who teach CSM find that additional meditations may be necessary when a person is under a special emotional stress such as the illness of a loved one, a financial crisis, or other conditions where a continued strain most be faced. Unlike the occasional use of mini-meditations to cope with a specific situation, this involves the scheduling of extra regular meditations over a period of time. Obviously this is a more serious matter than an occasional mini-meditation and should be handled with careful attention to its effects. Properly used, however, it can be extremely effective.

A patient of mine, who is a CSM meditator, faced a family emergency when his wife was rushed to hospital acutely ill. During her stay there, he put in many days of emotional strain waiting for her recovery. At the same time the pressure of serious decisions about the family's future and the total care of the children was weighing on him. During this period he found himself spontaneously meditating five or six times daily. Without this intense program of meditation, he says, he doesn't think he could have endured the strain of this crisis. With it he managed well, made sound decisions, and was able to plan constructively for his wife's eventual return home and subsequent recovery.

In teaching CSM, we have noticed that when a person is in a state of continuing stress, his first meditation of the day may seem almost futile, a mere drop in the ocean so to speak. Under such conditions these people report that this first meditation has merely scratched the surface, seeming only to skim off the uppermost layer of tension but no more. If the meditator then waits the regular half-day before meditating again, so much tension may have accumulated that he may experience the same thing with the second meditation; it too will seem to skim the surface.

If, however, the first meditation of the day is followed only one hour or an hour and a half later by another full meditation, this second meditation may have quite a different effect. It is as if the first meditation prepares the ground, and this closely spaced second one is then able to 'take hold' and may have a deep therapeutic effect. The final and third meditation, usually coming in the late afternoon or in the evening, will also be more effective under these circumstances. In this way the entire day may be affected because of the double morning meditations.

At times I have advised patients under unusually severe stress to do two 'double meditations' (that is, a pair of meditations separated by only an hour or an hour and a half) twice a day. These four strategically placed meditations each day during a time of intense emotional stress often work extremely well, as in the case of the man described above.

It is important, however, to watch how such extra meditations are affecting one's behavior, whether or not they lower alertness or result in any undue amount of tension-release. If so, they should be reduced. It is also important to discontinue the extra meditations once the emotional crisis is resolved, so that over-meditating will not develop into a habit.

Alternating Meditation with Rest

A striking instance of the use of extra meditations to handle an emotional crisis was reported to me by a psychologist colleague. He found himself in a severe panic because of certain distressing incidents which, while obviously upsetting, could have been better tolerated at another time in his life. He was experiencing sinking sensations, loss of identity, loss of control, and an eerie sense of unreality. These extreme reactions probably had, at least in part, some physical basis, but this was not clear at the time and it was obvious that some extreme measure had to be employed to break the rising panic.

Since he ordinarily meditates regularly and is familiar with the strategic use of meditation, he decided to try meditation to quell his panic. He first withdrew from all stimulation into a darkened room and meditated for twenty minutes, after which he lay down on his bed, half-sleeping and half-resting. He set his alarm clock, roused himself once more after an hour, and meditated again for twenty minutes. He continued to do this the entire day, remaining in a quiet, darkened room and alternating meditation with complete rest on an hourly schedule. As the day proceeded, he experienced immense relief as though he were being 'pulled out of a black pit' and as though 'pieces of a picture puzzle were being put together'.

Although this meditation strategy did not cure his basic condition – which involved some hormonal changes of middle age which later required medical treatment, change of diet and some psychotherapy – it did serve as an excellent emergency measure. In effect, it reversed what was a potentially dangerous psychiatric condition so well that it is a method worth considering under extreme conditions. Clearly, if such a radical measure is used, it should be discontinued once the severe condition is brought under control.

Meditation Under Catastrophic Circumstances

We do not yet know how people use meditation when under extreme duress involving a threat to their lives – as, for instance, when stranded in a lifeboat at sea, imprisoned in enemy territory, or facing other catastrophic situations. Systematic reports of such uses of meditation have not as yet been collected. It seems very much to the point, however, to consider some of the reports of persons who have used other relaxation techniques which, in effect, evoke a meditative mood, in order to comfort themselves and increase their strength and endurance under extreme conditions.

Several reports from autogenic trainees who used this technique to handle various catastrophes are reported in scientific journals and books. All these people were caught in situations where self-protection and survival assumed paramount importance. For all of them, the use of the relaxation technique had an important effect on both their minds and bodies and helped to support them so that they did not go to pieces. Instead, their egos were often strengthened under adverse conditions.

These reports range from isolated instances of persons who found their relaxation training helpful when they were being menaced by the Gestapo, to groups of soldiers in a POW camp where no medical assistance was available, to soldiers facing dangerous battle situations, and political prisoners in solitary confinement or during interrogation.

A particularly impressive example of the strategic use of a relaxation technique is the story of a middle-aged German-Jewish woman who happened to have learned autogenic training when she was a young girl in Berlin during World War II.[11] While hiding from the Gestapo, this woman at one point lived illegally for two and a half years, hiding wherever she could in order not to allow the authorities to know that she still existed. She was continually in immense danger, and suffered much anxiety and degradation.

During the air raids, when she had to stay alone upstairs in an apartment, often in complete darkness, she experienced her most difficult ordeals. It was then that her relaxation training proved to be crucial. 'How else would I have been able to stand this recurring terror?' she writes. 'I was not only afraid of being hit by a bomb, but even more so of the possibility I would get hurt and thus endanger the people who gave me shelter to save me from the Gestapo. As soon as the air sirens started, terrible feelings of anxiety developed. However, with the (relaxation) exercises, I could reduce these feelings to a relatively tolerable level, and somehow keep them away from me. I managed to remain calm and almost without fear until the attack was right close by.' At this point her relaxation training did not help anymore, but as the attack moved further on, 'I quickly regained my inner calm with the exercises . . .' This woman was convinced that it was in part due to her relaxation training that she managed to get through those years of terror and that she finally emerged with relatively little psychological damage. An exhaustive depletion of vitality did not occur, she said, because she was able to compensate for the repeated severe buildup of tension by inducing the comforting relaxation.

It is particularly interesting to note the limitations of relaxation training in this woman's account. The point at which its effectiveness seemed to break down was in the face of imminent threat to life – at the height of the bombings. In these moments the self-protective impulse to flee (which of course could not be acted upon under these circumstances) took over and the survival instinct became overwhelming.

What is also interesting is the fact that resuming the relaxation exercises again as the bombing receded helped this woman to handle her excess anxiety in such a way that restabilization could occur. As she indicated, the use of the relaxation exercises somehow prevented deeply disorganizing effects of these repeated traumas on her personality. This is an impressive account and there is certainly no reason to suppose that people well trained in meditation, which is similar in many respects to autogenic training, could not achieve much the same results if they entered a meditative state under similar circumstances.

Relaxation Under Physical Stress

In another interesting account of the strategic use of relaxation, a physician, H. Lindemann, has reported the manner in which he used his relaxation training while he was alone for seventy-two days in a one-man kayak-type boat crossing the Atlantic.[12] He would use frequent short periods of autogenic relaxation (similar to mini-meditations) to economize his energy, constantly promoting recuperation from stress. He claims that this helped him cope decisively with problems of fatigue and sleep while on this grueling journey.

Relaxation exercises coupled with self-suggestions were also effective in reducing his periodically recurring hallucinations. From time to time he would 'see' such things as a food store inviting him to buy food and then would experience a sudden powerful urge to jump overboard in order to get to the store. By quietly entering the relaxed state and repeating to himself that these hallucinations were not real, he was able to regain his equilibrium. His training also helped him overcome depressive states and desperate situations such as he faced after capsizing, by combining the relaxation with repeated suggestions to himself such as 'I am going to make it . . . my muscles can hold on, I am going to make it.'

Meditation and Self-Suggestion

Autogenic training is so structured that it can, when necessary, incorporate into its procedures various specific self-suggestions if these seem advisable. This feature seems to lend itself particularly well to dealing with emergencies such as those described by Lindemann.

We do not yet know if a meditative state can be put to a similar use. It seems entirely plausible, however, that a phrase such as 'I am going to make it' could be substituted for the repetition of a mantra. When repeated under emergency conditions it might fit into the rhythmic pattern already familiar to the meditator, established by long practice of repeating the mantra, and in all probability should be experienced as both comforting and reassuring. It is not inconceivable therefore that self-suggestion could be incorporated, when strategically necessary, into an existing meditative framework. At least, exploration of such a possibility should be undertaken.

As the examples in this chapter illustrate, one of the most important factors about meditation which makes it of potential use in stressful circumstances is the fact that it does not depend upon any outside person or force. It therefore seems particularly useful for people who face situations where they may be physically or emotionally at the mercy of some uncontrollable external threat. Using meditation strategically under such conditions could not only be an important contribution – it might be a lifesaving one.

Chapter 9

SOME INTRIGUING RHYTHMS

Some teachers of meditation suggest meditating at specific times of day in order to get the greatest benefits from this practice. TM advises morning and late afternoon meditation and devout Hindus meditate at sunrise and sunset. To find out what scientific evidence there is that meditating at one time of day is more effective than meditating at another, we need to look at how our body rhythms work.

Bodily Cycles

Human beings, like all other animals, and like the primordial oceans from which we sprang, are subject to cyclic highs and lows, so that we are literally a different person from one hour to another. On thousands of scores, we all change physically and emotionally in response to daily, monthly and yearly rhythms. We are aware of some of these rhythms – as when our hunger increases, our energy ebbs or flows, or we feel drowsy or wakeful – but we may be totally unaware of other changes in us, such as body temperature, which also take place in a cyclical manner.

The body temperature of human beings regularly varies from a low point in the small hours of the morning (whether we are awake or asleep) to a high point in the afternoon. This occurs in every person who is active by day and sleeps by night, and is such a persistent rhythm that even enforced inactivity over a long period of time can't alter it except under very unusual conditions – and then only partially.[1] Despite a regular daily fluctuation of one to two degrees in the body's temperature, however, we ordinarily don't recognize this change while it is occurring. In the same way, liver and kidney functions, brain chemistry, blood sugar levels, blood hormone levels and a host of other bodily processes differ markedly from hour to hour. Even sensitivity to taste and smell is different in the morning from the way it is in the evening, as are the effectiveness of our memory, ability to learn and capacity to make fine discriminations. Some of these changes may determine our resistance to stress at different times of the day. Pain tolerance can vary according to the hour, and allergies may follow a timetable, peaking at one time of the day and almost disappearing at another.

Daily highs and lows in adrenal hormone levels are closely related to the way we cope with stress. As Gay Luce points out, a certain dose of amphetamines can kill 77.6 percent of a group of animals when given at one time of day but the identical dose will kill only 6 percent of these animals when administered at another time of day.[2] The animals' times of high resistance to these drugs correspond to the level of adrenal hormones in their blood. Similarly, a medicine administered to a person at one hour of the day may have a different effect from the same medicine administered at another hour, a fact now beginning to be recognized by physicians.

Morning Versus Evening Meditation

Since we are not the same person from hour to hour, is meditation a different experience for us, depending upon what time of day we meditate?

While there is not an answer to this question based on experimentation, many people report sharp differences between their morning and evening meditations. One graphic example of this was my late husband's morning meditations. He described them as being like a vibrant muscle massage with a thousand invisible and gentle fingers kneading his whole body in rhythmic fashion, from his toes to his head. This was both invigorating and relaxing for him – a welcome waking-up-to-the-day. In the late afternoon, however, the very idea of these massage-like pulsations was unpleasant. His meditations at that time would take on a soothing, quiet, siesta-like quality, serving to waft him away gently from the cares and pressures of the day. During his second meditation, his sensation was at a minimum for him and mental quiet and drifting were his primary experience. Similarly, a colleague reports that his morning meditations tend to involve an awareness of the practical matters which must be handled in the day ahead, while his later meditations are more self-pleasing 'fantasy-trips'.

Meditation 'Readiness'

Most people experience certain moments during the day when they feel like meditating and other moments when they feel resistant to the idea. If they force themselves to meditate when they're not in the mood (something which may be hard to do) they report that their meditation tends to be superficial, restless or 'not really meditative'. Then they are likely to experience many organized thoughts and be less aware of their mantra or other meditational device. They may find themselves making plans or engaging in other typical 'unmeditative' preoccupations. They also often feel as though they are on the surface of the experience. Oddly enough, they may be relaxed following such a meditative session, despite its seeming superficiality. Because of this, an argument might be made for forcing ourselves to meditate at some regular hour each day, no matter how we feel about doing it.

Unfortunately, there is no easy answer to the question of whether or not we should be highly disciplined about meditation. Although making a routine of any habit is an advantage, forcing ourselves to meditate 'against the grain' can lead to just the kind of effortful striving that meditation is designed to counteract. The question seems to be whether we can hope to gain freedom by donning chains – even if the chains are said to be for our own good. I have talked with a number of people for whom meditation actually became stressful because it was approached in too rigid a manner. For the kind of person who makes everything into a chore, meditation can fit into this mold too, and this is clearly a disadvantage. If a basically permissive form of meditation is made into a virtual enslavement, it's not surprising that the meditator often escapes the whole process by abandoning it.

One of the main tasks when teaching meditation is to help a new meditator assume an easy, relaxed attitude toward the meditation process itself – not simple to accomplish of course if she happens to have a compulsive personality. As a general rule, I advise new meditators that it's better to skip a meditation altogether on a given day than to force it. It's the person who understands her own rhythms and respect her own wish not to meditate, as well as to do so, who will be most likely to stay with the practice and use it as a genuine growth experience.

One of my successfully meditating trainees put it very well: 'I've never really pushed myself into a meditation,' she said. 'I've never forced myself to do it when I had a feeling of "Ugh, it's the last thing I want," and for that reason, I've always come out of meditation smiling and with a lovely feeling of being refreshed and peaceful.' Some people, however, will postpone meditation indefinitely because they 'aren't in the right mood yet'. This is a different matter. I will discuss such blocks to continuing meditation later when we come to consider the problems which may arise in adjusting to the changes meditators find in themselves.

Yoga Scheduling

The fact that we feel more receptive to the idea of meditation at certain moments of the day may be obvious, but the exact pattern that meditation-readiness follows (if indeed there is a pattern) is not clear. The ancient discipline of Swar Yoga (literally, 'unification through breath') proposes a unique method for identifying recurring periods in the day when meditation is said to be suitable. According to Yogic belief, the 'correct' times for meditation correspond to those moments of the day when a person finds himself breathing predominantly through his left nostril. This can be easily ascertained by blocking each nostril in turn with the pressure of a finger. The nasal passage through which the air passes more freely is the dominant nostril.

When one nostril is dominant, the other is recessive, with a switch in nostril dominance generally taking place (in most people) at the end of every hour or hour and a half. The yogi masters believe that the left nostril concentrates energy in the right side of the body and brain, causing the person to be more passive, emotional, introverted and feminine in outlook.[3] According to Swar Yoga texts, meditation should be practiced only when the left nostril is dominant (that is, when the right side of the body and brain are considered to be active). If one tries to meditate when the right nostril dominates, the meditation session is said to be relatively ineffective and the person to feel restless and have many distracting thoughts.

This Yogic belief relates to what neurophysiologists are presently learning about the functions of the two cerebral hemispheres of the brain. The left hemisphere (controlling the right side of the body) has been found to control verbal activity and logical, sequential, practical thinking; while the right hemisphere (controlling the left side of the body) has been found to control space perception, musical awareness and the intuitive, holistic types of thought which characterize meditative and artistic states of mind.

Yoga theory concerning variations in meditation readiness with nostril dominance has points of correspondence with the reports of those meditators who contend that they find themselves quite unable to meditate at certain times of day but ripe for it at others. As yet no experiments have been carried out to test this Yogic belief. It would certainly be simple to have a group of meditators check nostril dominance before meditating and then record their 'depth' of meditation. If there is truth in the Yogic belief, it might have considerable practical application, since if nostril dominance happens to be 'incorrect' for meditation at a particular time, it can be voluntarily switched by lying down for several minutes on the opposite side of the body from the nostril one wishes to clear. Gravity draining the sinuses produces the desired nostril dominance.

The Basic Ultradian Rhythm

There is evidence from a different field which may supply additional clues about meditation-readiness. Scientists concerned with the rhythmical nature of biological processes have identified a short, ninety- to 100-minute cycle of rest and activity which seems to repeat itself throughout the day and which conceivably may relate to meditation-readiness (although this possibility has not been studied). This cycle is called the ultradian rhythm, from the Latin words *ultra*, meaning 'beyond', and *dies*, meaning 'day'. The word literally means 'outside the limits of our daily rhythm', in this case signifying a shorter time-span than the twenty-four-hour day.

It was not until the 1950s that the scientific world learned about such rest/activity cycles. At this time it was discovered that one phase of sleep was anything but 'peaceful' in the ordinary sense of the word, for it was accompanied by physiological changes indicating a very excited state. One of these was a rapid, spasmodic darting of the eyes beneath the lids which occurred in bursts during this time, giving the state its name of Rapid Eye Movement (REM) sleep. REM sleep, which turned out to be the time during which most of our elaborate vivid dreaming occurs, was found to recur throughout the night roughly every ninety to 100 minutes in adults and every sixty minutes in infants.

No sooner had this sleep cycle been discovered then Dr Nathaniel Kleitman, co-discoverer of REM sleep, noticed that human infants showed a regular sixty-minute rest/activity cycle during wakefulness as well.[4] On the basis of this he speculated that rhythmic changes in level of activation during the day may occur in a similar manner in adults. Perhaps, he reasoned, rest and activity regularly alternate in persons of all ages, 'around the clock'.

Exploring a Daydream Cycle

In 1966, my husband Harmon and I were involved in research on the functions of REM sleep. Working with theories involving the need for periodic stimulation of the brain during sleep, we were impressed by the unceasing alternation of quiet and active states during the night. Could it be that the same kind of alternation between restful and active states continues throughout the day (as Kleitman suggested) but that during the day the state of inner stimulation (we called it 'endogenous afferentation')[5] manifests itself in periods of heightened daydreaming?

To find out about this we conducted a preliminary study with a colleague cooperative enough to carry around a small portable tape-recorder strapped to his shoulders for fifteen hours as he went about his daily chores in a vacation cabin. During this time he whispered into the microphone every thought, no matter how seemingly trivial, that he could identify as passing through his mind that day. The only time he ceased talking was when he slept.

This pilot study resulted in a sketchy but consistent pattern. We saw that our colleague had shown proof of daydreaming roughly every ninety to 100 minutes during the day and that these daydreaming sessions seemed to alternate with periods of outwardly directed thinking of a more practical, logical nature.

Unknown to us at the time, however, this experiment was to be repeated with more sophisticated research methods several years later by other researchers. But prior to this, several lines of research had been slowly converging, all of them pointing to the existence of other kinds of daytime rhythms which also have a period of about ninety to 100 minutes.

The Oral Activity Cycle

In 1922, a Japanese scientist by the name of Toni Wada had conducted an unusual experiment. In order to study the timing of stomach contractions (supposed to be indications of hunger or readiness to eat) she had confined a group of subjects to bed for a whole day to measure these contractions. This she did by inserting recording balloons into their stomachs, which were then inflated slightly with air. In this way she was able to measure the quantity of air pressure within the balloon. Since the more forcefully the stomach contracted, the more it pushed air out of the balloon, she could obtain indications of stomach muscle activity. Recording these contractions, Wada found that they recurred with considerable regularity every ninety to 100 minutes throughout the day.[6]

Forty years later, two psychoanalysts involved in sleep research uncovered some evidence consistent with Wada's. Drs Stanley Friedman and Charles Fisher of Mount Sinai Hospital in New York City became interested in the question of whether or not 'oral' (mouth-oriented) activities might recur in roughly the same manner during the day as REM periods do during the night.[7] According to psychoanalytic theory night dreaming often serves to discharge 'oral' drives. If peaks of night-time dreaming recur every ninety minutes, they reasoned, perhaps this periodic 'drive discharge' might occur with the same regularity in the daytime.

To test this possibility, Friedman and Fisher decided to investigate people's tendencies to put things in their mouths. Would this tendency show a regular rise and fall throughout the day similar to the rise and fall Wada had found for stomach contractions? If so, would these fluctuations recur on a schedule similar to that of REM periods at night?

To explore this, the experimenters created a comfortable den where each volunteer was asked to spend a number of hours in isolation. The den contained a refrigerator stocked with food, an electric pot with a continually fresh and tempting supply of coffee, and books, magazines and cigarettes. The subjects were allowed to read, write or sketch during this time, but were kept isolated from other distractions and from each other.

Observing the subjects through a one-way mirror, the experimenters were able to record every object each person put into his mouth, every time he did so, and the exact time of day this was done. When these activities were later transferred to a time chart, the researchers saw a distinct pattern emerge.

The intensity of oral (mouth-oriented) activity reached a peak about every ninety-six minutes, at which time there was a much greater tendency for the subjects to reach for food in the refrigerator, take a cigarette, sip coffee, or whatever. This was followed by a gradual subsiding of oral activities until the next spurt of 'orality', which took place about ninety to 100 minutes later. Clearly, 'oral' activities were recurring regularly despite the fact that the subjects themselves were unaware of any such changes in their behavior.

Apparently Friedman and Fisher had identified a fundamental bodily rhythm. Since their experiment, animals have been shown to have a similar periodic waxing and waning of hunger during the day. A group of cats allowed free feeding have shown bursts of eating activity every fifteen to thirty minutes – a waking cycle that exactly corresponds with the typical cat REM cycle of fifteen to thirty minutes.[8] Other researchers have found that brain waves and muscle tone in monkeys recur around the clock in an ultradian rhythm similar to the monkey REM cycle at night.[9]

The Daydream Cycle Revisited

On the basis of the findings of the Mount Sinai group, two sleep researchers, Drs Daniel F. Kripke and David Sonnenschein at the University of California, began to wonder if in man, waking dreams (that is, daydreams) might occur in cycles similar to

REM cycles.[10] To find out, these researchers placed their subjects alone for ten hours in a comfortable room with no clocks, books or other distractions, and every five minutes during this confinement, a whistle was blown as a signal to the subject to write down a brief description of whatever he had been thinking about during the previous five-minute interval. During this experiment electrodes were taped to various parts of the participant's head and near his eyes so that both his brain waves and eye movements could be continuously recorded.

Since the subjects had little else to do under these isolated circumstances, as might be expected they reported a good many fairly extensive daydreams. But they also spent considerable time thinking about problems, looking around and moving around the room, so that two types of thought were fairly recognizable: organized, practical thinking on the one hand and extended reverie states on the other.

Analyzing the results of this experiment, Kripke and Sonnenschein found that daydreaming did indeed follow a ninety- to 100-minute cycle, as they had anticipated it might. At the peak of this cycle the subjects tended to have very emotional, sometimes even bizarre thoughts and images, while at the cycle's low point they thought about everyday problems and tended to make plans for the future, or organized their lives by simply observing their immediate surroundings.

Next the experimenters wondered whether these same ultradian rhythms would exist in a more natural environment. That is essentially the same question we had sought to answer when we asked our colleague to walk around recording his thoughts while engaged in daily activities at his mountain cabin.

Kripke and Sonnenschein conducted the second part of their experiment by asking volunteers to carry small cassette tape-recorders with them as they went about their daily routine. As the subject moved about, a timer connected to his belt activated a buzzer every ten minutes, signaling him to dictate a summary of his thoughts for the previous ten-minute interval.

In a naturalistic study such as this, we wouldn't expect subjects to have intense daydreams as often as under abnormal laboratory isolation conditions, but the researchers found that the ninety- to 100-minute rhythm of daydreams persisted none the less. Apparently, then, this ultradian rhythm is strong enough to continue despite distractions from the environment.

An Ultradian Rhythm for Meditation?

Although the implications of these studies for the scheduling of meditation have not as yet been explored, laboratory experiments to test the possibility that meditation-readiness, like daydreaming, fluctuates in an ultradian rhythm, would not be difficult to conduct. Perhaps, with future experimentation, we may find that the meditative mood, like the reverie state, tends to recur about every ninety minutes. If this proved to be the case, we might then want to ask some further questions.

If a person were to meditate when she happened to be on the outward swing of her ultradian cycle (moving into her period of activity) what would happen? Would this make her more resistant to meditation? Would it reduce the effectiveness of her meditation? Could such mistaken timing make a meditation entirely ineffective in certain instances, or perhaps even cause it to be an unpleasant experience?

In the other direction, we might wonder whether coordinating the timing of a meditation session with maximum inward swing of the ninety-minute cycle – those times when we naturally become ruminative, imaginative and physically quieter – might help us to realize the deepest possibilities of meditation.

While only careful research can answer these questions, in the meantime, observation of large numbers of meditators suggests that perhaps we intuitively observe our ultradian rhythms through our spontaneous choice of times to meditate, without realizing we are doing so. Many of us naturally vary our meditation time on any particular day. We may have been thinking of meditating for a half-hour or so, but it is only at some particular moment that we find ourselves actually making an active effort to do so. Are we perhaps instinctively timing our meditations to coincide with the inward swings of our own ultradian rhythms?

Until experimental answers to these questions are forthcoming, each of us has to discover, by trial and error, our own best hours for meditating each day. This we can do through respecting our feelings of readiness (or unreadiness) to undertake meditation at any particular moment of the day. We should, however, undertake such a self-experiment without, if possible, destroying the routine nature of our meditation. It is still a good plan to establish a regular meditation time for ourselves each day, and then vary it only if we feel strongly, on any particular day, that we're not ready for meditation at that time. This way both regularity and flexibility will be ensured.

There is obvious value in making meditation as much of a set routine as is genuinely comfortable. Linking times for meditation with some already established habit such as getting out of bed in the morning or traveling to or from work on a bus or subway, or connecting it with any other regular event in our lives, can be a help in doing so, since this increases the regularity of our meditation in an easy, natural manner.

Despite the desirability of routine, however, evidence points to the fact that such strategies are really useful in the long run only if the regular time of day selected genuinely feels comfortable. It is logical that meditation, which leads us back to ourselves, should be conducted in harmony with the tidal ebb and flow of our energy and moods. This way it can remain a gentle process, an interlude when we are truly kind to ourselves.

Influences of External Rhythms

The relationship of our internal rhythms to meditation is one side of this question, but there is another side that is equally intriguing: the effects of external rhythms upon this practice. Do changes in the earth's atmosphere or in the cosmos perhaps make certain clock times (that is, actual hours of the day) more appropriate for meditating than others?

Recent research shows that our inner production schedule is closely coordinated with the wider rhythms of nature that determine sleep and activity each day. The light/darkness cycle, the lunar cycle, changes in electromagnetic fields and other geophysical events – all these continually interact with our own in-built rhythms, forming part of a coordinated, oscillating system.

Solar Rhythms

As we increasingly recognize man's interrelationship with his environment, it is clear that the human being is intricately coordinated with the rhythms of the universe. Sunlight, for instance, a fundamental influence in our lives, appears to synchronize us with the rhythms of our planet.

The influence of the moon is also important but it seems to have a greater daily influence on nocturnal animals than it does on humans, who are diurnal (that is, active during daylight hours).

As Michael Gauquelin has pointed out, life on earth is particularly affected by the sun because the earth resides in a very real sense within the 'atmosphere' of the sun.[11] Not only can solar eruptions ('sunspots') interfere with electricity on earth, causing fade-outs in radio reception and accounting for intense geomagnetic storms that affect our weather conditions, but living things as widely different as fiddler crabs, chick embryos within eggs, and dry grain seeds have been shown to respond with incredible precision to the presence or absence of sunlight and to its varying intensities.[12]

While the normal response of plants and animals to the daily arrival of the sun has been impressively documented, one need only sit quietly in a garden in the early morning hours to experience the transformation that accompanies the approach of the sun. The isolated chirpings and warbles of the first birds, the intermittent moaning of the mourning doves, the distant whirr of the grasshoppers, gradually swell in pre-dawn to an oratorio as the sun approaches the horizon – and when it finally swings into sight, sweeping the land with its rays, the bird sounds triumph, enveloping us. Daytime has brought new birth.

The Sun's Influence on the Body

It is interesting that biometeorology, a branch of science which seeks to explore the influence of cosmic forces upon human and animal life, has documented, among other things, some of the unusual responses of organisms to the daily arrival of the sun. Particularly important from the point of view of considering best hours for meditation may be certain preliminary experiments performed in 1938 by a Japanese physician, Maki Takata, which suggest a little-known relationship between human blood serum and the sun.[13]

Takata, who is renowned for developing a test for the flocculation of the blood (this is the blood's propensity to curdle into small fluffy lumps when a chemical reagent is added to it in a test tube) found by chance that the 'blood flocculation indexes' of large numbers of Japanese people rose at times when sunspots were directing a concentrated beam of waves and particles toward the earth. The meaning of these changes in the blood serum with exposure to sunlight could not be determined, but Takata later demonstrated that this flocculation index regularly reaches an extreme low point in the early pre-waking hours of the morning. It then shows a sudden dramatic rise beginning about twenty minutes before sunrise, which continues at a somewhat reduced pace for about a half-hour following sunrise.

Going a step further, Takata then took subjects up in a plane to an extremely high altitude, where the 'atmosphere shield' against solar radiation is much thinner. As he had expected, he found that these subjects' blood flocculation indexes rose sharply as the plane rose into the less shielded atmosphere. With greater exposure to solar radiation, the blood showed more marked changes, supporting the idea that the sun was involved in these changes in a very direct fashion.

Takata's findings underline the importance of the great solar synchronizer in our lives. It is perhaps not surprising, therefore, that through the ages human beings have considered the moments of sunrise and sunset as having powerful, even mysterious properties, and that they have often linked religious practices and meditation with these times of day.

Primitive peoples, naturally rising before dawn, have often greeted the newborn morning sun with special ceremonies and worship. Until very recently, in fact, sunrise and sunset controlled most of humanity's waking life.

Even today, Hindus still awaken in the very early hours of the morning and perform prescribed purifications which include meditation and worship. Failure to meditate in the early morning hours is actually listed as one of the 'fourteen failings', and Sanskrit scriptures refer to pre-dawn as *Brahma Mahoorta* (time of pure consciousness) or *Amrit Bela* (time of the nectar of life).

In similar fashion, Moslems chant morning prayers at day's commencement and pious Jews, rising to pray in a meditation-like state, are instructed to wait until there is 'sunlight in the sky' to begin actual prayer. Sunrise prayer and meditations are also used as special spiritual exercises in Christian, Buddhist and other monasteries.

Down through history the meditative mood, manifested in

rituals, prayers or forms of meditation, has been prescribed to coincide with the rising and the setting sun. Countless observers in diverse areas of the world have found sunrise a time when they are moved to a sense of profound wonder and meaning. To a lesser degree sunset has been considered an hour for contemplation, meditation, prayer or solemn ritual. The rise and decline of the sun, it seems, deeply affects our life and our moods.

Does this mean that meditation is most beneficial if it is coordinated with the natural cycles of light and darkness?

The belief that it should be probably cannot be separated from the total view of life subscribed to by people who consider all activities in relation to the natural cycles of earth, sun, moon and universe. This point of view is particularly true of Yogic philosophy, where man, who is seen as part of the cosmos, is said to reflect the whole of which he is a part, and thus to contain within himself the pulsations and rhythms of the entire universe.

From this follows the concept that ill-health and emotional distress result from disharmony between man and the natural forces about him. When man is out of tune with the cosmos, he is thought to be like a fine instrument uncoordinated with other instruments in an orchestra. The notes he strikes are discordant, and the world appears to him as harsh and threatening because he is now paced differently from it, having broken contact with his roots.

In the Yogic system, as in many other spiritual disciplines, meditation is viewed as a means of re-establishing the unity between man and nature. It is thought to bring the individual pulsations of the human being into synchrony with the larger pulsations of the cosmos. For this reason Yogic tradition prescribes meditation at those times of day when the meditator can best synchronize his or her daily life with these wider cycles.

It may be that there is wisdom in such a concept, but unfortunately it has not as yet been tested in the laboratory. Folk beliefs, even if they are repeated the world over, are not prone to attract research interest or funding and may never obtain scientific verification for reasons that have little to do with their potential value. Hopefully this attitude will change with respect to the meditative traditions, so that controlled experimentation can contribute to our understanding of whether pervasive cosmic influences such as the solar and lunar cycles affect meditation-readiness.

Instructions to Meditate Morning and Afternoon

These ancient cosmologies are the source of the instructions given in certain Westernized forms of meditation such as TM, to meditate each day 'in the morning before breakfast and in the late afternoon before dinner'. Such instructions obviously differ somewhat from the traditions from which they originated since they have been tailored to fit Western life, but their derivation from ancient beliefs is obvious.

In the process of transposition to fit the needs of industrialized society, however, they may have lost some of their original meaning. It may be persuasively argued, for example, that we should pay attention to the natural cycles of light and dark because the actual moment of sunrise may have deep physical, emotional and spiritual significance for human beings. It is somewhat less convincing, however, to say that just before one takes coffee and orange juice, or just before one commutes to work, is necessarily the time when a person will be in greater communion with cosmic rhythms. Similarly, since 'late afternoon before supper' is not usually the time of the actual setting of the sun in temperate climates, does it make sense to look upon it as reflecting any 'correct' time to meditate? If we are not going to observe the ancient traditions in their original form, is there any point in observing them at all? There is, unfortunately, no direct experimental evidence relating to these matters and we must rely at present on the reports of meditating persons.

In my contacts with large numbers of people practicing the simpler Westernized forms of meditation. I have not seen any harm arising if a meditator has had to vary his daily meditation schedule so that it deviated from a strict 'before breakfast, before dinner' ritual. For thousands of Westerners who use practical forms of meditation, to have the first meditation of the day late in the morning, or even at lunchtime, may be completely satisfactory.

In the same manner, meditating late in the evening or just before retiring for the night can be extremely useful for those people who find this to be their only available uninterrupted time in the day. Such variations in routine may, in fact, make the difference between a person being able to fit in two meditations a day or not being able to do so. In light of this, feeling comfortable with such variations is extremely important.

Perhaps we can clarify this matter by making a distinction between those times of day when meditation is best, that is, when meditating brings maximum benefit, and those times when it is perhaps not best, but when it is nevertheless still possible to meditate quite successfully.

Adrenal Hormones and Morning Meditation

There is some evidence that suggests that there may be inherent wisdom in a 'pre-breakfast' meditation, if we are seeking an ideal time for our first meditation of the day. Human adrenal hormone secretion has been shown regularly to reach its peak in the hours between 4 and 8 a.m. Secretion of these hormones is related to stress, with adrenal hormones released in the bloodstream in high concentrations at times when the organism is facing intense stress, apparently in order to help the body cope. While it has not been demonstrated in man that emotional susceptibility is directly related to concentration of adrenal hormones, researchers have reason to suspect this may be the case.

At the Hartford Institute of Living, Dr Charles Stroebel and his co-workers observed monkeys to find out what time of day the monkeys showed the strongest fear responses and physical vulnerability.[14] They wanted to know whether the peak hour for fear would coincide with the peak levels of adrenal hormones in the bloodstream. They found that the monkeys responded with the most distress to danger signals in the environment in the early morning hours, just before and just after awakening from sleep – the exact same hours, in fact, when their adrenal hormone levels were at their peak. At this time, too, they were most vulnerable to physical distress.

Exploring this question further, the same group of researchers studied the manner in which rats responded to frightening stimuli at different times of day. Rats differ from monkeys in that they sleep during the day and are active at night. Like the monkeys, however, the rats reacted with most fear when their adrenal hormones were at their peak, which for them was just before and after awakening from their long resting period. At other times of the day, when these rats were showing their lowest concentrations of adrenal hormones, they actually took twice as long to react fearfully to the experimenters' warning signal.

If this cyclic emotional instability and physical vulnerability exist in human beings too, linking up with our peak hours of adrenal hormone concentration, then the hours between 4 and 8 a.m. should logically be the most vulnerable ones of the day for us. While we have as yet no direct evidence that human beings are actually more emotionally unstable at this point than during the rest of the day, we do have some indirect evidence – the fact that the greatest concentration of Rapid Eye Movement (REM) sleep of the night and therefore the highest concentration of dreaming take place during these same early morning hours.

REM Sleep as Stress State

As we have seen, REM sleep is a highly activated type of sleep and some researchers have viewed it as a time of stress. During REM the slow brain waves seen on the EEG in the quiescent sleep stage are replaced by a rapid, irregular, desynchronized pattern remarkably similar to that of the most alert wakefulness. Physiological changes indicating a highly excited state are also seen at this time. Heart rate, respiration and systolic blood pressure all show marked irregularity during REM with no discernible pattern appearing to govern their erratic fluctuations. In human males, penile erection is a regular accompaniment of the REM state. Paradoxically, muscle tone in head and neck virtually disappears during this state, with head and neck becoming limp, but the sleeper may make sudden thrashing movements or turn quickly from side to side. It is during REM that the ulcer patient is most apt to have his night-time ulcer attack, cardiac patients are most apt to experience heart attacks, and when a number of other illnesses affected directly or indirectly by stress seem to be aggravated. The REM state is generally a time of heightened physical vulnerability.

It is therefore interesting to find that REM sleep and hormone levels may be closely connected. Studying the levels of blood hydrocortisone (an adrenal hormone) throughout the night, Dr Elliott Weitzman of Albert Einstein Medical College noticed that this hormone did not seep steadily into the bloodstream of his human subjects during the night, as might be expected.[15] Instead, it seemed to increase in 'puffs', which were usually timed very closely with REM sleep. This suggested to Weitzman that REM periods and the secretion of adrenal hormones are related. Perhaps the increasing turmoil of the early morning sleep state does indeed reflect a generally unstable condition in man at this time.

From the standpoint of meditation, these studies suggest that meditating in the early morning hours might help people to start their day in a more harmonious manner. Meditation presumably is a peaceful and stabilizing influence which could be useful in counteracting this period of particular vulnerability.

While all this suggests that there may be an objective reason for having one's first meditation of the day before eight in the morning, the findings could also be interpreted in another manner. We might reason, for example, that since it is at the end of their daily resting period that human beings and lower animals alike show their lowest resistance to any kinds of stress, then whatever time we wake up (even if we are relatively late sleepers), we may well need a period of quiet stabilizing before we are fully ready to face the additional strains of daily living. There may therefore be considerable wisdom in the suggestion to meditate first thing in the morning, even if our waking hour happens to be later than 8 a.m. Certainly it seems appropriate to make one's morning rituals as gentle and supportive as possible.

Varying the Morning Hour

In many cases, however, we have to allow practicality to determine our choice of hour for meditation. While this may seem rather obvious advice, I have known a number of people who have discontinued the practice of meditation simply because they could not find a comfortable way to fit a pre-breakfast morning meditation into their schedule (or a late afternoon one) and erroneously believed that if they were not able to schedule meditations into their lives in this manner and no other, then meditation could not work for them.

The reports of large numbers of meditators indicate, however, that practical forms of meditation appear to be highly effective for most people on almost any reasonable schedule. A number of meditators who have said they cannot fit in their first meditation of the day until their lunch break have reported benefits from this practice equal to those of almost any pre-breakfast meditator I know.

For the sake of expediency. I have even advised some house-wives with young children to schedule their first meditation of the day in the mid-afternoon, when the baby is taking its nap. This is often the first hour of the day when these women are genuinely free from chores long enough to meditate. Of course the later the hour one does the first meditation, the later the hour the second meditation will have to be for the proper spacing if one is going to observe a spacing rule – that is, meditations should ordinarily be spaced no closer than four hours apart.

This rule, emphasized by the TM organization, seems to be sensible advice since it allows for a healthy alternation of medi-tation with one's active life. Again, however, the usefulness of putting a fairly sizable amount of time between meditations has not been *experimentally* tested.

Late Afternoon and Bedtime Meditation

There seem to be certain practical advantages in having one's second meditation late in the afternoon if that can be con-veniently arranged. Late afternoon meditation appears to serve an important function by breaking the day in half. Many people report that meditating at this time is an excellent way of 'washing away' the accumulated tensions of the day, giving the meditator a 'second wind' for the evening hours, clearly an advantage for many of us. Deciding whether to meditate in the late afternoon, however, inevitably raises the important question of whether or not it is possible to meditate late in the evening.

There are respectable precedents for late evening meditation. Many religions have prescribed prayer and meditation in the evening hours, and the 'darkest hour of the night' (midway between sunset and sunrise) is advised by Hindu scriptures as the time to meditate when faced with an insoluble problem.[16] If, say the ancient texts, one meditates upon a candle flame (the practice of *tratak*) at the darkest hour for forty consecutive nights, then the answer to the problem will be found. The belief that meditation is suitable for night hours is widespread and influences many present-day teachers of meditation. Richard

Hittelman, for example, writes that sunrise, sunset and before retiring are excellent times for practicing meditation.[17]

Curiously, TMers feel differently about this, standing firmly by their founder's belief that meditation at night, if not actually harmful, is certainly unwise. They teach that it will so charge the meditator with energy that she may be unable to sleep afterward. This is a reasonable assumption, of course, if one is the type of person who does become suffused with energy following meditation and cannot sleep after it.

Our research shows, however, that most of the people who have tried meditating just before retiring at night find it very useful and *not* stimulating. Some colleagues and I once distributed a questionnaire on meditation habits which was returned by eighty-six CSM meditators and thirty-four TM meditators – a total of 120 respondents. It included a question on whether meditators had ever tried meditating late at night and, if so, whether they had been able to go to sleep afterward. Two-thirds of the CSM meditators said they had tried meditating late at night (this is permitted in the CSM teaching), and of those who had tried it, 90 percent reported that they were able to sleep easily afterward, while 10 percent said that meditation had made them so energetic they couldn't sleep. By contrast, only two of the thirty-four TM meditators had tried meditating late at night, probably because they had been told not to. Both had found it possible to sleep easily afterward but had never repeated the experiment.

From a practical point of view, it seems wise for each person to discover for himself, by trial and error, just where they stand in this matter. If you find that you are one of the minority of people who react with renewed energy after a late evening meditation, then you should obviously not meditate late at night, unless you are studying for an exam or need to be alert and energetic during the night hours for other reasons. It is not wise to experiment with late evening meditation before your three-week adjustment period is up, however, since a person's reactions after first learning to meditate are often not typical. It is also useful to check on your ability to meditate late at night once or twice a year. Some people who are 'energizers' for the first few months or even for the first year after learning to meditate find that after they have been practicing meditation for a while they are able to meditate late at night very comfortably.

It is also a good idea not to meditate lying down in bed because of the need to keep meditation separate from one's ordinary sleep-producing cues. Some meditators in our survey, however, reported that they successfully meditate just before going to sleep at night by sitting propped up in bed against a pillow; and a few apparently do meditate actually lying down, either morning or evening, and find it helpful. Again, this is a matter of determining the individual's responses.

One other objection is sometimes raised by TM teachers about pre-sleep meditation. They feel that using it will eventually make the meditator come to depend upon meditation to bring on sleep, which is obviously undesirable. You might, so the argument goes, eventually train yourself so well to link up meditation and sleep that if by chance you do not meditate on a particular night, you could not get to sleep at all.

While this sounds reasonable from a theoretical point of view, I have not known anyone to report having had such an experience. None of those people who meditate just prior to sleep have indicated that they are unable to go to sleep on occasions when they may have forgotten or been unable to meditate at bedtime. Clearly this is a subject for further experimentation, preferably in a sleep laboratory.

Where We Stand on Timing

Perhaps this question of the correct hour for meditation can be summed up by saying that no matter what the requirements of one's schedule, personality characteristics will in all probability place certain limitations on what each particular meditator can do successfully. Since, however, it is possible to fit meditation time into even an unusual daily schedule and still derive benefit from it, I suggest to meditators that they try to find out how much changing around of their hour of meditation they personally can tolerate. There will be times when even the most conventional meditator may miss a late afternoon meditation. Those people who know they can meditate successfully at bedtime can easily make up the missed afternoon session at night, still achieving their two meditations of the day.

The cardinal principle with respect to timing seems to be that to be effective, meditation should be comfortable, fit into your life-style and be feasible. While you may conceivably be able to attain the maximum benefit from it by scheduling it at certain hours of the day rather than others (though this has not as yet been proven), it is better to meditate comfortably and well at another time of day than to give up meditation entirely because you can't fit it into certain time slots. Meditation at other times of the day, while it may not accomplish certain things, may do other jobs extremely well.

Chapter 10

THE MYSTERY OF
THE MANTRA

Do different mantras have different effects on personality? Are people ever assigned the 'wrong' mantra by mistake? Why do some meditation teachers select a secret mantra for their trainees? What happens if someone reveals their mantra to another person? These are some of the questions I am most frequently asked about meditation.

Of course mantra meditation is by no means the only effective form of meditation. As Robert Ornstein puts it, 'Almost any process or object seems useable and has probably been used. The specific object used for meditation is much less important than the maintaining of the object as the single focus of awareness during a long period of time. . . .'[1] Nevertheless, mantra meditation, as opposed to other forms, is particularly popular at present. We shall therefore look first at the basis of mantra meditation – the idea that sound can affect the emotions, the thinking, and even the physical well-being of human beings.

Impact of Sound

Obviously certain sounds have different effects from other ones. We respond differently to a Mozart sonata than to a rock concert. Some proper names seem soft and pleasing to us; others seem harsh and unpleasant. While our responses may be partly due to past experiences (our personal associations with different sounds) there are good reasons to suppose that we also have innate responses to certain sounds.

Most people react with comfort and relaxation to the sound of a bubbling brook, or to gentle rainfall on a roof; and tend to respond with discomfort and tension to the sound of a triphammer (even at a distance where its loudness is not a factor), or the sound of chalk scraped against a blackboard. Even sub-human organisms respond differently to different sounds. The use of certain types of music to stimulate the growth of plants, for example, is no longer viewed as merely a pleasant folk tale. Certain colleges of agriculture are now teaching their students to use music to foster the growth of healthy crops based on the results of experiments in this area.[2]

Actually the concept that specific mantras have specific effects does not presuppose any mysterious process. Since various sounds elicit different responses, it is logical to suppose that repeating one particular kind of sound to ourselves might have a somewhat different effect on us than repeating another one.

I have mentioned the modern Westernized technique of meditation developed by Dr Herbert Benson, the Harvard cardi-ologist (see Chapter 2). Consider Benson's choice of the sound which he asks his trainees to repeat during their meditation: the word 'one'. While he chose this word because it was 'euphonious' and did not have 'sharp' sounds (he considered the next number up the scale with such a pleasing quality to be 'nine'), the word is interestingly close to the Sanskrit mantra 'Om', which is traditionally considered to have powerful effects. Most of the other leading Sanskrit mantras also end in a res-onant nasal sound – in 'n', 'm', 'ing' sounds that tend to reverberate within the head even when we are merely thinking them.

Some research suggests, in fact, that we may be producing movements in the small muscles of the middle ear when we 'think' in sound. When Dr Howard Roffwarg and his associates at Montefiore Hospital in New York City studied the middle ear muscles of sleeping subjects, they found that activity in these muscles tended to occur during dream sequences involving *sounds*, and not to occur when there had been no imagined experience of sound in a subject's dream.[3] If muscles within our auditory apparatus can respond to an imagined sound in a dream just as they do to 'real' sound, then the emotional impact of imagined sounds may be similar to that of real ones.

If you'd like to conduct an experiment of your own to find out the effects of using different sounds as 'mantras,' you can try Benson's method of meditation using two different words.

To do this, sit comfortably in a quiet room, close your eyes, and begin mentally repeating the sound 'one' to yourself on every out-breath. The sequence goes like this: breathe in – breathe out 'one' . . . breathe in – breathe out 'one' . . . Keep repeating this sequence in your mind for about two minutes and then substitute mental repetition of the word 'two' on each out-breath.

You will probably find a difference in your responses to the two sounds, how great a one depending upon your sensitivity to specific sounds and your own preferences. If you intend to carry out this experiment, it's probably a good idea to do it before reading further, however. The following discussion might influence your observations.

In an informal test of these two sounds, many people have reported that thinking 'two' involves a slight, almost imperceptible twist of the tongue which has been trained to reach toward the front of the hard palate for the 't' sound. Thinking 'two' also made some people's stomach muscles tense slightly and it was often described as being somewhat sharp and abrupt in sound as opposed to being gradual, lingering and resonant (the qualities most often attributed to 'one'). The sound 'two' was more often felt as being light, superficial and at times even somewhat annoying, while many people felt the sound 'one' to be calm and steadying, giving them a sense of being 'pulled together' or centered. Those who found 'two' an abrupt sound sometimes found themselves becoming restless rather than quieted by their meditation.

Despite this, in trying this experiment some of you may have responded with greater calm to the word 'two'. What calms one person may excite another, and vice versa – another reason why meditation devices should be selected with the aim of suiting them to the individual.

You may also have noticed associations with these two words affecting your reactions. Mental associations with the word 'one' are quite significant for English-speaking people. 'One' implies unity and completion. It is the word for 'singular' and also the word for 'all', the phrase 'one world' meaning not so much a single world as a unified one. The word 'one' seems in fact to imply both individuality and totality at once, a concept which may be seen by some as having metaphysical implications. Repeating the word 'one' can affect the meditator, then, not only because of its sound but also because it evokes the thought of being 'pulled together' into one unified being. 'Two', on the other hand, has no such connotations for most people. In fact its associations in the English language are rather meager, although for any particular individual it may hold very meaningful personal associations.

Our mental associations with a word can even have an effect on our reaction to it if the sound is in an unfamiliar language such as Sanskrit. Certain traditional mantras, for example (depending upon how they are pronounced), sound like two short English words put together, and some meditators (myself included) will visualize these English words when they repeat such a mantra mentally. Such responses are of course likely to fade after a while and many meditators indicate that their mantras recede in their minds into a vague, pulsating beat rather than being identifiable as a word when they are having a particularly deep and restful meditation. On our meditation questionnaire, 45 percent of the CSM and TM meditators reported that they actually 'hear' the mantra as a word only 'occasionally or never'.

The Effects of Specific Sounds

This kind of consideration leads to the possibility of some interesting experimentation. We could, for example, make predictions on the basis of what we have so far informally observed about the response to different sounds using Benson's method. One such prediction might run as follows: 'For most people repeating the sound "one" is more soothing than repeating the sound "two".' Then, in scientific fashion, we could proceed to test this assumption, an elaboration of the experiment you have just performed for yourself.

At Princeton, researcher Douglas Moltz and I set out to investigate the effects of word sounds on mood in a more formal way.[4] We began with the simplest component of words – single syllables without specific identifiable meanings in English – sounds such as 'wys', 'grik', 'rahm', 'noi', and others. From a large pool of such nonsense syllables, a group of colleagues selected five sounds which seemed to them to be extremely 'soothing'; another five which seemed extremely 'jarring'; and five more which seemed neutral in their effects. Their choices were used to construct a list of fifteen nonsense syllables.

Our next step was to present this list to 100 college student volunteers and have them mentally repeat each one of the fifteen sounds and rate them on a seven-point scale from 'extremely soothing' to 'extremely jarring'. When we studied their ratings we found there was a remarkable agreement among these subjects. For example, the same two sounds were rated as 'soothing' by the overwhelming majority of subjects, with only three raters out of the 100 reporting a negative reaction to them. Likewise, the two sounds that were rated as 'jarring' were experienced as unpleasant so often that only two subjects out of the 100 had any positive feelings about them. One other sound was rated as 'neutral' most of the time. We were thus easily able to identify three sounds that had received very strong ratings.

We next asked another group of volunteers to repeat each of these three sounds silently in their minds for five minutes, and then to fill out an adjective checklist describing what their mood was like during the time they had been mentally repeating each sound. We wanted to see if certain word sounds would have different and specific effects on mood. This was an indirect way of testing the claim of the meditative traditions that particular mantras have particular effects.

We had guessed that some of the sounds might be more soothing than others but were unprepared for the dramatic results found. The experiment showed that moods can change in surprisingly specific ways according to the word sound the person is thinking.

For example, only one sound ('Lom') caused anger and hostility to be lowered in our subjects, while another sound ('grik') caused an angry, irritable mood to increase significantly. Repeating the harsh sound 'grik' also lowered depression (perhaps because it released anger), and the sound 'Lom' decreased 'sluggish' feelings. The sound 'noi' lessened feelings of being 'worn out' (a fatigue-related state), while 'grik' had no effect on either fatigue or inertia. 'Noi' was the only one of the three sounds that decreased tension and anxiety, but all the sounds reduced feelings of 'vigor' and 'activity', perhaps because repeating any sound long enough slows people down.

These results made it seem quite plausible that different mantras could be used selectively for lightening depressions; soothing an irritated patient; counteracting fatigue; lowering anxiety; releasing creativity; increasing energy; or for any number of other purposes. In fact, specific assignment of mantras to obtain special effects to suit individual needs has been practiced for thousands of years by masters working with the ancient meditative traditions, with claims of remarkable success. Since a suitable means of matching a specific mantra to a particular trainee has not yet been developed on a scientific basis, however, in its absence, our own inner wisdom as to which sounds 'feel' right to us to repeat mentally seems our best guide when undertaking any method of meditation without the assistance of a highly experienced meditation teacher.

Such self-selection of mantras can, in fact, work. At the New York Telephone Company the Clinically Standardized Meditation (CSM) method was used to train nearly 5,000 employees (see Chapter 18). A careful follow-up by the company revealed that all those who had learned the method were comfortable with the mantras they themselves had chosen – there was not a single report of adverse effects from repeating these mantras. This does not mean, of course, that a mantra assigned to a pupil by a master of the meditative traditions may not be more profound in its effects than one which a person might select for himself, but in the absence of a highly experienced meditation teacher, the latter seems the safest route to follow.

Margaret's experience illustrates this point. This woman, a stranger to me, had read my first book on meditation and had telephoned me seeking my advice for what she described as an urgent problem concerning meditation. She told me that she had been assigned a mantra by a meditation organization that had assured her it was 'exactly the right one' for her, although she said she had disliked it intensely from the beginning. Eventually she had had to abandon her meditation practice entirely because of the discomfort that thinking this mantra caused her.

Because her negative reaction to the mantra was so strong, it seemed to me that the particular mantra she had used might be the cause of her difficulty. The obvious next step was for her to try a new one and I presented her with the list of CSM mantras regularly given to those who learn this method.

At first Margaret couldn't comprehend how a sound which she had repeated *only in her mind* could cause so much difficulty, but when I asked her if an irritating tune had ever kept running through her mind even though she didn't 'hear' it played outside, and what effect it had had, she understood my point and was ready to cooperate. She chose a mantra from the list I dictated to her and started using it the following day. As soon as she did so, she was able to resume regular meditation. To her surprise her meditation sessions were now experienced as extremely relaxing, helpful and enjoyable. While her former mantra had been disturbing, her new *self-selected* one immediately had a calming effect.

It seems, then, as though sounds may have very specialized effects on people who repeat them, even when they are not pronounced out loud but only 'thought'. If the results of this experiment are borne out by future studies, it is possible that some day we may be able to predict accurately the effects of sounds on moods – something which could be very useful for therapeutic purposes. Conceivably different mantras might then be used selectively for lightening depressions; soothing an irritated patient; counteracting fatigue; lowering anxiety; releasing creativity; increasing energy; or for any number of other purposes. Specific assignment of mantras to obtain special effects to suit individual needs has been practiced for thousands of years by masters working with the ancient meditative traditions, with claims of remarkable success. Perhaps we are on the verge of being able to apply this ancient art of the guru in a scientific manner on the basis of laboratory experimentation.

If future studies show that simple nonsense syllables have specific effects on mood, then researchers may want to go a step further and design experiments to find out whether some of the traditional mantras, particularly the renowned Sanskrit mantras whose long-term effects can be predicted, are more effective for certain purposes than other, more 'prosaic' everyday sounds. This may well be the case, because these ancient mantras were selected and refined through a trial-and-error process lasting for thousands of years.

If we were to find that Sanskrit and other ancient mantras are indeed more effective than ordinary English words for certain purposes, we can visualize researchers working to identify the particular consonants and vowels and the combinations of these, or the particular pitch and length of beat, which gives the mantra the effect it has. Only through experiments such as these will we be in a position to make fully effective use of mantra meditation on a scientific basis. In the interim, we will have to resort to what is largely a trial-and-error process in assigning mantras to individuals, and must be alert to the reaction of each person to the particular mantra assigned to her – or which she has chosen, as the case may be.

The choice of the mantra certainly need not be a mysterious or secret process. On the basis of our study on the effects of sound on mood, and my own experience teaching meditation, it would seem that there are some objective criteria which can be applied in selecting a mantra, and I would strongly doubt that there is any such thing as the 'right' mantra for any one person. Our work suggests that there are more likely to be a number of different mantras which can be beneficial for each person and that the one which is finally chosen may need to be determined by the specific changes that the person seeks to bring about in herself. There are also likely to be a number of mantras which might be more neutral in their effects on the same individual, and still others which might be irritating or possibly even detrimental to her.

There are a few precautions which need to be observed when selecting your mantra, however. Certain mantras are what are technically known to Yoga practitioners as *bija* mantras. These are extremely powerful sounds which are thought to be unsafe for those whose nervous systems are not properly prepared for them, and to produce undesirable effects such as confusion, delusions, hallucinations or other symptoms of mental illness if they are not handled expertly. As a precaution I have eliminated all *bija* mantras from the list of mantras presented to people learning my CSM system, and I suggest that anyone who plans to self-select their own mantra – unless they are using the CSM recorded training which automatically takes care of the problem – check first with an experienced meditation teacher to be certain that the sound they have chosen is a safe one. Properly used, a suitable mantra can bring about deep positive experiences that can enhance both physical and mental health, but the latent power inherent in the mantra must be respected.

The Traditional Use of Mantras

Those of us in the field of meditation are still unable to answer many of the questions that are asked of us about the use of sound and mantra and therefore have to refer to teachers of the great meditative traditions who are expertly trained in the

ancient art of mantra. Traditional wisdom can tell us much that
is of use today.

Mantras are used by a variety of ancient spiritual traditions,
all of which carefully specify the ways in which they must be
employed. According to Yogic tradition, proper use of the
mantra rests on a number of conditions which cannot readily
be met in Western life. Each mantra is traditionally analyzed by
the master or 'guru' who dispenses it according to the sounds
used in producing it and the parts of the body or energy system
these particular sounds vibrate. The sound frequencies at which
the mantra is transmitted are said to determine whether higher
or lower portions of a particular energy center (or *chakra*) will
be affected. Yogic tradition stresses the fact that this process
depends for its effectiveness on the tonality of the teacher's
voice when imparting the mantra, as well as the pupil's ability
to reproduce that tone – out loud in the beginning, and later on
in the mind.

The instantaneous effect which a correctly pronounced
mantra can produce depends on the master's skill. An exact
and even inspired intoning of the mantra is apparently required
to put 'life' into the sound. Whatever secret there is in the
mantra seems to lie in how it is chanted. The word alone is
considered to be barren, much like musical notation which
remains mechanical and empty until enlivened by the feelings
of a musician. Just as notes of the scale played by a beginner
on the violin differ from those same notes played by a virtuoso,
so the effect of the mantra differs according to whether it is
conveyed by a well-meaning neophyte or by a person who,
with many years of practice, has mastered the particular sound
to be produced.

Such a skill is difficult to find even in India. While there
are many students of the *Mantra Shastras* (Hindu scriptures
describing the mantras) who understand their use, very few of
them are thought to know how to intone these mantras properly.
Even an expert may learn to pronounce only a few of them in
a lifetime. Since there is no notation system which conveys their
pronunciation, the 'notation' remains in each master's head,
passed down over generations by word of mouth.

A close relationship between master and pupil forms the basis
for the assignment of a traditional mantra by a teacher to suit
his particular student at a particular stage in that student's

spiritual development. The mantra may later be changed a number of times to correspond to the student's advancing spiritual growth. Since a mantra is assigned only after careful examination of the disciple and an exhaustive study of his condition, such precision cannot be duplicated by relying on general information such as a person's age, sex or socioeconomic status when determining the choice of a mantra, even though this is done by some contemporary meditation training systems.

I always advise people to be cautious about claims made by any large meditation organization that they can impart a 'personal' mantra to a trainee. This is not possible unless there is an ongoing and very close relationship between teacher and pupil, even though the large organizations may be helpful to a modern meditator in other ways.

The Sanskrit word 'mantra' actually means 'that which liberates the mind'.[5] In India mantras whose specific effects are known have been authenticated by highly trained practitioners over a period of several thousand years. Sri Shyam Bhatnagar, an internationally recognized master of sound and mantra who has been teaching his method of therapeutic sound in the United States and Europe for over three decades, indicates that in the Indian tradition, certain mantras represent the nature or innermost qualities of various energies or 'deities' that reside within us.[6] These energies are said to be evoked by properly repeating the mantra, which is often, though not always, the name of a deity. The concept that the power of a deity resides in its name is also embraced by the Judeo-Christian and Moslem traditions where the name of the Lord is looked upon as so sacred as to be unspeakable, or only to be repeated under special circumstances, because it embodies the very spirit of God.

Sri Bhatnagar also points out that mantras are not necessarily the names of deities – although they often are – but can be sacred phrases used to invoke the divine energy that is said to reside in all of us. Thus the name or 'verbal formula' (that is, the mantra) becomes the means through which a powerful connection is established between the devotee and the deity addressed, or the devotee and his or her own Higher Self, however one chooses to view this process. For this reason traditional mantras are never to be used lightly and must be assigned with great care.

A Sanskrit mantra may be one syllable, as in the case of the mantra 'om', or it may consist of many verses from the Vedic scriptures – sometimes it can have as many as sixty or more syllables. In Tantric tradition it may be 110 syllables of prose or poetry.[7]

Westerners are sometimes surprised to discover that in India mantras are dispensed by holy men or women to eager recipients for every conceivable purpose. There are mantras to be used for illness or physical discomfort. There are special mantras for business contingencies or for bringing wealth and blessings. There are mantras for social uses, and mantras for love, courtship and marriage. There are even mantras for use in sorcery known only to the 'Left' (less known, less reputable) branch of the Tantric tradition. The latter may be used together with talismans, secret rituals and other paraphernalia for casting spells, but these particular Tantric mantras are not used by serious spiritual aspirants nor taught by esteemed teachers.

The mantra is a highly potent intervention for spiritual evolution and can be used for the highest of purposes to which human beings aspire. It can also be used for therapeutic purposes and to enhance our sense of well-being and harmony. In my practice as a clinical psychologist, I have seen several of my patients undergo unusual and profound transformations through the dedicated use of a mantra. For me personally, intoning my mantra has become an essential part of my 'daily bread'. I have used my mantra as a simple stress-reduction device as in some Westernized forms of meditation, and also for a number of years have diligently chanted mantras especially assigned to me by my teachers to bring about deep and lasting inner change. I originally used the TM mantra assigned to me, and then for many years meditated with one of the CSM mantras. After that I elected to delve more deeply into the spiritual side of mediation and have been assigned mantras for my personal development by Sri Shyam Bhatnagar and his highly gifted associate, Dahliana Hohé.

In all instances my personal mantra has served me as an unusually faithful friend in times of hardship and an immediate consolation in times of trouble. It has acted as a determined sword in moments of profound transition and has always been a firm light of hope in my spiritual progress. As a person of today I am deeply indebted to the great traditions of the past for the valuable heritage which is the mantra.

The Admonition of Secrecy

Many meditators, expecially those who have learned TM, have been told by their teachers to keep their mantra absolutely secret. Some meditation teachers even imply that the revelation of your personal mantra will have dire consequences. They may have suggested that telling your mantra to someone else can ruin your meditation practice or rob the mantra of its effectiveness. Is there any truth in these warnings?

As with most complex matters, the answer is not a simple one. Certainly lightning won't strike you dead if you reveal your mantra to someone other than your meditation teacher, nor will this act bar you permanently from benefiting from your meditation practice. But there are certain consequences of revealing your mantra to another that may make you voluntarily decide to keep it a communication private to your own self. Here are some of the reasons for this.

There is a sound psychological principle that suggests that we reserve the mantra as a special sound to be used only for meditation as much as this is conveniently possible to do. The mantra is regularly repeated while we are experiencing a deep sense of inner peace and therefore soon becomes what psychologists refer to as a 'conditioned stimulus' for peace and relaxation. That is, it becomes a personal signal to become tranquil and turn inward and thus can automatically bring about a relaxed state because it has been associated with such relaxation in the past. Using a mantra which is specially reserved for this purpose can be an effective way of ensuring that your meditation sessions will produce the tranquility that you seek.

There are ways, however, in which one can render a conditioned stimulus ineffective. One way is to repeat the stimulus under different conditions than the ones you desire to bring about. If, for example, your mantra were 'Shanti' (a Sanskrit word meaning 'peace') and you went about saying to others, 'Please pass me the Shanti vegetables'; 'May I have some Shanti ice cream?'; and 'Let's go to a Shanti movie' (particularly if you used the word in a casual and superficial tone, not intended to deepen your awareness of the mantra), you might find that

'Shanti' had lost its significance for you – it would no longer be a signal to *turn inward*.

Another reason for not telling your mantra to a casual acquaintance or talking about it under conditions which are not genuinely serious or respectful is its highly personal nature. If you have a special mantra that has been assigned to you (or which you yourself have selected from a list of mantras) it eventually becomes a part of you. It can even symbolize your own identity. For some people, refraining from sharing this special word with others can therefore be an extremely important step toward inner independence. Such people may have always felt compelled to share everything they think or do with others. Their mantra now becomes one part of themselves that they can clearly call their own.

Ancient Views on Revealing the Mantra

There are some ancient views about sharing one's mantra that may explain some of the mystery that has traditionally surrounded this subject. These traditional views may not apply to many of us in the Western world but may nevertheless explain the secrecy stand taken by some contemporary meditation groups.

In India, for example, the traditional approach to secrecy concerning the mantra depends on the use to which a particular mantra is put. Many mantras are freely divulged in India, but these do not include the very powerful mantras used to reverberate specific energy centers in order to further the spiritual evolution of a student. Those mantras are considered part of a sacred trust and represent a special sort of communication between teacher and student.

There is a particular type of master–pupil relationship which is cemented in India by the giving of a 'devotional' or 'guru' mantra. This guru mantra ensures the discipleship. It is considered to bind master and pupil together forever, being almost in the nature of a spiritual 'marriage contract'. A guru mantra *must* be kept secret at all times, it is never to be known by anyone save the master and pupil. Just as a married person would not lend her wedding ring to a friend, so the guru mantra is to be shared with no one else. If it is revealed, then master and pupil are 'divorced', their spiritual bond broken. Possibly those meditation organizations which demand strict secrecy concerning the mantra are following the tradition of the 'devotional' or 'guru' mantra.

As for my own position on secrecy of the mantra, when I teach CSM, I advise trainees not to tell their mantra to others often, if at all. It is best, I suggest, not to use it as an everyday word. It should be kept as a special word used exclusively to turn inward. I advise this because being discreet about the mantra is undoubtedly sound psychology.

I also point out a more subtle reason for keeping one's personal mantra confidential. In the act of meditation we are alone with our own selves in a way that doesn't involve action or 'doing' in the ordinary sense. At that time we are not viewing ourselves as a person-in-action but are instead contacting the deepest core of ourselves, the inner being which simply 'is'. Our personal mantra therefore brings about a communion with a subtle yet profound aspect of ourselves which is often obscured by our daily whirlwind of activities. Since the mantra is a call to our deepest self, when we reveal it to another person (other than a meditation teacher) we are, in a sense, giving away part of our own essence. We all have need of an island of purely personal awareness. Our mantra gives us access to this.

Each one of us must therefore decide if we want to share the intimate experiences that our personal mantra affords us. I personally have elected to keep my mantra confidential except when discussing it with my meditation teachers. This has worked beautifully for me but you alone will decide what is best for you. I suggest that this decision be based on respect for the mantra and for your own true self, and that your guide be your wish for inner growth rather than any attempt to observe the letter of the law. This way you can attain true freedom in meditation.

Chapter 11

A FEW NAGGING QUESTIONS

There are a number of instructions on how to practice meditation which many people take for granted simply because they were given by their meditation teachers. Some of these are questionable, however. What do we really know, for example, about such things as postures for meditation, about suiting a particular meditation technique to a certain person, or about the meaning (and perhaps the value?) of temporary vacations from meditation?

Correct Postures for Meditating

It is often said that the lotus position is the ideal posture for meditation, even though it is certainly not easy for many Westerners. However, while it is the prescribed posture for persons studying advanced forms of meditation (often with the aim of furthering spiritual development), unless someone has been carefully trained in Yoga or Zen, it is usually more satisfactory for people to meditate sitting in a chair.

Even in a chair, however, the question of posture in meditation remains important. An uncomfortable sitting position can distract a meditator so that it cancels out the benefits of meditation. Some chair-sitting meditators complain, for example, that their head involuntarily drops forward when they go into a deeper meditation state, which in turn pulls on the neck muscles and can increase an already existing back or neck problem. This can quite effectively spoil a meditation session. For such people one solution may be to sit in a chair with a high enough back so that their head can rest comfortably against it when meditating, or if they like to sit on the floor, leaning back against the wall may be a good solution. TM teachers, however, feel that one should not support the head because this may encourage sleep; teachers of Zazen feel that one should not lean against walls or backs of chairs;[1] and writers on Yoga meditation advise their followers not to lean back against the furniture while meditating because it is 'important to your health'.[2] People who have tried supporting their neck because they felt they needed it, however, have not reported that this made their meditation any less effective or that they felt in any way more sleepy. Once again, this seems to be an individual matter as far as practical meditation is concerned.

As for meditating lying down, this position is associated with sleep and for many of us dropping off to sleep is an automatic response to lying down quietly with eyes closed. Nevertheless, the classic Yoga posture, salvasana, which clearly evokes a meditative mood, is performed lying on the back, as are many of the autogenic training exercises. Baba Ram Dass, for example, advises his students to lie down for certain meditations if reclining does not lead to sleep.[3] It is therefore certainly possible to consider lying down when meditating if this becomes necessary. This is important to realize, because occasionally people find that meditating while lying down, or partially lying down with head and back just slightly propped up, is for them the only feasible position. People who feel they must meditate this way seem the least likely to fall asleep during meditation when lying down. Perhaps such people are intuitively aware of certain physiological or psychological needs which make lying flat their best position.

As indicated, this advice refers only to the practical forms of meditation. Spiritual meditation always requires a certain prescribed posture, usually the lotus position or some variation of it, and the very process of mastering it becomes a form of meditation for the devotee. Since so many of the great meditative traditions insist on the importance of the proper grounding of the person in the pyramidal shape before 'true' meditation can be said to take place, it is possible that certain deep states can only be obtained this way.

The practical meditator, however, should decide for herself what goals are appropriate for meditative practice and select the form and level of the discipline that best suit these aims. An average tennis player has no need of a four-hour workout every day if he simply wants to play on weekends with friends. A tennis pro, on the other hand, may have to practice more than this, and this practice will be highly specific and designed to overcome special problems. Meditation postures follow the same rules – the higher one sets one's sights in terms of personal and/or spiritual development, the more rigorous and exacting the postures must be. In the *practical* forms of meditation there are many options with regard to the best position. Ultimately each meditator must decide for himself which is most suitable.

Vacations from Meditation

In our previously referred to meditation questionnaire, one of the questions asked was whether meditators had ever taken a 'vacation' from meditation. If so, for how long, and were they later able to resume meditating regularly?

More than half the meditators who answered reported having temporarily stopped meditating at some point – the longer they had been meditating the more likely meditators were to have taken time off. Sometimes these 'vacations' were only a day, a few days, or a week in length; sometimes several months or longer. In a few cases they involved stopping meditation for a year or more. The people involved had all spontaneously resumed meditation afterward, and most of them said they were able to be fairly regular in their practice of meditation after the vacation. Occasionally, though, they reported having had difficulty resuming the practice because they felt 'guilty' for having stopped.

Just why people feel they need these breaks from meditation is an interesting question. There may be a number of different reasons why they occur and why at times they may even be helpful.

Certain people are aware of why they temporarily stop meditating. A patient of mine who stopped for three months was in the process of dissolving a marriage which had ended two years before, but which only now did she have the strength to terminate legally. During this period of her life she stopped meditating, although she considered the practice extremely valuable to her and one of the contributing factors in her decision to make a new life for herself. She reported that meditation had increased her sense of independence and her wish to be entirely on her own. Since it was not yet feasible to put these positive plans into action, the meditation sessions during this interim period left her with a painful sense of frustration. To avoid this, she simply abandoned meditation temporarily. She said that the knowledge that meditation was still 'there', however, should she really need it, gave her security.

Other people stop meditating temporarily because another activity is substituting for the meditation. Some vacationers, for example, find that meditating in natural surroundings is an exalting experience, but others find the opposite. For the latter, fragrant mountain air, the whispering of a brook, the smell of the sea or a pine forest, or other experiences which naturally bring about the meditative mood, are so compelling that they find that they no longer use formal meditating while on their holiday, but will usually resume regular meditation on their return to 'civilization'.

Similarly, at certain points during their artistic work, some people will find so much excitement in the act of creation that they may temporarily forget to meditate or may feel that meditation slows down their intense creative drive. Such people may stop meditating during the height of their productivity. A number of creative people, however, report the opposite, as we shall see when we consider meditation's contributions to the creative process. For these people, meditation seems to enhance their work, freeing and strengthening their creative drive. Clearly this is an individual matter, sometimes not even predictable for the same person from one project to the next.

An occasional meditator may also stop temporarily because he finds that when under heavy stress, meditation increases anxiety, rather than being calming. As one student puts it: 'At times I've stopped meditating when I've been particularly stressed – when I'm under too much stress meditation can be very annoying – and so I just can't meditate at such a time.'

Stopping is usually the only solution for such a person at this point. Merely reducing meditation time under such circumstances seems to do little. Closely related to this reaction is one described by a CSM meditator who found that when she was under severe emotional stress due to the impending death of a parent, her meditations lost their value for her. She now could not fit meditation comfortably into her pressured schedule and was finding herself becoming irritated and tense during meditation instead of calmer. In order to avoid what is known as 'counterconditioning', whereby meditation might become a 'signal' for tensing *up*, she stopped meditating entirely during this period. After her parent's death and following a period of mourning, this woman was able to resume meditating with the same beneficial results she had originally obtained.

Many of the same reasons that lead people to stop meditating entirely cause others to take vacations from it. Various blocks to meditating, foremost among which is guilt at allowing oneself to have pleasure, can result in frequent intermittent breaks from meditation. When this happens it is usually the reflection of an internal struggle; a wish to meditate and enjoy the benefits of this practice is counterbalanced by an equally strong need to escape from meditation and the anxiety or guilt it entails. The solution is 'on-again, off-again' meditation. The person meditates until too much guilt accumulates, takes a vacation from it until the guilt subsides, and then starts again with a temporary feeling of well-being – until guilt builds up once more.

Other people may stop not because of any deep-seated problems but rather to establish a sense of independence in relation to the practice. They have a need to prove to themselves that they are not rigidly controlled by the routine of meditation but that they can freely elect to practice it. A student expresses this clearly: 'Sometimes meditation becomes too much of a routine – too confining – too restrictive – so on occasion I have stopped for a few days.'

For the fairly sizable number of people who occasionally stop meditation in order to establish their sense of independence from the practice, these breaks are often effective and do establish the meditator's autonomy. Under such circumstances, the vacation can be considered to have been a healthy move. Essentially we should never meditate because we have to, but because we want to. If we have to stop meditating temporarily to make this point clear to ourselves, then that is a wise decision.

Some people may have to take more radical steps to restore power to their technique, however. Shifting temporarily or even permanently to a different type of meditation may be for them the only answer to this problem. Even if we use a different meditational technique only occasionally as a change of pace, it may 'recharge' our original technique, lending it new life. Many people have a strong emotional attachment to the meditational device they were originally taught to use. This is understandable, for the device can become in time an intimate reflection of our deeper self. We therefore usually gravitate naturally back to it when it is sufficiently enlivened so that its effectiveness has been restored. The process is like that of recharging a battery which has run down. There is no need to throw away the battery, but sometimes a special process is required to make it work again.

Another constructive reason for vacations from meditation is a phenomenon which is recognized by educators. If someone studies a subject such as a foreign language for a number of months, and then stops studying it or even thinking about it, it is not unusual to find on a test taken several months later, that the person has an even better grasp of the subject than he did directly after the period of intense conscious effort. The implications of this are that some form of learning has been going on during the 'rest' period. By stopping the active process of forcing ourselves to learn, we sometimes allow learning to consolidate, to become a natural part of us; something which would not happen if we were to keep our 'nose to the grind-stone' all the time. Do people continue to develop from meditation even during those intervals when they may not be actively practicing it?

This does not seem to be the case with the physical results obtained. When hypertensive subjects who have reduced their blood pressure through meditation stop meditating, their blood pressure gradually starts to rise again, showing that the effects of meditation are wearing off. This process can only be reversed by resuming meditation.

On a psychological level, however, it is not at all certain that the effects wear off in this manner. Some evidence suggests that the meditative attitude may continue as an important part of one's life, even if one takes a vacation from meditation. Meditators who are not currently meditating will report that they nevertheless find themselves spontaneously entering medi-tative moods during the day when formerly they might have been tense and over-directed in their attitudes. Meditation can change the way a person lives her life in a rather fundamental respect, a change which is not likely to be easily reversed.

A final reason for vacations from meditation is the fact that any routine, no matter bow beneficial, can be wearing after a while. We sometimes need a vacation from the best things or the most important people in our lives. Time spent away from them can result in our being all the more enthusiastic about them when we return. Perhaps this is so with meditation. Most people come back to meditation after their 'time off' apparently no worse for the experience and sometimes with a newfound sense of freedom about their meditation.

Certainly, given the frequency of vacations from meditation in the general population of meditators, no one needs to feel guilty about taking some time off or feel that because she has done so, she is a 'failure' at meditation. Guilt about such a vacation can make for serious difficulties, even if the vacation itself does not, because the guilt makes the meditator define herself as a failure. This in turn is likely to make her hostile to the entire endeavor of meditation. It is those people who cannot forgive themselves for taking a vacation from the practice who are most likely to stop meditating permanently following their vacation.

Suiting the Technique to the Person

While the permissive forms of practical meditation work for a surprising number of people, some people are unable to adapt to them. Permissive forms of meditation such as CSM or TM may be too 'free' for these people. If so, practicing them can increase their anxiety level, rather than reduce it. Not everyone wants or needs maximum flexibility in their meditative technique. On a questionnaire given out at Princeton University on meditation practices, college students gave interesting opinions when asked to evaluate various meditation and relaxation techniques:

> Zazen meditation was very interesting. I think it provided a necessary alternative to TM. Sometimes TM is too free and open – a more rigorous meditation is necessary.

> My easy-going mantra meditation technique may not have been as effective for me since I'm an ordered, logical individual who may have needed a more structured method.

> I think progressive relaxation suits my character better than mantra meditation. I'm a fairly nervous person and progressive relaxation does more to relax me on a physical level.

Clearly the wrong meditation technique can create difficulty.

One patient of mine was unable even to talk about learning TM without becoming anxious. Many of her friends were practicing TM successfully and although she 'wanted' to learn it, she had an obsessive fear of losing control during meditation. Since she was unable to contemplate going to the TM center with her friends, I decided to try teaching her CSM. Despite my attempts to teach her in a quiet, non-forcing manner, however, she was unable to meditate without becoming more anxious than she was before trying and was particularly worried about meditating 'incorrectly'.

We did not try meditation again until a year had passed and she had shown considerable progress in her adjustment to many aspects of life. Since she still kept saying that she longed to be able to 'meditate', I decided to teach her Benson's method – meditators using Benson's method or any of the other breath meditations can always tell whether they are doing it 'correctly'.

Teaching her this method turned out to be quite effective. She preferred Benson's to a more open-ended approach, although she could not practice even this form of meditation for longer than three minutes and ended up using it only for 'mini-meditations' when she felt tense.

While the art of suiting the meditative technique to a particular person in their present stage of development is as yet unexplored, it may well be one of the most important areas for future investigation.

Atmosphere of Instruction

To be taught to meditate by a person who takes the experience seriously is essential. The meditation teacher gives trainees 'permission' to contact their own self deeply: the act of instructing a person in meditation is therefore in a sense to sanction an inner rebirth. For this reason, the actual moment of learning meditation is frequently deeply meaningful. It is a milestone in the person's life and even the appropriateness of some form of simple ceremony is often intuitively recognized.

The spirit of meditation can certainly not be conveyed by describing the outer trappings of the practice. Meditation does not consist of the devices used to foster it, it is a way of being. Unfortunately, however, some people are taught how to 'meditate' in an offhand manner by room-mates, friends or family members. 'All you have to do is just sit down and keep saying this word over and over to yourself in your mind,' they may be told, or other similar easy phrases. While sometimes the instructions they get in this manner are even technically correct, they do not teach the person how to meditate. Glibness in teaching meditation fails to convey the spirit of the practice. The meditation experience may therefore be shallow, boring, or even make the new meditator feel ridiculous. If it does, this person may never meditate again.

Because it relies upon the evocation of a particular mood, over the ages meditation has been transferred from person to person with an attitude of quiet respect: a *feeling* as well as a technique has been transmitted. This process can be looked at as a long procession of people stretching back through time into antiquity. We might imagine each of these people holding a small lighted candle with which, in turn, she can reach out to ignite the candle of a new learner. The process continues over the centuries until, at a particular moment, someone leans forward and ignites the candle flame within you – and you, too, become a meditator – an endless procession of humanity sharing with humanity down through time.

To teach meditation without recognition of this profoundly human element is, I suspect, to leave out a vital part of the practice. Even if meditation is taught in a book or by recording, this should be done with respect and concern for new meditators and a sense of genuinely sharing an experience with them. Every attempt should be made to convey the spirit as well as the technical aspects of the practice. Meditation imparted mechanically, casually, jokingly, as a parlor game, or in a too impersonally conducted experiment, is cold by contrast.* It is something like the presumed test-tube baby of the future. All contingencies may have been taken care of in a practical sense

---

* I have mentioned the strategic teaching of a meditation exercise to a class before an exam (see Chapter 8). Such simple centering exercises as these do not constitute the 'teaching' of meditation unless the instructor specifically indicates he expects those learning it to be able to adopt it as a regular practice. If so, the instructor should teach it quite differently with careful follow-up instructions about meditation routine, possible side-effects, ways of adjusting the meditative process to suit the trainee, and so forth. The instructor should also prepare the trainees more carefully for their first meditation and offer them a fuller, more emotionally satisfying initial experience.

but this baby will never have been bathed in the waters of the womb or have known the comfort of any other heartbeat than its own.

Meditation is therefore a delicate process. Managed correctly, it may lead toward self-realization. Handled carelessly or without proper flexibility, it may be ineffective, perhaps even detrimental to those who learn it. The way in which practical meditation, when properly managed, does contribute to personal growth is the next thing we will discuss.

Part 3

MEDITATION AND PERSONAL GROWTH

Chapter 12

A NEW
PARTNERSHIP

In the 1950s and 1960s, middle-class Westerners became aware that while they were relatively well situated with regard to material benefits, something of fundamental importance seemed to be lacking in the way they led their lives. This something has been variously defined as love, creativity, meaning, personal growth, self-fulfillment, or spiritual values. Whatever the term used, it is clear that such values would formerly have been considered quite beside the point for psychotherapy. The psychotherapist was someone whose job it was to 'cure' a patient of an illness. But now there began to be an increasing number of mental health practitioners who viewed their role quite differently, taking what has been called a 'humanistic' approach to psychotherapy,

This newer approach lays emphasis upon self-fulfillment. It sees people as longing to realize their full human potential and as ultimately striving to do so if given the least opportunity. It emphasizes the importance of individuality. Each person, by virtue of their own particular background and experience, is treated as unique and important. It accords a central role to values; people are not seen as biological machines but as thinking, feeling, judging human beings capable of directing their own destinies. It is essential that each person gain a clear sense of self-identity, discover who they are and who they want to become, so that their potential may be fully developed.

The humanistic approach is positive in nature. Despite the violence, cruelty and horror that humankind has perpetrated throughout history – the undeniable capacity of man for evil as well as good – he is not seen as necessarily evil. While he may sometimes operate almost totally in terms of his negative potentials, he still retains the possibility of realizing his positive capacities as well.

Such a viewpoint has an impact upon the way psychotherapy is approached. The humanistic psychotherapist focuses on helping patients to perceive themselves as they really are, to accept their weaknesses and strengths, to be fully themselves. If they learn to do this, they will then drop their defenses and be open to experience; they will 'live' in the true sense of the word. The result is a new attention to the creative and healthy side of human nature – a contrast to psychotherapy's former emphasis on personality disturbance and repair.

This approach is not only appropriate for treating disturbed individuals, but deals with the failure of 'normal' people to realize their potentialities as well. It addresses itself to the great mass of human beings who feel alienated and at odds with their own nature. It seeks to help people be themselves, more fully and joyfully – to live their lives with meaning.

In this aim meditation and humanistic psychotherapy join hands. Meditation, working on its own level, helps the self grow naturally without impediment, to flower in its own way and at its own pace. It can be therapeutic in that it often serves to counteract specific psychological or physical problems, yet it fosters a more pervasive change than the mere absence of symptoms. Recognizing this, some psychotherapists are finding meditation a powerful ally in their work with patients, and a new and exciting partnership is born.

The Hartford Experience

I first became interested in the possibilities of using meditation with psychotherapeutic patients in 1972. At this time, the Wallace–Benson studies were beginning to appear in the scientific journals. Perhaps, I thought, this technique could be of help to people with incapacitating anxiety. It looked promising, and a working relationship between meditation and the mental health professions seemed a possibility.

Others in the psychiatric field were also sharing my curiosity. The venerable Hartford Institute of Living, one of the oldest and most prestigious psychiatric hospitals in the country, had decided at that time to launch a three-year research study on the effects of TM on hospitalized psychiatric patients.[1]

Originally, Dr Bernard Glueck, Director of Research, and Dr Charles Stroebel, Chief of the Institute's Psychophysiology Lab, had set out to compare three groups of patients to find out which of several types of relaxation training would be most useful in advancing the progress of psychotherapy: TM, alpha biofeedback or progressive relaxation. All three techniques looked promising because they had the advantage that once learned, they could be self-administered, something particularly useful for psychiatric patients, who are often prone to expect hospital authorities to provide them with a 'cure'. The investigators felt that if these patients were able to do something for themselves to improve their own state of mind, this in itself might prove therapeutic.

While the original plan was to compare three groups, as so often happens in scientific research, the plan did not work out. Soon after the studies started, subjects began dropping out of the biofeedback and progressive relaxation groups in large numbers and the statistical value of the study was being negated. The alpha biofeedback subjects reported having difficulty in making practical use of their alpha state or even in understanding its purpose. Patients who had learned progressive relaxation almost unanimously reported that they found this process both tedious and dull. In contrast to both these groups, almost all the patients who had learned to meditate continued to do so regularly. They generally enjoyed the practice and recommended it to their friends in the hospital. In fact a long waiting list developed to learn meditation.

The loss of these two comparison groups posed a problem for the researchers. To whom could they compare their meditation subjects? The solution they decided on was to match up each meditator with a 'twin control' chosen from the hospital population at large. The twin control was another patient of the same sex, roughly the same age, and with a similar personality profile to that of the meditator. Both groups of subjects were to be evaluated on a number of levels.

The evaluation procedures were extensive. One was a periodic readministration of the Minnesota Multiphasic Personality Inventory (MMPI), a personal self-report form which the patients filled out to indicate the degree and type of emotional disturbance they were experiencing. In addition, each patient in the study kept a daily record of the quality of their sleep, moods and eating habits. There were also objective measurements of change: brain wave recordings and other physiological measurements, nurses' daily computerized reports, psychotherapists' progress reports and hospital records.

Studying the first group of meditating patients to be discharged from the hospital, the researchers looked at the records showing their psychiatric condition at the time of discharge. The condition of the meditators had improved significantly more than had that of all the other hospital patients discharged that year. They had also improved more than their 'twin controls'.

While these are the only statistical findings released, the research team had informally noted other changes. The meditating patients often required lighter dosages of tranquilizing drugs and other forms of psychotropic medication after commencing meditation. A number of patients who had difficulty sleeping reported that their sleep had improved. In many instances, these people's sleeping medications could be reduced or entirely eliminated several weeks after they commenced to meditate.

A preliminary look at the MMPI results showed encouraging changes in the way patients reported their own condition after they had been meditating for a while. The average scores of the meditating patients on the MMPI seemed to show a steadily improving psychiatric condition. These self-reports were also supported by the nursing notes which suggested that with the practice of meditation, anxiety, depression and unacceptable behavior on the wards tended to decrease.

Despite this encouraging report from Hartford, I needed more specific information before feeling ready to recommend meditation to my patients. I wanted to know which kinds of psychiatric disturbance are likely to respond to meditation; what, if any, are the undesirable side-effects of this practice; if there is any type of patient for whom meditation may prove dangerous. To find out the answers to these questions, I traveled to Hartford to consult with the research team at the Institute, and while there I had an opportunity to observe the effects of meditation on hospitalized patients.

Meditation was being used in the Hartford experiment with all types of psychiatric patients. The researchers had even taught a number of schizophrenic patients to meditate successfully,

with beneficial results. Dr Glueck talked about one schizophrenic woman who was so ill and whose thinking was so
confused that they initially doubted she could learn to repeat the
mantra or understand the purpose of meditation. With careful
attention from specially trained teachers, however, this woman
had been able to learn the technique and was now showing
excellent improvement. I also had an opportunity to talk with
a teenage paranoid schizophrenic boy who was having his brain
waves monitored as a routine part of the study. He was definitely pleased with his meditation and told me that he was
feeling 'less paranoid' since he had commenced meditating.

The researchers showed me the brain wave recordings of
psychotically depressed patients who had learned to meditate.
They had even taught meditation to two patients who had
suffered serious brain injury as a result of accidents. While
meditation obviously could not cure the physical damage these
patients had sustained, it was helping them to adjust to their
altered brain functioning. They were now less anxious, more
cooperative, and easier to get along with than they had formerly
been.

I discovered that the Institute's program for teaching meditation was quite different from that typically used outside of
the hospital. Two TM teachers, who were full-time members
of the hospital staff, were on the premises at all times, spending
as much time as necessary with each new patient learning the
technique.

The teachers checked the patients' meditation practice every
day for the first three weeks, meeting with them individually.
They also met with them as a group once a week. After the first
three weeks, the patients were usually left on their own to
meditate (except for the required group meetings), but at any
time of day or night, if a meditating patient had a question
about meditation or any anxiety in connection with it, a teacher
was available at short notice.

Obviously this is the best arrangement for a psychiatric
program using meditation, but it raises certain questions. Is it
possible that some of the improvements found in these patients
were due to the fact that they had someone (their TM teacher)
who was deeply interested in them during their stay at the
hospital, someone willing to guide them and give them extra

attention? In other words, could the special attention by these TM teachers have created a placebo effect?

The researchers doubt this, pointing to the fact that the improvements these people showed were sustained well beyond the time when most placebo effects fade. Two years after the commencement of the study, a questionnaire was sent out by the staff to all patients who had originally learned meditation. Of those who responded (about 70 percent of those contacted), 68 percent reported that they were still meditating and obtaining good results from the practice. All the people in the follow-up study had been discharged from the hospital and were now living at home. Encouragement by the hospital TM teachers was therefore not a factor at this point.

To my many questions about possible undesirable side-effects of meditation, the researchers replied that they had found no unfavorable effects of meditation on the patients in their study, possibly because of these special instruction methods and precautionary procedures. A few patients who had dropped out near the beginning of the study had indicated that as a result of having learned to meditate, some of their thinking was 'clearing up' so rapidly that they feared they might lose all their familiar defenses if they continued. They were apparently not prepared emotionally for such rapid change, a problem which, as we shall see, others have noticed in their patients as well.

The research team was also acquainted with occasional difficulties which arose from the use of TM in the community outside the hospital. In all those cases which they had investigated, the trouble seemed to have been caused by the fact that the person involved had been using meditation incorrectly. Excessive over-meditation seemed to be the major cause of damaging side-effects.

In general, the Hartford researchers felt that it appeared that most seriously ill psychiatric inpatients *could* learn to meditate successfully, provided adequate attention was given to the various problems that may arise during the first several weeks of meditating.

Reducing Anxiety

Anxiety is not only a driving force behind most severe psychiatric conditions, but one of the chief stumbling-blocks to their effective treatment. The highly anxious person is frequently afraid to talk about the very things which are most important for him or her to face. Unmitigated anxiety leading to panic is so painful an emotion that it is usually avoided at all costs, even if the costs be the undermining of the patient's psychiatric treatment. Any auxiliary therapy that can lessen anxiety is therefore of help, one reason why tranquilizers are so widely prescribed.

In observing patients who are meditating, my psychotherapist colleagues and I have noticed that anxiety is lessened in a majority of them as they continue in their practice of meditation. These people now worry less about their jobs, their families and a host of anticipated dangers which formerly paralyzed their initiative. They seem protected or cushioned from these strains.

As their anxiety lessens, they also tend to be more relaxed and proficient at handling many tasks. This increased 'coping ability' is different from that which we usually see in patients on tranquilizers or anti-depressant medication. Drugs may restore a patient to feeling more 'normal' – 'I feel like my old self since I've been taking my tranquilizer' – but the drug is not likely to foster personal growth or help the person experience life in a new way. By contrast, after commencing meditation, people often find themselves reacting in ways they have not done before. The practice of meditation tends to open up new horizons rather than restoring a former state of affairs. For this reason some psychiatrists familiar with meditation will recommend to patients that they try learning meditation, before prescribing tranquilizers for them.

Another advantage of meditation over drugs is the fact that the meditator does not ordinarily lose alertness or become groggy. People taking high dosages of tranquilizers, on the other hand, often complain that they feel dull or sleepy and that their reaction times are slowed down. Because of this, people taking these kinds of drugs are regularly cautioned not to use machinery or engage in other activities where quick reflexes are required. By contrast, meditators are frequently more alert, nimble and aware of their surroundings than they were before.

The very fact that meditation is something which patients can do for themselves also builds strength and confidence. People who meditate when anxious and thereby regain a sense of calm, sense that they are in control of their own life and that no drug is doing the work 'for them'. One lesson of meditation, then, is that one can bring physical and mental processes under one's own control, a basic step in coping with anxiety.

Combating Addiction

Whether anxiety causes forms of addiction such as alcoholism or drug dependence is uncertain. These kinds of behavior are often strongly influenced by the stratum of society in which the person grows up, their early home situation, and perhaps certain inherited biological characteristics. If anxiety cannot be said to be the cause, however, it is certainly an effective trigger for severe bouts of addiction.

If meditation reduces anxiety, can it then help to control forms of addiction? This question is worth exploring when we consider the magnitude of addiction in our society and the inadequacy of most of our present treatment methods to deal with it. In 1971 researchers Benson and Wallace sought to find out if meditation might have some effect on drug usage. They studied 1,862 TM teachers-in-training who had been practicing meditation for at least three months and often for longer, in an effort to find out how much marijuana, amphetamines, barbiturates, or hallucinogens (such as LSD) these people were still taking after their considerable amounts of meditation.[2] On an anonymous questionnaire these teacher-trainees reported having all but eliminated drug abuse since commencing meditation, and even moderate use of such drugs was greatly reduced.

Whether this was due to meditation alone is hard to tell, however. TM teachers-in-training belong to a tight-knit community. They live together in residential training centers for many months, undergoing an intensive regime of meditation-plus-instruction. While there, they experience strong group pressure to abandon drugs in favor of meditation; 'successful meditators' are thought of as being non-drug takers. However, even if the results Benson and Wallace found were due, in part at least, to a need to conform to group standards, this in itself tells us something important about how drug abuse might be controlled. It suggests that a meaningful social community can exert pressures which may effectively reduce drug intake.

In the six-month period before they started practicing meditation, about 80 percent of these prospective teachers had used
marijuana, and of these, about 28 percent had been 'heavy users'
(that is, were using the drug once a day or more). Six months
after commencing meditation, only 37 percent of the teacher-
trainees were using marijuana and of these, only 6.5 percent
were still heavy users. Among those trainees who had been
meditating for twenty-one months or more, only 12 percent
were still using marijuana and only one individual remained a
heavy user. The decrease in the use of LSD was even more
marked, and similar results were reported for other hallucinogens, narcotics, amphetamines and barbiturates.

These seemingly anti-addictive effects of meditation also
extended to other areas. In the Benson–Wallace study, the percentage of teacher-trainees who drank hard liquor (either
occasionally or often) *before* commencing meditation was 60
percent. This figure came down to 25 percent for the group who
had been practicing TM for twenty-one months or more.

Much the same kinds of result were found for regular cigarette smokers: 48 percent of the teacher-trainees said they had
smoked before starting meditation and 25 percent described
themselves as having been 'heavy users' (that is, as having
smoked one or more packs a day). After twenty-one months of
meditating, these percentages had decreased to 16 percent who
were still smoking and only 5–7 percent who were still 'heavy
users'.

What does this study tell us? Did these results occur because
people who were more or less ready to stop taking drugs
anyway signed up to learn TM (this would leave hard-core drug
users out of the picture)? Did the serious drug abusers among
the meditators happen to dropout of meditation before the questionnaires were handed out, and so were not included in the
study? Do drug abusers in general shy away from becoming
TM teachers? Are the people who stay with the practice of
meditation the type of people who would be more likely to
become drug-free in the first place? In other words, does this
study apply to a select group only or are its results typical of
the general public?

There are as yet no answers to these questions, but some
of my psychotherapist colleagues and I have seen impressive
decreases in the use of drugs in patients who do not become

TM teachers, and whom we have observed both before and after they learned to meditate. It was, in fact, clinical observations of this sort that led Dr Mohammad Shafii and his associates at the University of Michigan Medical Center to design a study which attempted to overcome some of the drawbacks of the Benson—Wallace one.

The Michigan group felt it essential to have a 'control group', something which the Benson–Wallace study lacked. For this they chose people who used drugs but who were not meditators so that they could find out to what degree non-meditating people naturally cut down on drug usage over time. Because the Shafii group used this additional experimental safeguard, and because they used regular meditators, not TM teachers, as subjects, the results of their investigation are more informative.

The Shafii study showed a striking reduction in the amount of marijuana the TM group was still using after they had been meditating from one to thirty-nine months.[3] The number of marijuana users was now reduced to nearly one-third the original number, while the figures for the control group stayed approximately the same, dipping only slightly.

As to regular cigarette smoking – a habit which when it is compulsively followed is classified as an addiction – 71 percent of those who had practiced meditation for *more than two years* reported a significant decrease in their use of cigarettes, and 57 percent had totally stopped smoking by that time, while cigarette usage for the control group remained almost the same.

Drinking of alcohol was affected too. Within the first six months after commencing meditation, 40 percent of the meditators who had been meditating regularly for more than two years had stopped drinking either beer or wine, while no control subjects had stopped. After three years of meditation the figures were even higher – 60 percent of the meditators had now stopped drinking beer and wine. In addition, 54 percent of this last group (as against 1 percent of the control group) had also stopped drinking hard liquor.

And newer studies support these findings. When Ann Royer studied the effects of meditation on cessation of smoking over a two-year period,[4] she found that 51 percent of those meditators who had adhered closely to their meditation program and been regular in their practice had successfully quit smoking by that time. By contrast, only 21 percent of those meditators who had only partially adhered to their meditation program and were irregular in their practice had quit the habit. Her results also suggested that the benefits of meditation were cumulative – the regular meditators' smoking had *continued* to decline (or to cease altogether) over the twenty-four months of the study. In addition, once they stopped smoking, very few of the meditators ever resumed the habit.

Such studies as these suggest that meditation can be effective in preventing certain forms of addiction providing that a person is sufficiently motivated to continue meditating regularly for a long enough period of time. There seems to be a definite relationship between the amount of time a person has been meditating and the effectiveness of this practice in lessening drug consumption – the longer, the better.

Perhaps we have come to the point where we no longer need questionnaire studies which ask people what their drug usage was in the past. Instead we need more studies that follow a group from scratch, studying the same people before they start meditating and then again one or two years later. Although such studies are difficult and expensive to conduct, some have been done and the results of such longitudinal studies have been positive.[5] There are also some interesting clinical observations which extend over time.

In my own practice I have observed five patients smoke less marijuana after commencing meditation, four patients reduce their use of alcohol, and another three stop smoking cigarettes with little, if any, nicotine withdrawal effects. This represents a large proportion of my patient population who were heavy drug users since only very few of my patients used drugs heavily to begin with. My clinical observations therefore seem quite consistent with the reduction percentages in the Shafii study.

Interestingly, I have seen one patient take up smoking marijuana for the first time after she resumed her regular practice of TM. She claimed, that her freedom to use marijuana stemmed from the fact that meditation made her feel less guilty and she could now allow herself to experiment. Her behavior in this respect was part of a more general change. She had been a rigidly conventional woman, afraid of being spontaneous in any way. Now she was branching out into new activities in many areas of her life. She did not, however, develop an addiction to marijuana as a result of her easier attitude toward it. Her interest in it seemed to level off and eventually subsided, and at no point was her use of the drug more than a very occasional one.

A questionnaire survey on meditation and drug abuse conducted by Dr Leon Otis has also indicated that a very small number of the meditators questioned (6 percent) reported that they increased drug use after commencing meditation, although the majority (68 percent of those who had been meditating for less than two years) reported a sharp *decrease* in the use of drugs.[6] It seems, however, that any increase in drug use with meditation, when and if it occurs, is sufficiently rare to be of minor significance compared to the pronounced trend toward decreased use of drugs with meditation.*

Why Is Meditation Anti-Addictive?

Since meditation lowers anxiety, it may simultaneously lessen the need to take in an addictive substance to counteract anxiety. This is certainly a possible explanation for the effects of meditation on addiction. It may not be the only explanation for those anti-addictive changes we see with meditation, however.

Dr Andrew Weil, a physician and author whose report on the effects of marijuana usage is a milestone in this area of experimentation, considers drug use an expression of a natural and universal drive to achieve altered states of consciousness[7] – a drive which leads children in every culture to engage in activities such as whirling in circles until they fall to the ground, dizzy yet exhilarated by the new and different form of consciousness they have achieved. According to Weil, the drive to reach such unusual states may be behind the universal use of drugs such as alcohol, tobacco or caffeine, as well as common mind-altering drugs and even the more powerful opium and morphine derivatives. It does not, he feels, explain the *abuse* of such drugs, but only their *use*.

While drugs may satisfy the natural need for altered states of

---

* Unfortunately Otis was not able to obtain information on how extensive these drug increases were when they occurred, which specific drugs were involved, whether the increases resulted in use or abuse of the drugs, or the role that the drug increase may have played in these people's overall emotional adjustment.

consciousness, Weil feels this need can also be met, perhaps even more satisfactorily, through the use of meditation, changing, special exercises and other drugless techniques. A natural 'high' is not lost, as when a drug wears off. It is also under one's own control, with the person being aware of his own role in bringing about the desired state.

Weil comments that people who begin to move in a spiritual direction in connection with drug experimentation sooner or later look for other methods than drugs for maintaining their experiences:

> One sees many long-term drug users give up drugs for meditation ... but one does not see any long-time meditators give up meditation to become acid heads.* This observation supports the contention that the highs obtainable by means of meditation are better than the highs obtainable through drugs.[8]

By 'better' Weil does not mean morally preferable, but simply more effective.

A report on meditating patients at the Manhattan Psychiatric Center's Alcoholic Rehabilitation Unit seems to support Weil's theory. CSM was taught to twenty-five alcoholic patients in this unit by trained staff members. The patients were chronic alcohol abusers, classified as being in the most 'hopeless' 5 percent of the alcoholic population with respect to the seriousness of their addiction. These men lived as derelicts when not in the hospital and can be considered one of the least promising groups for any new habit formation such as regular meditation. Their lives are ordinarily haphazard and without any routines at all when they are not in hospital.

At first these patients showed great resistance to learning meditation; they wanted no part of it. Then two of the patients on the ward rather cautiously agreed to try it. As soon as these two had started, the word spread through the unit that meditation was the 'best experience these men had had since they had gone off alcohol'. It was considered the only thing available in the hospital that could give them a somewhat similar feeling.

---

* As we have seen, there may be some instances where drug usage has increased with meditation, but we have no indication that such people gave up meditation for drugs or that they became 'acid heads' or otherwise seriously addicted.

The staff members who taught CSM reported that the reaction of these alcoholic patients to their meditation had a special quality. Rather than simply having a quiet rest during meditation, these people had 'trips'. Many fantastic images and sensations occurred. Meditation was clearly being welcomed by these patients because it was recognized as a substitute activity. It was, in fact, the only therapy capable of calming them in the absence of alcohol.

As with many other in-hospital treatments, this gain did not continue when the patients were discharged into the community. As soon as these men returned to their previous environment, they typically stopped meditating, started drinking again, and eventually had to be hospitalized once more for alcoholism. When they were rehospitalized, however, many of these patients requested renewal instruction in meditation.

I feel that the interchangeability of different kinds of altered states of consciousness should be studied carefully. People who have been heavy users of hallucinogens before learning meditation will often report quite different experiences during their meditation than people who have never used drugs or who have not used them heavily. As one meditator explained:

> I get these really far-out experiences during meditation – but then of course I'm familiar with that kind of experience from my drug trips. If I hadn't learned to handle them without anxiety when tripping, I would probably be very scared now and I imagine I would more or less suppress this kind of experience.

This does not mean that former heavy drug users make the 'best' meditators or have the 'best' meditative experiences. Differences in the degree of positive response to meditation seem to be a purely individual matter – but it does highlight the interrelationship between different types of altered states of consciousness. Experience in one does seem to affect experience in others – different altered states do seem to interact. It has been shown, for example, that subjects who can concentrate well on a simple meditative task are in general more easily hypnotized than subjects who are highly distractible during meditation. This interchange or linkage between different methods of altering consciousness should be studied further.

Combating Physical Illness

I have already spoken of Dr Herbert Benson's work. His interest in meditation commenced because he envisioned its possible use in combating the 'fight or flight' response, a physiological reaction which releases emergency mechanisms in the body which speed the flow of blood to muscles, thereby preparing the animal or person either to fight an enemy or to run from danger.[9]

We need this hair-trigger survival response if we are jungle dwellers, are on a battlefront, or are facing any other situation involving an immediate threat to our life. This emergency response is *not* appropriate, however, in dealing with most everyday problems. The tensions that civilized people face usually cannot be physically fought or taken flight from – they are continuous. Our 'enemies' are all too often such things as concern about holding onto a job, about managing difficult relationships, about finances, about measuring up to competition, or other present-day stresses. Effective handling of *these* threats are hampered by physiological reactions such as a pounding heart, too rapid breathing, or spiraling blood pressure – the hallmarks of the fight or flight response.

Incorrectly used over a period of time, this response can be very harmful. When the body repeatedly mobilizes itself to deal physically with threats from which it cannot escape and which cannot be fought physically, this eventually results in permanent changes to the body which may damage health.

For example, the blood vessels may become more constricted and remain that way if the fight response is too often evoked in situations where fight is impossible. The person with chronic high blood pressure (hypertension) seems continually geared for a fight or a flight that cannot be made. This means that those emergency responses of the body, which were so useful under primitive conditions, have now become a disadvantage.

Because of these dangers, Benson reasoned that a technique which might relax the inappropriate fight-flight reaction and allow a natural counter-reaction (he called this the 'relaxation response') might be an effective way of altering the unhealthy physiology of the hypertensive patient. He pointed out that the relaxation response appears to be as much a part of our inherited equipment as is the fight-flight response although it is not easily evoked in a high-pressure society that demands that its members move at a fast pace, continually punch real or imagined time clocks, and constantly measure up to invisible yet threatening demands.

Benson was impressed when the studies on meditation which he conducted with Wallace showed that a profound state of relaxation could be brought on simply by practicing TM. Later he was able to demonstrate that this same state of deep physiological relaxation could be induced by using his own form of meditation. To date he and his associates have studied the effects of both TM and his own meditation method with hundreds of hypertensive patients, and many other researchers have studied meditation's effects on hypertension as well.[10]

While many of these patients have shown significant and sustained decreases in their blood pressure after about two months of meditation practice, others have shown only slight effects, if any. In Benson's studies, the patients' systolic readings (the blood pressure during the contraction of the heart) dropped on average about ten points and their diastolic readings (the blood pressure during the expansion of the heart) about five points – scarcely dramatic results but in the right direction. Many borderline hypertensive patients (whose blood pressure reading is just on the upper limit of what is considered the normal range) have achieved normal blood pressure after they have learned to meditate and a few patients have even been able to reduce the dosage of any anti-hypertension drugs they have been taking.

Benson emphasized that regular practice was essential in order to maintain these good results. Those hypertensive patients who responded well to meditation were able to keep their blood pressure down only if they continued to meditate regularly. If for any reason they discontinued the practice, their pressure would gradually drift back up again. Meditation seems to be like a change in diet which eliminates symptoms *only as long as the diet is faithfully adhered to*. It is therefore a preventive measure rather than a 'treatment'. It must become a permanent way of life if a person is to gain lasting benefits.

Since bronchial asthma is also recognized as a tension-related disease, researchers Honsberger and Wilson reasoned that it too might respond to meditation.[11] When they studied a group of asthmatic patients in the University of California Department of Medicine, they discovered that after beginning the practice of meditation, 94 percent of these patients showed improvement in their asthma symptoms as determined by measurements of their 'airway resistance' (a test of free breath flow). The personal physicians of 52 percent of them also rated their patients' conditions as 'improved', and 74 percent of the patients themselves reported their own condition to be 'improved'. Another group of asthmatic patients who simply read material about meditation for twenty minutes every day (but did not learn to meditate) showed no improvement. These were promising results.

Meditation is also frequently used to combat tension headaches. It has proven effective in a number of cases of headache that I have treated, and research studies have shown similar results.[12] I have received reports from psychotherapist colleagues on about a dozen patients who have learned meditation because they hoped to rid themselves of incapacitating tension headaches and in each of these cases, the headaches improved with meditation. In many instances they were eliminated. Once again, *continued* regular meditation seems crucial. If these patients stopped meditating, their headaches returned.

Migraine headaches (very different physiologically from tension headaches) may not respond as well to meditation. According to Benson, of seventeen patients suffering from severe migraine headaches studied at Boston's Headache Foundation, only three were helped by the regular practice of TM and one subject was actually 'made worse'.[13]

Counteracting Insomnia

One of the most common symptoms of anxiety is trouble with sleeping. When we are anxious we are apt to find it difficult to get to sleep or experience sleep as genuinely restful when it comes. We may awaken tired, irritated and tense rather than refreshed. Since meditation often serves to reduce anxiety, does it help to overcome sleeping problems?

It does, although it is not clear what the exact effects are. Together with some of my psychotherapist colleagues, I have treated a number of meditating patients with sleep problems and have noticed that these patients more often than not report improvement in sleep habits after commencing meditation.

Sometimes the improvement is dramatic. At the Institute of Living, the researchers found that their meditating psychiatric patients required far less sedation as their chronic insomnia was replaced by a normal, restful seven to eight hours' sleep. For a number of these meditating patients, in fact, sleeping medications could be eliminated.[14] This is a striking effect and coincides with our clinical observations. We so often see improvement in the sleep of patients who commence meditation that I now routinely recommend to any patients who have difficulty sleeping that they try meditation.

Improvement in sleep is also one of the benefits of meditation reported by a large number of people who learn the technique and who are unaware of having sleep problems. Researchers Matthew Silverman and Ernest Hartmann sent out a questionnaire to practitioners of TM who were not insomniacs or people with particular sleep disorders, but an average sampling of meditators. Many of these meditators reported they were sleeping better and needing less sleep after they had been meditating for at least four months.[15]

When the same researchers studied eight meditators in the sleep laboratory over a four-month period they found that these people could now fall asleep faster than they could before meditating. While the subjects in this study did not have any particular sleep disturbances to begin with – even before learning to meditate it took them on average only thirteen and a half minutes to fall asleep, a time so short as to be the envy of all those who experience difficulty in falling asleep – after they had learned to meditate even this modest waiting time was reduced. Now on average they required only eight and a half minutes to fall asleep.

Several systematic investigations have been done where meditation has been used with people who actually suffered from insomnia. At the University of Alberta in Canada, researcher Donald Miskiman found that after commencing meditation, people with insomnia could fall asleep more quickly.[16] These particular subjects had had so much difficulty in falling asleep to begin with that the change was considerable. Before learning TM it had taken these insomnia sufferers on the average about an hour and a quarter to get to sleep at night. After learning to meditate, they fell asleep within fifteen minutes after lying down in bed.

Such results are not confined to TM. Other forms of meditation work equally well. At Rutgers University a research team headed by psychologist Robert Woolfolk compared three groups of severe insomniacs, people who, on average, took about an hour and a quarter to fall asleep at night and who reported other serious difficulties in sleeping.[17] One group was taught progressive relaxation; another, a form of meditation which Woolfolk devised; and the third was not taught any technique.

The technique taught to the meditating subjects was basically the same as the breathing meditation described in Chapter 6. The only difference is that when they had mastered the meditation itself, Woolfolk's subjects were then requested to select some specific mental image to focus upon while repeating this exercise.

At the end of four weeks, when the subjects' daily sleep records were studied, the researchers found that both meditation and progressive relaxation had been effective. The subjects who had practiced these tasks were now able to fall asleep within about a half-hour after going to bed and the whole process was much easier for them. The do-nothing control group's sleep habits had not changed. What was even more encouraging was the fact that a follow-up study done six months later showed that these gains were not only retained but, if anything, improved. Some subjects had by then even further reduced the time it took them to fall asleep.

Meditation, therefore, seems to be effective in dealing with some of the problems that are major concerns for the mental health professions: persistent anxiety, stress-related illness and sleep disturbances. But does it go further than this and affect attitudes, the traditional cornerstones of psychotherapy? We will look at this question next.

Chapter 13

MORE OPEN TO LIFE

Many people conduct an inner dialogue in which they criticize themselves for not behaving 'properly' or doing things 'well'. An important change frequently brought about by meditation is that meditators will be begin to be more patient and understanding with themselves:

> During meditation, I do not clutch to engage. I do not make an effort to cope. I do not try either to succeed or to fail . . . Although distant music and memories may uninvitedly flow into my ken, there is no effort to define what I see or hear . . . In meditation I float rhythmically, effortlessly, almost totally divorced from the nagging of commands and 'shoulds'.[1]

If this newfound self-acceptance begins to affect their everyday life – and it often does – then meditators may find themselves becoming more tolerant of their own weakness, life may be seen in better perspective, and they may become more efficient since their actions are no longer hampered by unproductive self-criticism. Easing of self-blame also makes it easier for the meditator to accept certain thoughts that otherwise might be difficult to face without guilt or anxiety.

Dr Bernard Glueck has pointed out that when meditating, thoughts come into awareness that would ordinarily cause a person alarm, but that during meditation the reactions to them are different. Distress in the face of this usually anxiety-producing material is markedly reduced or almost absent.[2] My colleagues and I have noticed similar reactions.

One meditating patient, before getting married, became extremely anxious because her mother's several disastrous marriages had left an indelible impression on her. During this pre-marriage period in her life, her meditations became filled with mutilating images that were so vivid and realistic they would have horrified her under ordinary circumstances. These images would 'whiz by' during the first ten minutes of her meditation and then fade as she 'really got into meditating', but at no time did they cause her pain or distress. Because she reviewed them during meditation *without fear*, she was able to discuss them freely in psychotherapy and as a result to resolve some deep-seated fears.

Another meditator experienced anger during his meditations which ordinarily would have been alarming but was not so in the meditative state:

> In meditation today I began to realize, to visualize my anger. It was colossal, unholy, soul-searing. It looked and felt like all the fires of hell fused into one ball of broken china, of crashing glass, of steel mills on a gigantic scale... These images then blended with tornado-smashed cities, with cyclones and hurricanes and battle-fields which flooded the universe and hurtled through space with calamitous force... Then something happened... As my meditation went on, a feeling of love seemed to dissolve the pain... Something was set to rest within me.

Resolution of an uncomfortable emotional reaction during meditation is not unusual. When this occurs, the person may feel more emotionally alive outside of meditation too. This can mark the beginning of a new era in the meditator's life, a deeper awareness of who he really is.

A Repression Lifts

Closely related to the greater ability to accept emotions calmly when in meditation is the dramatic lifting of repression which sometimes occurs in meditators, permitting long-buried memories to come to the surface. One of the most impressive effects of meditation I have seen involved release of forgotten, terrifying memories in a woman who had for many years effectively banished them from awareness.

Adele initially came to the guidance clinic for help for her young daughter, who was suffering from severe anxieties which hampered her at school, but she denied the need for any psychotherapy for herself although she was obviously tense. Her voice was high-pitched, her breathing rapid, her speech pressured. She had a chronic heart condition for which she took medication several times a day and she suffered from high blood pressure and a thyroid condition. Soon after her daughter began to be seen for psychiatric treatment, Adele complained that she was unable to cope with the child and entered a mothers' guidance group which I was leading.

When she joined our group she was fearful about whether or not she would 'fit in' with the other mothers, and it seemed at first as though she was trying too hard to be liked by them. Because she was so tense, I decided that meditation might be a useful aid to her treatment.

When Adele learned CSM, her immediate response was a powerful one. She reported that during her first meditation she had felt as though she were a bird gliding freely through the skies, experiencing a wonderful sense of freedom as she drifted over the countryside. During this first meditation, too, she spontaneously shifted from using the mantra which she had chosen from the list of CSM mantras, and substituted for it a phrase of her own which suddenly popped into her mind – 'inner peace'. She continued to use this self-made mantra from then on and found it a most effective calming device.

Some effects of meditation on Adele's life were almost immediate. Within two days of commencing this practice, her heart became slow and regular and she was able to dispense with her heart medication within the first week of learning to meditate and has never returned to it.

During the first few weeks, her meditations involved images of floating and drifting in the sky among nature, flowers and other peaceful symbols. Soon, however, these pleasant 'floating' sensations began to alternate with frightening ones in which she would see atomic explosions or other cataclysmic happenings during her meditation. At this time Adele requested an individual psychotherapy session with me.

Because she seemed unusually tense, I suggested that she and I meditate together before commencing her therapy session. We had been meditating for about ten minutes when the session was interrupted by loud, almost hysterical laughter. Adele explained that she had had a sudden fantasy during meditation: she had imagined she was on a boat with her mother and she had pushed her mother off into the water. It had given her so much pleasure that she could not restrain herself from bursting out laughing.

She confided in me that this fantasy was an 'incredible thought' for her and wanted to know if it were 'normal' for her to have such thoughts. When I assured her it was normal to have many mixed feelings about a parent, a floodgate opened. Up until this point she had insisted that her parents were 'fine and wonderful people – no one could ask for better'. Now she revealed that she had been a battered child living in terror of a psychotic mother. One memory after another came to the surface in this session, some of them memories which she had managed to push out of her mind since childhood.

Adele had been born without the sanction of the church of which her mother had been a devout member. Because of this, Adele's mother viewed her daughter as having been born 'in sin' and developed a mental illness shortly after the child's birth which lasted during the girl's entire childhood.

The first buried memory to surface during a meditation session was an early childhood incident that Adele had long tried to forget. When Adele was three years of age, in a fit of rage, her mother had grabbed a dish towel, twisted it around the child's neck, and tried to strangle her. It was only when a neighbor across the alleyway, seeing this attack through the window, rushed to the door to intervene, that her mother, in a daze, had let go.

Another meditation session brought to light a different incident which Adele had not recalled for almost thirty years. When she was very young, her father had given her a toy dog as a gift before leaving on one of his all too frequent business trips. She had carried this toy about constantly when he was away and, perhaps because of its comforting presence, cried out, 'I'll tell Daddy!' the next time her mother started chasing her in order to catch her and beat her. In retaliation for Adele's 'answering back', the mother had dragged her into the cellar of their home, locked the door, and told Adele that if she ever revealed to anyone, especially her father, the mother's beatings, she would push her into the furnace. To illustrate this point, she threw the toy dog into the furnace and forced Adele to watch it burn.

Despite the intense difficulties in her life, Adele had managed to save herself from destruction. As soon as she graduated from high school she joined the armed services, determined to learn effective methods of self-defense such as karate and judo. She did learn how to defend herself, and later worked, married, had several children, and lived a generally constructive life, although her many tension-related illnesses attested to the fact that her traumatic early life was still having its effect on her.

As she began to discuss her mother's mistreatment of her in individual psychotherapy, her meditations became filled with hostile fantasies toward her mother. At one point she vividly pictured an atomic bomb killing her parents but sparing the rest of the population. So many painful memories were beginning to surface during her meditation sessions, in fact, that Adele began to be afraid of meditating, while at the same time she did not want to stop because it was obviously benefiting her heart condition. At this point I advised her to reduce her meditation time to three to five minutes per session to slow up the tension-release. This worked well and Adele was soon ready to share her painful memories with the mothers' group in which she participated.

This was an important step. Her mother's childhood threats about the terrible punishments that would follow if she told anyone about her mother's mistreatment were still deeply engrained in her. When the other women in the group accepted her painful revelations with understanding and support, it was a source of new strength for her. Following this, her attitude toward her own mother began to change. She was now able to accept the fact that her mother had been mentally ill and probably should have been hospitalized during those years – that, in effect, she had not been responsible for her actions. This realization so relieved Adele that she was able to return to meditating for a full twenty minutes twice a day, a schedule she has been able to maintain ever since. Memories now stopped flooding her meditation sessions which were once more filled with largely pleasant fantasies, with only occasionally a momentary violent scene.

From then on Adele found herself less harassed about many things. When her children started yelling at each other around the house, it no longer upset her. Her compulsive nail-biting stopped. Life-long nightmares receded to almost zero. It was also instructive to see her lose her need to prove to the world that she was 'self-sacrificing'. She was now easy-going and casual in the mothers' group and had stopped trying to solve everyone else's problems for them. As she worked through her painful relationship with her own mother, she also found herself able to play with her little daughter for the first time, and to thoroughly enjoy doing so.

Adele says that if she had not had individual psychotherapy sessions along with meditation, she would have been so frightened by the upsurge of painful memories that she would not have been able to continue meditating. I agree that had she not had my support and later the encouragement of the group to help her handle her anger at her mother, she almost certainly would have had to discontinue meditation in order to escape unbearable anxiety. I doubt, however, whether psychotherapy *alone* could have helped Adele resolve these problems. She was initially too fearful of facing the painful areas in her life to have allowed herself to enter individual psychotherapy of the type where free association might have been used to recover repressed memories. Meditation, however, enabled these memories to surface within a remarkably short span of time so they could be constructively dealt with in her therapy.

Sense of Self Increases

As we have indicated, the contribution of meditation to personal growth does not stop with removing symptoms, even such crippling symptoms as the repression of crucial memories or an inability to come to terms with anger in oneself, but reaches further, effecting a change which has to do with the unfolding of a sense of personal worth, a growing awareness of one's true self. A meditator expresses this in his journal:

> When I meditate I go into myself. I come into myself. I apprehend myself as an entity separate from every other entity, separate from every other thing. I am not my house, nor my car, nor the clothes I wear. I am not the rules I live by nor even the words I say. I am me. How strange! This is what it feels like to be me![3]

The ability to view ourselves as separate from our surroundings is called field independence by psychologists. This capacity frequently increases with meditation, an important consideration since people who are 'field independent' are apt to see themselves more distinctly, more clearly, and in a more sharply detailed fashion. They tend to be inner-directed rather than outer-directed, asking themselves, 'How does this feel to me?' rather than, 'How does this look to others?' Those with a less developed sense of identity, who tend to rely on other people to shape their attitudes and judgments, are known as 'field dependent'.

These aspects of personality are particularly interesting because they have some highly reliable testing instruments available to measure them. One is the Embedded Figures Test, a refined version of those puzzles given to children where they are asked to find the 'little pictures' hidden within the larger picture. The more 'field independent' a person is, the more rapidly he can isolate the little figures from the big one that embraces them.

In the Rod and Frame Test, the person has to perform a physical task: straighten a rod viewed in a somewhat tilted frame. People who are more 'field dependent' tend to straighten the rod by aligning it so that it is parallel with the vertical edges of the frame; they use outer cues when performing their straightening task. Those who are more 'field independent' tend to straighten the rod by aligning it with the vertical of their own body; they use their own self as the reference point. The Embedded Figures and Rod and Frame Tests are considered very 'stable' measures; the way a person approaches these tasks tends not to change over time once she has reached adulthood.

It is all the more interesting, therefore, to discover that these tests often show positive changes in people who have been meditating. In a study conducted with Zazen meditators, for example, researcher Melissa Hines found that her subjects scored significantly higher on the Embedded Figures Test after they had been meditating for ten weeks than they had before learning to meditate.[4]

When psychologist William Linden taught a group of third-grade children from an underprivileged background a form of Zazen meditation, he found much the same thing.[5] These children were tested with the Embedded Figures Test before they started meditating and again after a period of thirteen weeks during which they had practiced meditation in school for a few minutes each day. At the end of the experiment, their scores showed that they were significantly more 'field independent' – a finding of importance to people who are concerned with fostering individuality and independence in young children.

The results using the Rod and Frame Test are impressive because no matter how often a person performs this task, his score will not improve with practice. Using the Rod and Frame Test, the Embedded Figures Test and a task which measures the tendency to perceive the apparent movement of a spot of light in a darkened room, psychologist Kenneth Pelletier of the University of California School of Medicine tested a group of subjects before they learned TM and again after they had been practicing it for three months.[6] He compared them with control subjects over that same time interval. At the end of this period, the meditators' scores had improved significantly on all three measures, while those of the non-meditators had not improved at all. Basic perceptual measures such as the Rod and Frame Test and the Embedded Figures Test had therefore changed with meditation.

In a study done at Princeton University, researcher David James later showed that field independence, as measured by the Embedded Figures Test, can even change over the *short term* if a person meditates during the interval between testings. A group of subjects improved significantly more on scores of field independence after twenty minutes of meditating than another group of subjects who simply rested for twenty minutes.[7] In fact, the scores of the 'resters' remained unchanged over this interval. This finding is surprising since it had previously been thought that field independence could not fluctuate on a short-term basis. It suggests a strong immediate influence of meditation on our interaction with the environment.

The findings on meditation and field independence may have important practical implications when we consider the desirability of field independence for certain types of work. The practice of meditation has, for example, been shown to enhance field independence in art students from two universities,[8] a result which may explain some of the increased creativity frequently reported in meditators. This is a subject we will look at more closely when we come to discuss the relationship between meditation and creativity.

The increased field independence seen in mediators may also be related to the interesting fact that meditators often report that they have developed a greater sense of their own identity since they have been meditating. They tend to sense their personal rights in situations where formerly they might have been unaware of them, or can now withstand social pressures without abandoning their own opinions. They may also find themselves becoming more decisive and expressing ideas more openly.

A patient of mine, Richard O., is a successful professional man who grew up in a home where the family members tended to deny their emotions. They rarely showed anger or sadness, always acting 'reasonably'. Richard learned to exert a tight control over his own emotions and eventually almost lost awareness of them. Now, more often than not, he could not tell when he was angry or when he was sad, or identify any other strong feeling. He could only reason that maybe he *might* have felt a particular way. One of the few times when genuine feelings were available to him was when he had had some drinks, and drinking was becoming a problem for him. One of the first tasks of psychotherapy was to help Richard get in touch with his own feelings and, among other therapeutic approaches, I suggested that he learn CSM.

On emerging from his initial meditation, Richard said he had felt as though he were 'in another world' and would have liked to have stayed there for a long time; in fact, indefinitely. When he phoned me the following day to report on his meditation (a routine procedure) he asked me if he might be allowed to meditate more than twice a day, because he found it such a 'pleasant experience'. I suggested that he not increase his meditation time because this might release tensions too fast for him to handle comfortably.

After meditating for one week, Richard returned for his psychotherapy session already showing changes. He no longer compulsively interrupted his sessions to go outside and grab a cigarette (and never again had to interrupt a therapy session to smoke), he was more relaxed in his posture, and he now talked about different subjects. Before he had been businesslike and intellectual, speaking in a highly organized fashion about his relationship with his wife. In this session, he talked about himself in a somewhat musing fashion, bringing up thoughts about his childhood and his own inability to enjoy himself or to 'play' in life. He seemed to have a new interest in exploring his own reactions and for the first time expressed a desire to use therapy to enrich his own life rather than just as a tool to improve his marriage.

The following week, while traveling on a plane, he was meditating and had the impression that he heard his own voice saying, 'Empty yourself of your desires!' This rather mysterious statement was followed by an experience of exaltation and the further words: 'I can have a drink or smoke a cigarette if I want to – but I don't have to.' This seemed to him to be a startling revelation, giving him for the first time a feeling that he now had a choice of whether or not to drink.

Richard had always found it extremely difficult to know what his own wishes were. After meditating for about three weeks, he reported an 'unusual incident'. His children had asked him to stop at a roadside stand to buy ice cream. His usual response to such a request would have been to buy the same ice cream for himself as for the others, not realizing that he, too, might have preference for a particular flavor. This time, however, he found himself saying, 'Fine, I'll get you what you want – then I'm going to get chocolate ice cream for myself.' Seemingly a small thing, this was important: he had sensed his own need and stayed with it.

The experience of a new and convincing sense of self during meditation often forms a base of self-awareness which can be built upon to advantage in psychotherapy. Archimedes, the ancient Greek mathematician and physicist, is reputed to have said: 'Give me a place to stand and I will move the world.' Certain patients seem unable to move ahead in therapy because they appear to lack a base of self on which to stand in order to produce change. In these cases even deep psychological insights may build on quicksand, as it were. Meditation often makes an important contribution to therapy by building into the person a new, deeply convincing, but largely wordless experience of self.

Another meditator illustrates this process. Jack was an intelligent although extremely withdrawn man who had been in psychotherapy of one sort or another for nineteen years. Being meticulous in his habits and extremely responsible, he was able to hold onto various administrative positions for a long period of time, but at home he led the life of a recluse with few friends or relationships. Although he was in his mid-forties he had had virtually no sex life. Jack's relationships were fantasy ones. His life was filled with daydreams of dating attractive women but these were always followed by obsessive worries about how he might, even timidly, approach such women should he meet them.

At his therapists' suggestions, he had attended marathons, encounter groups, group therapy, and even undergone a full course of 'systematic desensitization' by a behavior therapist – all to no avail. The behavior therapy had even made his symptoms worse because as he tried to imagine dating in the context of being deeply relaxed, instead of feeling calmer he became more anxious and developed palpitations. His increasing tension made him abandon this form of therapy.

His present therapist suggested to him, almost as a last resort, that he learn CSM. Jack, who usually returned sneering after having tried out some new method that had been suggested to him, agreed to learn it.

Surprisingly, meditation worked. Jack was enthusiastic about it, and according to both him and his therapist, it 'remade' this man's life in many ways. He was deeply impressed with the technique from the beginning and became a regular meditator. After beginning meditation, his attitude toward experimenting with relationships changed markedly. He was soon able to try out new forms of relating to others. He initiated some tentative sexual relationships, and his progress along these lines continued.

For years people had been making constructive suggestions to Jack about things he might do to 'change his life-style'. Some of these suggestions had been daring, some mild; but he had not been able to act on even the simplest of them. As he put it, 'Even though I could recognize that their advice was good, there was nobody present in me that could respond to it – now there is a me to listen, and respond, and move on these things. Meditation has given me a center to myself.'

The 'center' which Jack refers to seems to be an 'inner ear' that is sensitive to his own being. It is a center of the self that can mobilize and begin to take action. The result is that where before he seemed to have no 'backbone' or substance, now he had a new assertiveness and for the first time was able to make progress in his psychotherapy.

Through meditation, people begin to see themselves as self-determining beings, separate from their surroundings. At the same time they also begin to feel more intimately connected with all that surrounds them. An entry in my late husband's meditation journal expresses this:

> During meditation I am me, not 'you', not your values. I am me, and my values are reconstituting me. . . . A tree is not a slave, its growth is its own. In meditation I grow as a tree, I live with the sun and the earth, and am my own ten commandments. . . .

Greater Openness to Others

Just as meditation can increase one's sense of individuality and lead to self-assertion, allowing one to feel close to one's self, by the same token it often increases one's sense of closeness to others. As Erich Fromm has pointed out, love of self and love of others are but two aspects of one fundamental capacity for loving.[9]* It is interesting to see meditators become more individualistic and, at the same time, more cooperative and friendlier to others than they were formerly. The openness and ease with people which often come with meditation and the increased friendliness and greater tolerance for the weaknesses of others, parallel the easing of the meditator's attitude toward himself.

It is a common psychological observation that as self-blame lessens, so does the tendency to blame others.[10] In the same way, if we can experience joy in our own aliveness, we will support the aliveness of others, the reason why psychotherapists begin by helping their patients to accept *themselves*. Relationships with other people seem automatically to improve as this occurs.

Another byproduct of growing certainty about one's own identity is that having become the center of their own awareness, meditators may find themselves having less need to be

---

* Fromm makes a sharp distinction between self-love and 'selfishness'. The 'selfish' person is said not to love himself, but hate himself. His lack of fondness and care for himself then leave him empty, frustrated, and anxiously concerned to wrench from life whatever satisfactions he can. This makes him seem to care too much for himself, but he is actually making an unsuccessful attempt to cover up and to compensate for his failure to care for his real self, and therefore to be able to care for others. People who have genuine self-love, on the other hand, have the capacity to love *both* self and others.

the center of attention in a social gathering; it is no longer necessary to prove an identity and self-importance which are now self-evident. This may lead the meditator toward a more natural relationship with other people. She may become more genuinely aware of others for their own sake because she is no longer concerned with how she is 'coming across'. Meditators' families frequently report that they have become 'much easier to live with'. Their friends often say they are 'easier to talk with', 'friendlier' or 'warmer'.

I recall an immediate change of this sort which I noticed in a patient within a few days after she had learned meditation. This woman had behaved in a critical, argumentative and suspicious manner in her treatment sessions with me, but in this hour she was different. Her face was relaxed and more attractive. She looked directly at me when she spoke. Her speech was quieter. For the first time since she had come into therapy I felt that I was facing a friendly human being, one with whom I could work in a constructive give-and-take fashion.

It was significant that in this session she reported a change in her relationship with her little daughter as well. Since she had commenced meditating, she was finding herself no longer so 'hard' on the child and she realized that in the past she had been taking out feelings of anger at her husband on the little girl. Now, she said, she could quietly instruct her daughter without commanding her to do things, and the child was responding by becoming more emotionally open with her mother.

Several research studies support these observations on the fortunate changes in human relationships that frequently occur with meditation. Studying the social effects of teaching meditation to high school students, educator Howard Shecter reports that meditating students showed a significant increase in 'tolerance' scores on tests of social attitudes given to them before learning TM, and again fourteen weeks after learning it.[11] Along similar lines, researcher David Ballou, studying the effects of meditation on the personality of prisoners, found that when a well-known clinical measure of personality, the MMPI, was administered to two groups of prisoners – one group which was taught TM and the other which did not learn to meditate – the meditators improved significantly on the 'social introversion' scale, moving toward the more 'socially outgoing' end of the scale, while the scores for the control group remained unchanged.[12]

In another prison study, researchers found that prison records kept on meditating prisoners showed that the number of positive activities these people participated in, such as sports, clubs and education, had doubled after they started meditation, while the number of prison-rule violations was reduced. Non-meditating prisoners, on the other hand, did not change in their behavior over the same period of time.[13]

While such studies need to be carefully evaluated in terms of other possible factors that may have influenced changes in the prisoners – such as the positive attention they may have received from meditation instructors or the expectations they held for the technique – the fact that they correspond with what I and other psychotherapist colleagues have seen in patients, suggests that they probably reflect genuine changes in social attitude and relationships with meditation.

As the anecdotes described in this chapter illustrate, the improvements we see in meditating patients are not merely clinical ones; that is, meditation does not just result in the solution of an emotional problem, although this can certainly happen. Equally important is its capacity to expand the ability to live life more fully and to savor the sense of self. For this reason, meditation has many benefits to offer numerous meditators who will never need psychotherapy.

Chapter 14

THE CREATIVE
MEDITATOR

When asked whether meditation makes people 'more creative' I find it somewhat difficult to respond. The answer is both 'Yes' and 'No'. Meditation helps some people develop certain characteristics we identify with creativity; but this does not make them artists, inventors or creative scientists if they do not have the interest in or ability for this sort of work. Meditation also helps others already in creative fields to develop their abilities further. On the other hand, many meditators who benefit from meditation in other respects have not become more creative, and some people already doing creative work do not want to meditate or do not continue meditating if they learn.

The relationship between meditation and creativity is difficult to pin down because 'creativity' does not seem to be a single characteristic. It is a combination of character traits or abilities which are only loosely linked and our methods for detecting even one of these qualities are not as yet exact. Despite such problems, however, when psychologists Marie Dellas and Eugene Gaier, of the State University of New York, reviewed the literature on creativity they were able to arrive at a composite picture of the 'Creative person'. It sounds surprisingly like someone in a state of meditation.[1]

According to their study, the creative person is capable of an unusually flexible *inwardly directed* awareness which permits a much greater than usual use of 'primary process thinking'. Primary process is the name given by Freud to the laws governing those unconscious processes which operate differently from familiar conscious thought. They are the 'stuff that dreams are made of' – a type of thinking using symbolic, often pictorial ways of expressing deeply buried needs and desires.

The primary process tends to surface in drowsy states where the mind is unhampered by logical restrictions. It can produce bizarre images: the 'absurdities' we sometimes see in dreams, or the strange forms that hallucinations may take.

Creative breakthroughs which have occurred in dreams and other altered states of consciousness where primary process thought is prominent abound: Robert Louis Stevenson received his inspirations for most of his books from his dreams; the material for Chagall's paintings was taken directly from his dreams; Howe was inspired by the idea of the needle with the hole at the bottom – an insight which enabled him to complete an operable sewing machine – from a dream; a reverie and a dream revealed to Kekulé the structure of the benzine ring, and to Crick the DNA molecule. There are many other examples which illustrate that contact with primary process is an important factor in the creative process. This is significant because meditation encourages primary process thinking. Like the creative person, a meditator drifts from idea to idea and image to image during meditation, unhampered by the restrictions of commands or 'shoulds'.

Ability to experience primary process thought is not in and of itself an index of creativity, however. This contacting of the unconscious must also be controlled; it needs to be integrated with and regulated by the conscious mind. Apparently it is neither the conscious nor the unconscious mode of functioning which is most useful for creativity, but rather the smooth interaction of these two different modes which leads to success in creative endeavors.

There is some research which has demonstrated this relationship between meditation and the ability to use primary process thought in a controlled fashion. Psychologist Terry Lesh used the Rorschach inkblot test as a means of measuring the amount of primary process thinking each person was able to use *in a constructive manner*. The subjects were psychological counselor trainees who were tested before and again after they had been practicing Zen meditation for a period of four weeks. At the end of this time, the ability to make constructive use of primary process thought had increased in the meditators, but had not changed in the non-meditating counselor trainees.[2]

In another study, psychiatrist Edward Maupin discovered that the more effectively his subjects handled primary process thought and visual images during their meditation, that is, the more comfortably they were able to experience this 'free-wheeling' kind of thought without either suppressing it or allowing it to run away with them, the more satisfactory they afterward judged their meditation sessions to have been.[3]

Increased openness to experiencing emotion, and the ability to allow oneself to respond to problems on an intuitive level, are two additional personality traits which Dellas and Gaier found distinguished creative people from the average. Again, both these traits are frequently increased by meditation. Many meditation teachers encourage their students to adopt an intuitive approach rather than logical thinking. A Zen archer, flower-arranger, painter or poet is taught to allow his art simply to 'happen'. He is to respond with a delicately attuned awareness to what is occurring, rather than to impose rational rules on the process. In the same way, a Westerner learning modern forms of mantra meditation is taught not to clutch at the mantra, but to allow it to 'come to him' in a natural, easy manner, without effort or planning.

The koans (riddles) used in Zen and the manner in which they are resolved also illustrate the way in which intuitive thinking is employed in meditation. Time after time the Zen student reaches an *intellectual* solution of the riddle, only to have it rejected by his Zen master, until finally an inner crisis is reached. Realizing that intellectual skills are worthless to solve the problem, the student then gives up the fight for a rational solution, lets go, and is said to 'throw himself into the abyss'. It is then that 'enlightenment' occurs. Solving the koan, therefore, involves the ultimate rejection of the logical, linear intellectual approach in favor of an intuitive grasp of a problem. This letting go and 'plunging into the abyss' seems to correspond to the 'creative leap' which artists must make. Many creators report that much of their production takes place in an 'egoless' state similar to that during which a Zen student solves his koan.

Creative people also have access to a relatively unfocused kind of attention which Dellas and Gaier have called 'perceptual openness'. This is the opposite of our usual ways of perceiving. What we ordinarily notice is almost always strongly limited by certain factors. Among these are our needs of the moment. If we walk down the street when we are hungry we will generally notice many restaurants and food stores but few, if any, movie theaters or shoe stores; children selling newspapers will not capture our attention, while those eating ice-cream cones will; the smell of a rose garden will go unnoticed while that of a barbecue will seem to fill the air.

In the same way, our past experience ordinarily limits what we perceive. When we walk down a particular street every day, in all likelihood we rarely notice the buildings on that street because we are familiar with them. We will, however, generally notice a *new* street, or a new building on a familiar street, immediately. Our perception of the unfamiliar tends to be keen. Because of this selective process, most things with which we come in contact are never fully registered in our consciousness. We see what we want to see, what we need to see, and by and large, what we expect to see.

A look at the history of certain creative breakthroughs suggests that this tightly programmed, limited mode of perception is not as typical of the successful artist or scientist as it is of the ordinary person. These gifted people's thought tends to seek the unknown and move freely about, unrestricted by narrow goals. Creative people are said to be tolerant of changing situations and easily able to adopt fresh ways of seeing things. They are more 'perceptually open' than the rest of us. Because of this they will be aware of many things in their environment that may escape the so-called normal person, and they may also be able to remember and make use of this information more effectively.

Art is often an unusual presentation or arrangement of familiar objects, an ability to 'make strange' ordinary objects. This makes it possible to notice them as we would if they were entirely new to us. A Campbell's soup can or a box of Morton's salt is nothing when seen in the kitchen cabinet. If it is not presently needed, it goes unnoticed. Placed in a gallery, however, it becomes something startling. The artist who first puts an ordinary object into a painting is considered 'creative' because he has seen the object as no one has seen it before. The Zen masters would say he has been able to view it with 'the eye of the beginner',[4] a valued achievement in the Zen tradition.

Scientific discoveries as well as artistic ones require the ability to view an old problem from a new perspective; as do practical discoveries, those 'inventions' we all make when we meet a novel situation with an innovation in our everyday life. Instead of filing away a piece of information into a familiar 'cubbyhole' in the mind, the person in the process of inventing allows it to connect mentally with seemingly *unrelated* pieces of information. A wine press, for example, was used over the ages but inspired only thoughts of fragrant flowing liquid and revelry, until printing from wooden blocks was developed at the dawn of the fifteenth century. These diverse processes had never been connected in anyone's mind, but Johann Gutenberg saw a wine harvest in a new light. Watching the power of the wine press, it occurred to him that the same steady pressure might be applied by a seal onto paper and the *pressure* could enable printing to take place. This inspired the invention of the printing press. While not all, perhaps not even most, unusual combinations of previously unrelated information turn out to be this useful, when they do they can be trail-blazing.

As psychologist Rollo May points out: 'Obviously if we are to experience insights from our unconscious, we need to be able to give ourselves to solitude.'[5] Meditation can be described as a state of inner solitude. During it, perceptual openness similar to that characterizing the thinking of creative people often seems to occur. The Hindu meditational tradition advocates the opening of the 'third eye', seeing more and more from a new vantage-point, and the Sufi sect of Persia views meditation as a means of developing an added perceptual organ which is said to enable one to overcome the limitations of the normal perceptual system. In addition, one of the general aims of traditional schools of meditation is a state called 'non-attachment', in which one is said to exist 'without desires'. This state has some similarities to the attitude of creative persons who are not goal-bound but freer than most people to scan a vast field of impressions without becoming caught up in any one of them.

The opening-up of perceptions through meditation is, however, more than a momentary thing. It often influences a person's general manner of responding to stimuli, both inner and outer, when he is not in meditation. As we have seen, yogis and Zen masters failed to habituate to clicks outside of meditation, indicating that they were unusually open to stimuli during their ordinary waking lives.

Even people who have been meditating for a relatively short period of time can experience increased perceptual openness.

In a survey conducted as part of our research at Princeton University on the effects of meditation on personality, 73 percent of the subjects reported that they had improved in 'awareness of external and internal environment' after having meditated for three and a half months.

While meditation can affect certain aspects of creativity, it is unlikely that all the traits which cluster together in the creative person are affected by meditation. Some of them seem to be the result of heredity or personality drives so strong and fundamental that they are unlikely to be created or destroyed by any outside intervention. Three important aspects of creativity which *do* respond to meditation, however, are: productivity, originality and stamina, or 'staying power'.

Increased Productivity

Increased productivity often depends on the ability of ideas to flow easily and rapidly. Meditation may bring about such a release of ideas. As I described in Chapter 1, within a week of learning to meditate, my late husband was able to write a forty-page scientific paper that he had been postponing for six months. In contrast to his previous difficulties with it, his ideas now flowed unhesitatingly, a change he traced to the free-floating thought of meditation, where images and ideas drift unhampered by self-criticism.

Within the first week of learning meditation, one of my patients discovered that she could do crossword puzzles with great ease, something she had never been able to do before. Her previous inability to do these puzzles was related to the fact that she had always had difficulty in any situation (such as an examination) where she was required to 'switch perspective'. She would arrive at an exam having studied the course material thoroughly from one viewpoint only to find herself unable to tackle it from the different perspective required by the test. In the same way, when trying to do a crossword puzzle she used to 'get into a rut'. Seeing one possibility for a word, she could not abandon this when it did not fit so as to enable herself to scan her memory for other words, a necessity for creative puzzle-solving. Meditation, however, seemed to unlock her ability to shift gears mentally. She was now free to reshuffle ideas into new combinations.

One of the most impressive effects of meditation on blocked productivity which I have witnessed occurred in a college student. Susan was a brilliant young woman and an outstanding scholar, but when she was an undergraduate at Princeton she was so self-critical and perfectionistic that she was unable to write more than a few pages of her junior paper (a key require-ment at the university) without tearing it up in disgust. Although she had completed research for the project, she faced the equivalent of the familiar writer's block in preparing it. Her six months of work resulted in continual frustration and she was in danger of failing her junior year because of this stalemate.

When her visits to the counseling service on campus and my considerable encouragement as her adviser failed to help her, I suggested that she learn meditation. Susan agreed, went to learn TM, and for two weeks after that did not contact me. At the end of this period, she walked into my office and handed me a thirty-five-page typed manuscript, a complete draft of the paper. When I read it I realized it was more than a draft; with little change it could be submitted as a solid piece of research, more than fulfilling her junior independent work requirement.

Susan later told me that the reason she had finally been able to write her research study was that meditation had literally 'opened up the floodgates', permitting her ideas to flow again. A particularly important aspect of this incident is the continuing effects meditation had on her. She was now able to handle her studies with ease, and began to realize her full academic poten-tial. A year later, she graduated from Princeton, Phi Beta Kappa, and received highest honors.

Aside from anecdotes such as the above, there is some experi-mental evidence suggesting that meditation may help to increase productivity. In Melissa Hines's study on meditation and creativity conducted at Princeton University, she found that what psychologists call 'ideational fluency', a tendency for mental associations to flow easily, rapidly and productively, can be influenced by meditation.[6] There was a significant increase in ideational fluency in the Zazen meditators she studied over the ten-week period, while the control subjects' ideational fluency was unchanged.

Curiously, this improvement in the meditators took place almost entirely in the *last four weeks* of the study. During the first six weeks, there was relatively little improvement. This suggests an accumulative effect of meditation on certain mental processes connected with creativity. Perhaps the *longer* a person has been meditating, the more likely it is that she will have personality changes in the direction of increased perceptual openness and ideational fluency. Since a number of people report an almost immediate 'opening up' of productivity after beginning meditation, however, it is obviously not necessary for *everyone* to have been meditating a long time for this to occur.

Improved Quality of Creative Work

Some people have reported striking changes in the nature of their creative work which they themselves have attributed directly to meditation. Probably the most impressive instance of this is a former patient. Tony found psychotherapy an exceedingly painful experience. He had been to several therapists before coming to me and during the time that he and I worked together, this sensitive, gifted young man found it so anxiety-provoking to talk about his problems that he would lapse into silence a good portion of the time.

Since Tony showed an interest in drawing and painting, I decided to use art therapy in his treatment. When crayons and a large pad of paper were made available, he readily 'drew his feelings' on paper and we were able to discuss them. Sometimes he would alter his drawings to reflect newer, more healthy attitudes toward himself. His artwork was not outstanding, however. He was a rather awkward beginner and I viewed his drawing simply as a therapeutic maneuver.

Tony then left for another city. While he had improved his outlook somewhat, he was still far from comfortable in therapy and had yet to bring under control a lifelong tendency toward intermittent depressions. Some months after moving, he phoned me to request that I recommend a new therapist in his vicinity. Knowing his past difficulty in opening up in therapy, I suggested to him that he first learn TM near where he lived, practice it for three months, and then recontact me at the end of that time.

Tony followed through on this suggestion and as soon as he learned meditation he found it had a profound effect upon him. His meditation sessions were, from the first, deeply compelling experiences. More impressive, however, were the effects they had on his life. His troublesome depressions came under control and remained stabilized thereafter. He became a regular and enthusiastic meditator, almost never missing his two sessions a day.

At the end of three months of meditating, Tony felt ready to re-enter therapy and so I referred him to a therapist in his new vicinity. Because of the changes brought about by meditation, he had now acquired a different outlook on psychotherapy. He no longer felt that therapists were 'all-powerful'; and in searching for his new therapist, he found himself sensing his *own rights* in the situation. When he started his new course of therapy he was able to talk freely and productively and use the experience to great advantage. Since the anxiety which had formerly all but paralyzed him in his treatment sessions was greatly lessened as a result of meditation, during this new course of treatment he made excellent progress.

Particularly surprising was the change in the quality of his creative work. Meditation seemed almost immediately to release a wellspring of creativity within him. Soon after learning this technique, he was completing four to five paintings a week, while at the same time holding down a full-time job as a cabinet-maker. Although he sometimes ran into fallow periods, for the most part he was astonishingly productive.

When I had the opportunity to view a showing of his paintings a year after he had stopped working with me, I was startled to see the difference in his work. His painting style had changed from an awkward, constricted, amateurish one to a powerful, artistic expression. Here was an artist with integrity, strength and surprising technical mastery. His fantasy figures, somewhat reminiscent of Chagall's, were at the same time his own unique statements. Tony has, to date, exhibited his paintings and his figured pottery (which is equally original) in a number of galleries. He remains absorbed in his artistic work and continues to meditate with absolute regularity. In this instance, I witnessed a flowering of a vital talent which had not been evident before the artist began meditating. Obviously, meditation did not create his talent, but it seems to have released it at a strategic point in his life.

Verified anecdotes of this sort are to me more impressive than the few statistical studies presently available which deal with increased creativity as a result of practicing meditation. Means for measuring creativity on a wide scale are far from adequate at this point. We can select a few components of the creative process and identify them, but the elusive quality that makes the true artist can still only be identified by viewing his artistic *work*.

One study measuring changes in 'creativity' with meditation is worth mentioning, however. Researchers at California State University compared a group of people who had been practicing TM for several months with a group about to learn the method. Both were given a test for creative thinking.[7] The people who were already meditating did better on this test than those who were about to learn meditation and, as in the Hines study, the meditators showed greater ideational fluency. They also showed more flexibility and more originality in their thinking than did the non-meditators. This study, of course, has some of the flaws seen in all meditator versus non-meditator comparisons. We do not know whether these meditators might have scored better on creativity tests even *before* they learned to meditate.

Strengthening of Staying Power

Another link between meditation and creativity lies in a different realm. Meditation may contribute to the *stamina* of the artist, to her ability to sustain long periods of creative work. Here the results are clearly promising, although they are entirely anecdotal; I know of no formal studies in this area.

Arnold Schulman, the successful screenwriter and playwright and twice an Academy Award nominee, is an interesting example of this since he bases his method of writing on meditation. He has practiced Zazen meditation much of his life, having studied with an outstanding Zen master, Miura Roshi, head of the Rinzai sect in Japan. The Rinzai school of Zen Buddhism is famed for its use of koans in achieving enlightenment

Schulman originally learned meditation in order to cope with his problems in writing. In an interview with me he described himself before beginning to practice meditation as having been disorganized, inept, undisciplined and 'chaotic' when writing. He followed no logical work sequence. He would often stay up all night writing and then sleep all day. He was frequently unable to get started for days on end and had no orderly work habits. Already a successful writer at twenty-three years of age, he realized then that he actually could not continue writing if he did not change his approach to work, which was, he says, filling him with self-contempt. He experienced growing depression. Schulman's psychoanalysis was helping him with some other problems but could not seem to bring his writing under control.

Accordingly he cast about for auxiliary answers. First, he taught himself to concentrate thoroughly on *one thing at a time*. He found the ability to exert a gentle, firm control over his mind to be the first thing which brought about a change in his approach to work. He now seemed to have a handle on the creative process and could begin to shape it to his own ends.

He then went deeper, commencing to work with teachers of meditation and subjecting himself to the rigorous discipline of classical Zazen training. Meditation has subsequently become a way of life for him. As he puts it, 'I could no more do without meditation than I could do without air or food. It has become essential.' By this he does not mean that he is hooked on it, but that it is so inwardly strengthening that denying it to himself is inconceivable.

Schulman regularly programs his writing efforts to take place in a meditative mood. His work is always done sitting on the floor in a Half-lotus position. He works on a low table a few inches off the floor, writing either by hand or on an electric typewriter. Every night before going to bed, he sits in a semi-meditative state and reviews the story he is working on up to the point where he stopped writing, then he respectfully requests his 'unconscious' to have the next sequence ready the following morning or at midnight or at four in the morning – whenever he plans to begin work again (it is, he says, important to give an exact time).* Having done this with complete faith that the unconscious, a 'loyal servant' whom he treats with the utmost gentleness and dignity, will fulfill his request (an attitude toward work which he learned from a teacher of Raja Yoga), he then dismisses the problem from his mind and usually goes

---

* This is Schulman's own system. Others might disagree with his procedures or even with this use of meditation.

immediately to bed and to sleep. At the time he told me about this he no longer had to sit in the meditative position to do this. It had become so engrained a pattern that he now could direct his next day's writing while in bed, the very last thing before dropping off to sleep.

When Schulman starts working in the morning, he unthinkingly begins writing. He does not know what will come, but simply 'lets it happen'. The new sequence invariably presents itself in full as the writing unfolds and, when it does, he accepts it completely and unquestioningly. Later, in the editorial stage of his work, he will view it critically and decide how 'good' or complete an answer it was.

When working on a screenplay, he sleeps at the most three or four hours a night and when awake works continuously with only brief breaks from the routine. After rising from sleep he always meditates for one full hour. Later he may do some Raja Yoga or some *asanas* (Yoga postures) if he feels tired. A half-hour of these postures, he claims, will substitute fully for sleep. He works sitting in a half-lotus position and maintaining to the greatest degree possible his meditative mood. This enables him to establish a 'direct pipeline to the unconscious'. His words flow forth onto the paper, 'mindlessly and fully'. He describes this phase of work as 'achieving orbit'.

The problems of creativity are, Schulman feels, much like the problems of space travel. One must first get enough thrust to break out of the atmosphere into space. 'I can only function when in orbit,' he says. His means of pushing off the launching-pad and breaking through is meditation. Not only does he begin his day with a long meditation, but when there is any interruption whatsoever (such as a phone call) he brings himself back into the creative mood by meditating once more, perhaps this time for fifteen or twenty minutes.

His workday thus involves a series of meditations as needed. This way he is able to sustain as much as twenty hours of highly creative work at a time. He does this without fatigue and in an almost unbroken rhythm until his writing assignment is completed. He explains that he must sweep through to the conclusion of any creative project 'all in one breath'.

In addition to enabling him to sustain this unusual productivity, Schulman feels meditation has assisted him in his work by eliminating the paralyzing anxiety a writer so often feels when faced with a blank page; the fear that can lead to endless postponement. Because meditation is not working with the conscious, logical, critical mind, he thinks this eliminates the prejudgment and fear of failure that can cause writer's block. In the meditative mood the writing flows – clearly, openly, effortlessly – and without anxiety.

It is important to remember, however, that Schulman's unorthodox use of meditation was undertaken under the supervision of highly skilled meditation teachers with whom he had worked for many years. As we will discuss in the next chapter, it is not advisable and can in fact be dangerous for a person to meditate for long periods of time in a single day if this practice is not carefully supervised by a highly experienced teacher.

We might consider this sustaining aspect of meditation an indirect contribution to creativity. It is an important way in which meditation can assist the creative act. For some people meditation fosters the opening-up of unrealized potentials. There still remains, however, the question of which people it will do this for and under what circumstances. When is meditation effective and when not? We will look at this problem next.

Chapter 15

SOME PROBLEMS ARISE

Meditation is not a panacea. Not everyone wants to learn it and not everyone who learns it benefits from it. Some people who do benefit from it discontinue the practice. It is also possible that other people do not need meditation because their life-style already supplies them with something equally satisfying.

Dr Mihaly Csikszentmihalyi and his research team at the University of Chicago have a fascinating theory of pleasure based on their study of people involved in deeply gratifying activities.[1] This concept, which they call 'flow', has many things in common with the meditative mood.

According to the Chicago group, flow is present when the person is so totally involved in whatever he is doing that there is no time to get bored or to worry about what may or may not happen. They studied this holistic sensation that people feel when they act with total involvement – as *flow* – in structured interviews conducted with a large number of individuals involved in a wide variety of activities.

Careful analysis of these interviews revealed that games are obvious flow experiences and play is the most complete form of all. Yet playing a game is no guarantee that one is experiencing flow – it is the ingredients of the experience that count. If the person is totally engrossed, 'lost' in the game, then she may enter flow.

Flow is often present in creativity. People as diverse as composers and dancers, rock climbers and chess players, surgeons involved in medical research and mathematicians working in the frontiers of their fields, all experience flow. When they do, it is usually so enjoyable they are willing to forsake many other things for it, including money, fame or comfort. In a certain sense, flow is the essential joy of living, beside which all other considerations are insignificant.

The Chicago group was the first to investigate this human experience with the methods of science and to identify what they believe to be its main elements. They describe these as follows:

> Flow is a state of total absorption. As an outstanding chess player describes it:
>
> The game is a struggle, and the concentration is like breathing – you never think of it. The roof can fall in and, if it missed you, you would be unaware of it.[2]

> Flow involves centering one's attention on a limited stimulus field – with all else shut out. A professor of science who climbs rocks says:
>
> When I start on a climb, it is as if my memory input has been cut off. All I can remember is the last thirty seconds, and all I can think ahead is the next five minutes.[3]

Flow involves a kind of self-forgetfulness. This does not mean that the person in flow loses touch with his or her own physical reality or sense of existence, they may be more exquisitely aware of them than ever. What is lost is the artificial 'self construct', the awareness of social roles and role-playing. The sense that 'I am such and such a person, with such and such a name and status who is taking action', fades and a far more fundamental sense of self takes over. In flow there is no social 'me', no learned awareness of 'self', no ego-sense, to stand as a screen between each person and total experience. An outstanding composer says:

> You yourself are in an ecstatic state to such a point that you feel as though you almost don't exist. . . . I just sit there watching . . . in a state of awe and wonderment. And it (the music) just flows out by itself.[4]

A chess player says:

> Time passes a hundred times faster. In this sense, it resembles the dream states. A whole story can unfold in seconds. . . . Your body is nonexistent – but actually your heart pumps like mad to supply the brain.[5]

In flow the person is in control of his actions and his environment – he or she can cope. A dancer says:

A strong relaxation, and calmness comes over me. I have no worries of failure. . . . I want to expand, hug the world. I feel enormous power to effect something of grace and beauty.[6]

For flow to occur, the demands of the situation must be *clear-cut, predictable, and not contradictory.* In flow the person must be able to know at any moment where she or he is with the activity. Rules of a game, specific training in certain skills, or rituals which are to be followed, make flow possible. They allow people participating in it to evaluate how they are proceeding without having to think about it at all, without needing to break the absorption. A basketball player says:

I play my best game almost by accident. . . . If I'm having a super game I can't tell [whether I'm playing well] until after the game. . . . Guys make fun of me because I can lose track of the score.[7]

Flow involves no goals or rewards external to itself. A young poet who is a seasoned rock climber says:

You get to the top of a rock glad it's over but really wish it would go forever. . . . The justification of climbing is climbing, like the justification of poetry is writing; you don't conquer anything except things in yourself. . . . You are a *flow.* The purpose of the flow is to keep on flowing.[8]

By this definition, many meditation sessions are also a form of flow. When the person is deeply into meditation, thought follows upon thought according to its own inner logic and needs no conscious intervention by the meditator; attention is strictly limited to only a few basic matters; activity is totally absorbing. The meditator is also in complete control of his actions and is protected from decisions by the ritual involved. During meditation there is little distinction between self and environment, between stimulus and response, between past, present and future – attention is riveted on the intensity of the moment.

What does the concept of flow teach us about the need to meditate? Will a skier who regularly enters a state of flow in her downhill glides, experiencing ice and wind in perfect balance and existing in moments outside of time, still feel like meditating later that same day if she is a regular meditator? Is the need for flow ever-present, or does it wax and wane? Is there a need to balance one type of flow with another? Do people seek to alternate active flow experiences with those which are passive and receptive in nature – the age-old need to experience both aspects of life: repose and tension, the feminine and the masculine, Yin and Yang?

These are crucial questions which must be answered if we are to discover whether other activities can supply the same ingredients as meditation and if they can make meditation superfluous for certain people – or perhaps for all people at certain times. It is at least plausible that some people do not need to meditate because they live with a pervasive sense of harmony in their lives. Who these people might be and why they should feel this way, however, is as yet unknown.

We do know, though, that certain people whose lives are apparently unfulfilling, people who are tense and driven in their behavior, are also frequently disinterested in learning meditation. Such people will not sign up to learn it even when meditation is offered free as part of a curriculum, or at a guidance clinic. They remain disinterested even if their family or friends are enthusiastic about the practice. It looks as though such people are actively avoiding learning it.

Although no research has been done of tense people who avoid meditation, some clinical reports on patients who have persistently resisted suggestions that they learn to meditate give us some clues about the reasons for such resistance.

Refusal to Learn Meditation

Meditation may run counter to some people's life-styles. This is particularly true of ambitious, driving people who hesitate to slow down their pace even momentarily. Such people are usually difficult to slow by any means. If their physician tells them they need a good rest for their health, they are apt to take the rest, if they agree to it at all, in their own way. They may manage to be constantly interrupted by business phone calls during a vacation: may take a dictation unit with them; or spend their holiday making business contacts. Whatever way they find to distract themselves, they are not apt to let down or become tranquil and are usually threatened by such an idea. Their self-esteem seems to rest on a vision of themselves as accomplishing something at all times: constantly measuring up to high standards, and untiringly beating out the next one in line.

Suspecting that meditation might slow them down, they usually resist learning it.

Other people seem not to want to learn meditation because it means being alone with oneself. These are the types who tend to remain constantly occupied in order to avoid confrontation with their own selves. A patient describes this dilemma:

> When I first learned to meditate I was frightened of being alone with myself. I think that's why people set up all the things they do, all the activities in their lives, the sports, the bridge games and this and that, in order to run away from being alone with themselves. To be alone and not responsible for *doing* anything? – my first feeling about it was – 'No!'

People who are overly dependent on the response of others to supply their sense of self-worth may also be afraid of sitting still with eyes closed. Without seeing others, they come face to face with a stranger in their midst, their own self. Such people are reluctant to 'let go' of the outside world and seem automatically to shy away from the meditative disciplines. Some of them will go so far as learning meditation, but soon drop the practice.

It may be useful for such people to keep their eyes open the entire time they are meditating so that they can remain in contact with the outer world upon which they depend. They may also find a form of moving meditation comforting.

People needing to be in control at all times may also be threatened by meditation. They often shy away from the new and unexpected in life and cannot conceive of themselves meditating because this practice is both unstructured and uncontrollable. A former patient was bothered by the relationship of meditation to hypnosis, for example, because he had always feared losing control under hypnosis. No amount of information about the differences between the two techniques mattered. He continued to view meditation as some sort of 'mind control' that would 'take over' and rob him of his right to be in the driver's seat. Needless to say, he never learned meditation although he suffered from severe symptoms of tension.

Added to these deep-seated reasons for not wanting to meditate are some incidental ones. I have known people who were urged so forcefully to learn meditation by overenthusiastic meditators in their family or among their friends that they resisted doing so on principle. For others it may simply be the wrong time in life for them to learn. These people may become ready to begin meditation at some point in the future.

Those Who Learn Then Quit

Perhaps more surprising than the people who do not want to learn meditation in the first place are those who learn to meditate and then quit. Their actions are often difficult to understand when taken at face value. While some people stop the practice because they are having difficulty with it, many stop just when they seem to be getting excellent results. There are a variety of reasons for dropping out, and our meditating patients have provided an opportunity for us to explore some of them.

Certain people seem to become disappointed with meditation because they have built up too many expectations around it. In their fantasy they might have seen meditation as a sort of 'ideal helper', as though it were a genie or a fairy godmother on whom they could depend. This is understandable because meditation is an intensely personal experience and the comfort it brings when it is working right is rather like the soothing of a kindly parent. If it does not go right for some reason, we are all somewhat disappointed. But the person who sees meditation as a 'magic helper' does not just feel disappointed when it is not going right, he feels crushed, devastated. He may then react like a hurt child having a temper fit or one who has gone to sulk in the corner.

A patient of mine, Rochelle, thoroughly enjoyed meditation. After she commenced meditating she felt cushioned for the first time from the harsh accusations of some of her family members and began to interact with them more positively. She was more hopeful and experienced a sense of peace which she had not known before. She began feeling so well, in fact, that she hailed meditation as a major contribution to her life. But this picture changed when she came down with a severe case of the flu. At this time she became so weak that she was unable even to lift a glass of water to her lips. Although she tried repeatedly to meditate during her illness she found herself unable to summon up the energy to do so, even when lying down. She simply could not mentally repeat the mantra in her mind.*

As a result Rochelle felt that meditation had 'deserted' her just when she needed it most. This made her bitterly angry. From then on she resented meditation and refused to resume the practice after she had recovered from her illness. She could not justify this decision on logical grounds since meditation had been extremely beneficial to her, but her negative feelings were so strong she could not overcome them.

Fortunately Rochelle had an opportunity to work on this problem in psychotherapy, where we were able to explore the reasons why she had turned against meditation so strongly. She had been one of eleven children brought up in relative hardship on a country farm. When she was ill as a child, her overworked mother, finding a sick child in the family an extra burden, would remove herself emotionally from the child. She would order her to her room and rarely, if ever, visit her there. To the little girl this meant that the time when she needed parental comfort and support the most, she was abandoned.

This painful experience had shaped Rochelle's life in important ways and now, many years later, when, as an adult, she found herself ill and entirely alone (she was divorced at the time) and tried to meditate to comfort herself, meditation too seemed to be 'indifferent' to her. As a result she experienced a resurgence of the despair she had felt as a child when she lay in her room ill and alone. It was as if the meditation had changed at that moment from an ideal 'good mother' (which it had felt like up to this point) into an indifferent 'unavailable mother'.

It was only as Rochelle's feelings of abandonment and personal unworthiness began to change through therapy that she found herself once again interested in the idea of meditating. To get her started meditating, however, it was necessary for me to meditate with her. She appeared to need my encouragement and support in this experience – the presence of a sort of 'mother-therapist' who cared enough about her to stay with her.

---

* Some physically ill patients find themselves unable to meditate although others seem to be able to do so successfully. The ability to meditate when ill seems to vary both with the person and the type of illness (see discussion in Chapter 8).

Gradually she once again began to look upon meditation as positive and resumed the regular practice of it, with good results.

Another person who had a highly personalized reaction to meditation was a man who became enraged at his TM mantra because it would not readily enter his mind when he sat down to meditate. He was particularly angry because he felt he had spent a considerable sum of money for the mantra and it 'should' come to him when he wanted it!

This man was acting toward his mantra as one might toward another person who refused to cooperate or come when called. He began to work on this problem in his therapy and soon remembered that as a child he had experienced a similar fury at his mother when she paid attention to his brothers and sisters and was not available when he needed or wanted her. He had not been able to control his 'mama' the way he wanted to; now he could not control his mantra the way he wanted to – both seemed to evade him. His reaction was to reject meditation as though saying to an imaginary mother, 'If you're a bad mother and don't come to me when I want you to, then I will desert you.' The result of this personalizing of the mantra was that this man stopped meditating until the problem of his mother could be worked through in therapy, after which he returned to practicing meditation with a fair degree of regularity and satisfaction.

Some people, however, stop meditating for a different reason: they have made the meditation ritual into a tyranny for themselves. Such people tend to be overexacting about their meditation. They tell themselves that they must do it in a certain way, at a certain time, and are intolerant of the least infringement on their own part of their own rules. It is scarcely surprising that they eventually rebel and dismiss meditation as 'just too much trouble'.

I have found that people who react this way tend to be puritanical and harshly self-disciplining in many other respects as well. They seem to be experts at making that which is inherently pleasant into something difficult. Simple instructions of when, where and how to meditate are interpreted by them as authoritarian commands which they deeply resent. Showing such people how to vary their meditation ritual to introduce a bit of freedom into it may do some good, but I find that in most instances insight into what they are doing is the best solution. If they can understand that they themselves are responsible for their supposed 'enslavement' by meditation, and if they can begin to ease up some of their rigid demands on themselves, then they may be ready to return to meditation.

Other people may react adversely to meditation because of personal associations with the process. A friend of mine found herself becoming alarmingly depressed whenever she had to sit still with her eyes closed for TM. Because of this she soon discontinued meditating. When talking with her about this afterward, I asked her what 'sitting still' brought to mind. She volunteered that as a child she was punished by being made to sit absolutely still without speaking, a condition which she had dreaded. While it is not certain that this was the reason for her depression when sitting still during meditation, it is possible that this early training may have caused her to have an antipathy to any situation which involved enforced sitting in silence. Under the circumstances, assigning her a form of meditation where she could move about and keep her eyes open might have been a solution to the problem. It is also possible that she should have been instructed to meditate for only very brief periods at a time.

It is apparent that 'what is one man's meat may be another man's poison'. The stillness which is such a welcome part of meditation for most people may be a frightening aspect of it for others. We have discussed tension-release during meditation. This occasionally causes someone to stop meditating entirely because deep emotions or bizarre and dreamlike thoughts during tension-release may be so intense that they cannot be tolerated. If reducing meditation time does not remedy the situation, then there seems no alternative for the person but to abandon the practice altogether, and it is probably a wise idea to do so. We do not know at present what it is that prompts such occasional 'allergic' responses to meditation, but it is sensible to treat them like any other allergy – by avoiding the source of the irritation.

As Maupin discovered with creative people, it may not be the appearance of strong emotions or bizarre thoughts that is important, but the degree of control one has over them that makes the difference. Those who feel, for whatever reason, that the process of tension-release is out of control in meditation may become alarmed and quit. On the other hand, meditation may help to make strong feelings manageable for the first time in a way they have never been before. One meditator describes her experience:

> I find that in meditation I am in tune with my feelings. I wouldn't listen to them before ... Now I find that I can experience the most devastating feelings, but meditation somehow gives me a sense that I'm in charge of them. They're not out of control, I have control of *them*.

Resistance of Self-Image to Change

The changes in outlook or behavior that result from meditation may not involve the deepest layers of personality, as we shall see, but they can be more sudden and dramatic than those which usually occur in psychotherapy. Meditation can change behavior so rapidly in some respects, in fact, that the person may be unprepared for the 'new self' that develops. No matter how positive the changes, new ways which do not fit old ways can be threatening. Unless the meditator gains some understanding of what is happening, he may stop meditating.

A patient of mine, Margaret, had cleared up her tension-related symptoms of gastric ulcer and colitis with psychotherapy, and her depression had lifted, but her chronic tension headaches had not lessened after a year and a half of treatment. Because of this I decided that meditation might be worth trying and referred her for training in TM (I was not at this time teaching CSM). After commencing meditation, Margaret's headaches cleared up within the first few weeks and she was headache-free for the next four months – the first respite of this sort in years.

During this period she began to notice some personality changes in herself which disturbed her, however. These, she claimed, were directly due to meditation. She had formerly been self-sacrificing, playing the role of 'martyr' to her husband, children and other relatives. Now she was finding herself more aware of her own rights and compelled to stand up for herself in circumstances where formerly she would have given in.

When placed under extreme pressure at work, she used to be submissive, swallowing her resentment (and often developing a headache). Now she found herself fighting for her own point of view and certain things around the office were getting changed as a result. At home she marshaled the courage to obtain a legal separation from her long-estranged, mentally disturbed husband, and stood up with strength for the first time to her teenage sons and demanded that they stop calling her 'the old lady'. Apparently her manner showed that she meant what she said, because the boys treated her more gently after that, making fewer scathing comments. Clearly Margaret was becoming more self-assertive, more able to mobilize self-defensive anger when necessary and to express it in an effective manner.

Despite the possible advantages of this new behavior, however, she began to be alarmed at the unfamiliar forcefulness of her own responses and complained that meditation was making her into 'a hateful person'. Her relatives, she said, especially her elderly parents, were complaining that she was no longer the 'sweet' person she had been when she was more pliable.

Margaret also noticed another change in herself. She used to talk almost continuously at any social gathering, often becoming the 'life and soul of the party', but after commencing meditation she lost this compulsion to talk and would even remain silent for long periods. Because of this she now became aware for the first time of her deep sense of social uneasiness which she had hidden beneath her compulsive chatter. This too made her anxious.

Soon Margaret stopped meditating and was not able to force herself to resume the practice by any exercise of willpower, even though her tension headaches returned in full force. The personality changes brought about by meditation had been too extensive for her to assimilate. She was unprepared for them.

Before she could return to meditation it was necessary to trace, in therapy, the origin of her pervasive need to deny her own rights. As we delved into this facet of her personality, Margaret discovered that her competition with her older sister, Helen, was at the root of much of her difficulty. When they were children, Helen had been considered by their parents to be a 'saint', undoubtedly headed for a religious life and certain to be a credit to the family. Margaret, on the other hand, was looked upon as a troublesome, irritating child. When she was very little, she had keenly felt this difference in attitude toward Helen but she could do nothing about it. On reaching adolescence, however, she found a 'solution'. At this point she developed an intense need to prove that she was more 'saintly' than her exalted sister, although often this meant total sacrifice of her own wishes or needs for those of others. When Helen began to disappoint the family (she did not become a nun as expected and showed personality problems) Margaret moved into the position of being the 'good' one in the family. Although she received relatively little recognition for this new role, she strove ever harder to prove how self-denying she could be.

Years later, when she learned to meditate, the 'self-indulgence' of meditation threatened this vision of herself as being self-sacrificing. As meditation made her more assertive in many situations, her saintly image of herself was on the verge of being shattered. It was at this point that she stopped meditating.

After working through some of her problems in therapy, Margaret was finally ready to resume meditating. For quite a while, however, she was only able to meditate once weekly without building up too much anxiety. She and I would regularly meditate together for twenty minutes before her psychotherapy sessions.

This maneuver worked well because by meditating comfortably in her presence, I was demonstrating that meditation was a good and acceptable activity. Much later, looking back on this period of her treatment, she commented: 'For you to say to me, "We'll meditate together" – that was granting permission for me to meditate – it was taking the whole problem out of my hands. I was relieved, and I could go ahead with it.'

These weekly meditation sessions were deeply restful for Margaret. Her headaches once again disappeared and she began to experience personality changes typical of regular daily meditators, such as a richer and more enjoyable fantasy life. In this moderate dose, she was able to handle the gradual changes in her self-concept which were occurring.

After a year at this pace, Margaret was able to return to meditating on her own once a day and has continued doing so ever since. In general she is now a more independent, self-confident, happier person who is able to accept the positive changes which have taken place in her.

Depression and Meditation

People who suffer from what is known as 'chronic low-grade depression' – a lingering sense of gloom and joylessness in life – may respond well to meditation, regaining a feeling of well-being after they commence practicing it. Those with more severe depressions, however, more often than not react in a different way. Even when meditation may help them feel better, these deeply depressed persons usually stop practicing it. It may threaten their self-image or run counter to a disturbed life-style. On the basis of research at the Hartford Institute of Living, for example (see Chapter 12), Dr Bernard Glueck reported that TM had not proved useful in the treatment of patients with severe depressions when they were in what is known as a retarded depressed state, a state where the person is apathetic. The Hartford researchers noticed, however, that meditation did help to reduce anxiety in an agitated depression, a state where the patient is highly tense and restless even though depressed. Under these circumstances improvements would often occur if the patient could be helped to meditate regularly. Once a patient wanted to come out of a depression, he could both meditate regularly and benefit from the usual responses to meditations.[9]

I have noticed that severely depressed people frequently resist suggestions that they learn meditation in the first place, sometimes with flimsy excuses that can barely be convincing even to themselves. One depressed patient spontaneously told me that she did not want to learn meditation because 'it might make me feel better and in a way I might not want to feel better'.

Another patient is an example of those who quit meditation because it threatens a 'depressive' life-style. Anna, a woman in her thirties who suffered from chronic (long-term) depression, was obsessively indecisive about her marriage relationship. Although she found life with her husband 'unbearable', she made no effort to remove herself from her painful home situation, even temporarily. She remained in her house, barely able to do housework, and otherwise tearful and inactive.

Anna talked little during her therapy sessions with me, attempting to force me to solve her problems, while at the same time resisting any constructive suggestions I might make. In the hope that meditation might replace her attitude of resignation with a more active and cooperative one, I suggested to her that she learn TM in her hometown. To my surprise, she consented, took the training, and found to her own bewilderment that she began to feel decidedly positive effects from meditation. Her mood lightened, her compulsive crying spells ceased, and she began to make decisions of a meaningful sort. She also reported that she was feeling more energetic and was becoming more active. She said that meditation was making her feel 'much better'.

At this point, however (it being summer), both she and I left for vacation. During her month-long holiday, Anna stopped meditating entirely. Later she explained this was because she had become 'angry' at meditation because it was 'making me cope' and also because 'it made me feel so calm that I could no longer cry or feel sorry for myself'. Feeling that she must cry and must continue complaining, she had discontinued meditation and was then able to resume her despair, weeping and self-pity. In her own words, 'I had my own feelings back again.' Anna never returned to meditation, nor, in fact, did she continue long with psychotherapy, but eventually received anti-depressive drugs from a physician which enabled her to get along somewhat better without essentially changing her behavior in any fundamental manner.

There seem to be several factors in Anna's wish not to continue meditation. By letting her go on vacation (and by leaving myself) I was clearly requiring her to become more independent. She may have resented this and rejected meditation to 'retaliate' – I was the one who had suggested that she take it up in the first place. She was also a person who tended to make every new activity into an enslavement and meditation soon seemed to be a new 'ordeal' or 'duty' which she had to perform.

Probably the most important factor, however, was the fact that meditation threatened to rob her of her role as a 'helpless' being whose misery was being used (unconsciously) as a club with which to control others – her husband, friends and myself. In effect, the meditation may have been working 'too well' by fostering a genuine change in attitude for which Anna was not ready. Since she did not have the personal resourcefulness, persistence and inner strength of the previous patient discussed (Margaret) and her emotional illness was far more serious, the only choice compatible with her neurotic pattern was to abandon meditation.

This inability of Anna's to tolerate the pleasant aspects of meditation brings us to another curious reaction. Many people seem to abandon this practice precisely because it is making them feel too good.

Fear of Pleasure

Enjoyment constitutes a problem for many people. The idea that we should occupy our time with 'useful' pursuits is widespread. A businessman may come home to rest over a weekend, only to find himself compulsively catching up on chores around the house, and may end up spending the entire weekend working. Even if he plays golf or tennis, he may make 'good use of his time' by trying to improve his game or make business or social contacts. Many people work themselves into exhaustion while supposedly playing. At that point they feel harassed, cornered, and may try to escape from the whole process by 'knocking themselves out'.

Drinking is one escape from such tension. Attaching oneself to a TV set or newspaper is another. Our society has any number of escape devices which help us lapse into total passivity and be relieved of responsibility. They are necessary safety valves for us if living is merely a mechanical duty rather than a joyous process.

Meditation stands quite apart from this round of work versus escape. It is a moment of actual presence, an aliveness which exists for its own sake and needs no justification. It goes beyond the requirements of mere survival, either material or social, and opts for joy.

The Indian spiritual leader Bhagwan Shree Rajneesh suggested that existing in the material world is but an 'emergency measure' and that the true goal of man 'is always to come to the flowering of the potential of all that is meant by you'. This flowering can only come about if you add a new dimension to your life, the dimension of the 'festive':

> [Meditation] is not work; it is play ... in business the result is important. In festivity, the *act* is important ... any moment can be a business moment; any moment can be a meditative moment. The

difference is in attitude. If it is choiceless, if you are playing with it, then it is meditative.[10]

It is precisely what Rajneesh calls the 'festive' attitudes – free and playful spontaneity, doing things for their own sake – that is often condemned in our society. The old dictum 'Satan finds mischief for idle hands to do' may be outdated, but its spirit lives on. It is not at all unusual for meditators to report that they feel they have no right to feel as 'good' as they do when they are meditating, or afterward. It may even be frightening for them to feel happy and at peace. Such people may believe they stop meditating because of practical reasons, but the underlying cause usually becomes clear if you discuss their practice with them. Their attitude about meditation is quite different from that of those who stop meditating because they find it unpleasant – typically, these people have nothing but praise for meditation.

People afraid to experience the fulfillment that meditation offers often manage to put themselves into a position where it is impossible for them to meditate properly. One woman who had learned meditation and claimed to enjoy it thoroughly, consistently complained that she could never obtain a peaceful meditation at home and therefore rarely meditated. On questioning, it turned out that when she did meditate it was always in the family room of her house at a time when her husband and children were present. A peaceful meditation under these conditions was impossible and by selecting this time and place for her meditation she was depriving herself of a fulfilling experience. She could have gone to her bedroom and locked the door, or she could have meditated in the early afternoon when she first returned from work to an empty house, or even late at night, but she did none of these things. What was more, she resisted any suggestion by her meditation teacher or friends that she handle her problems constructively. She was an intensely self-denying woman – meditation promised too much happiness.

The psychotherapists I know who use meditation with their patients have all reported observing certain patients who cannot tolerate the pleasantness of this state. Dr Bernard Glueck, for example, noticed that some patients in the Institute of Living study seemed unable to accept the pleasurable feelings which

resulted from meditation and that they frequently stopped meditating rather than face the guilt that this practice brought to
them.[11]

Because meditation is so inherently pleasurable, certain
people may even stop meditating in order to punish themselves.
A meditator describes this process when she speaks of meditation as being a form of reward:

> It's the same way you would reward yourself with candy or
> whatever.... Meditation is gentle, it's a good thing, a journey
> within. But if you feel you've behaved badly, you will use medi-
> tation as a weapon and say to yourself, 'No! You will not go to
> meditate! You don't deserve it! You have no right to feel that
> good!' ... You don't even meditate badly at such a time. You don't
> meditate at all . . . .[12]

The pleasure-giving aspects of meditation may also cause
special anxieties in people who have been taught to feel guilty
about masturbating. It is possible unconsciously to view meditation (an experience where one is alone and gives oneself
pleasure) as a 'forbidden' experience, similar to masturbation.
For people with masturbation guilt, something all too common
in our society, meditation may be avoided because when practiced it may now create anxiety rather than bring about
relaxation.

If allowed to continue long enough, of course, meditation
itself often helps to lessen even these deep-seated guilts, because
it tends to reduce self-blame. If a person allows herself to keep
meditating for months or years, the meditation may automatically lessen her guilt about enjoying life or about sexual
fulfillment. Of course it also may not do so. In this case, professional help in handling these problems should be sought.

These are some of the reasons we have discovered so far for
people dropping out of meditation. It is instructive to look at
the research evidence on this subject. One investigator who has
studied this problem is Dr Leon Otis of the Stanford Research
Institute. His research suggests that those who start meditating
and then quit may have very different personalities from those
who stick with the practice.[13] In the first part of Otis's study,
questionnaires were sent to two groups of people who had
previously learned TM – one chosen at random from the TM
organizations records, the other composed of TM teachers in

training. In the second part of the study, the subjects were people who had volunteered to learn TM at the Stanford Research Institute. The questionnaire used asked about a person's history in practicing TM, any physical or behavioral changes experienced since starting it, and any changes in basic aspects of personality that the meditator had noticed since commencing to meditate. The basic personality changes were judged from the words a person chose, from a long list, to describe himself.

The results of these studies showed that the dropouts from meditation tended to think of themselves as withdrawn, irritable and anxiety-ridden. They checked adjectives such as moody, worried, impatient, insecure, defensive, self-conscious, perplexed or 'a loner type' to describe themselves.

People who had been meditating for less than six months and who were continuing to meditate, described themselves positively, however, and thought meditation had helped them. They tended to see themselves as being excitable, prompt, zestful, self-controlled, ambitious and alert people.

The meditators who had been practicing meditation consistently for eighteen months or more had a still different view of themselves. They described themselves as being peaceful, alert, determined, attractive, secure, self-confident, considerate, renewed, pleasant, candid, precise and warm – very positive attributes indeed.

Is this because meditation produced all these changes in the long-term meditators, or did these two groups differ from each other even before they started learning meditation? Otis's results suggest the possibility that it is only those people who are strongly attracted toward the calm way of life in the first place who will tend, once they commence meditation, to stick faithfully with the practice. More insecure or troubled people may abandon meditation, perhaps because it is not helping them or perhaps because they cannot assimilate the help it does have to offer. It certainly does not take as much dedication, strength of character or predilection for a practice to continue to do it for six months or less, as it does to remain regularly with it for a year and a half or more; many people will start things, but relatively few stay faithfully with any discipline over a long period of time. Is this perhaps the reason why the six-

months-or-less group showed such different personality characteristics from the long-term meditators?

The Otis study showed that different people respond differently to meditation, stay with it for different amounts of time,
and report different benefits from it. His results, taken together
with our clinical observations, suggest that no blanket statement
can accurately describe the situation. To assume that everyone
can, needs to or even wants to meditate seems unwarranted. At
the same time, it is becoming increasingly obvious that meditation is extremely useful for many people.

Chapter 16

THE MISUSE OF MEDITATION

Blocks to meditating represent one type of problem with which all of us working with meditation must deal. An entirely different difficulty arises, however, when meditation is embraced, but for the wrong reasons, or when it is used in an undesirable fashion.

While some people shy away from meditation, others take it up with too much intensity. If twenty minutes twice a day is beneficial, then two or three or four hours of meditating per day should be correspondingly better – or so the reasoning goes. As with any therapeutic dosage, of course, this is not the case. If one pill is prescribed, taking the whole bottle is not a good idea.

While the proper meditation time may be highly beneficial, anything over that amount may have adverse effects. As we have seen, for some people, even fifteen or twenty minutes of meditating at one time is too much. When I speak of over-meditation, however, I mean a much longer amount of meditation. For the average person practicing practical meditation, this might be defined as meditating more than one hour a day for the first year, and after that for more than one hour at a single sitting, or more than two hours on the same day – keeping in mind the fact that the 'safe' limit may be considerably lower than this for certain individuals.

As we saw in Chapter 7, tension-release during ordinary meditation can produce side-effects which, at times, can make for difficulty if they aren't regulated. If meditation is prolonged for a matter of hours this process of tension-release can be magnified many times. When a person spends this much time meditating, powerful emotions and 'primary process' (bizarre) thoughts may be released too rapidly to assimilate and the meditator may be forced into sudden confrontation with long-buried aspects of himself for which he is not prepared. If he has enough inner strength, or is doing the extra meditation under the supervision of an experienced teacher, he may weather such an upsurge of unconscious material and emerge triumphant. If he has fewer inner resources or has a past history of emotional disturbance, he may be overwhelmed by it, fragile defenses may break down, and an episode of mental illness occur.

This eventuality is guarded against by most responsible teachers of meditation who strictly limit the amount of time the meditator is advised to spend at his practice. TM, for example, is limited to no more than two twenty-minute sessions daily; Benson gives the same directions for his method; and we similarly limit CSM. Those who choose to meditate against these explicit instructions are usually people with deep-seated personality problems who make use of meditation in a very special way. We will discuss this way in a moment as we look at some examples of people who have over-meditated.

Over-meditating seems to be similar to other forms of addiction. Studies of drug usage have shown that those who tend to abuse drugs, as opposed to those who simply use them, show many more signs of severe personality disturbance, social withdrawal, and the like. In the same way, those who consistently over-meditate, when studied psychiatrically, most often turn out either to have a previous history of addiction to drugs or to have other psychiatric problems of a serious nature. Taken in heavy doses in a person with an unstable background, meditation can be dangerous.

Problems from Over-Meditation

The following anecdotes illustrate some of the difficulties which may arise from over-meditation. While these examples may seem severe in terms of the psychiatric symptoms involved, they are typical of the over-meditator. To my knowledge there is no such thing as a mild case of true over-meditation. When a person comes to the point where she is meditating many *hours* a day, on her own and without supervision, that person usually has a disturbed emotional adjustment to begin with.

The people I will describe here already had deeply troubling personality problems. Over-meditation increased their difficulties, however, and appeared to push these people over the brink, as it were, precipitating a serious psychiatric condition.

Kaye was a withdrawn young woman who consulted me when she was already in a state of incipient mental breakdown, because she had heard that I was 'sympathetic to meditation'. She reported that she was losing her sense of identity and was haunted by sexual terrors. Her life was chaotic. She could barely handle the simplest practical tasks and shied away almost totally from contact with people.

Kaye's experience with meditation was based on a lifelong problem. She had been an extremely shy girl with a painful sense of inferiority about her own body, which she felt to be 'deformed', although this was not in reality the case. Upon graduating from high school she had found refuge from the challenges of social life by entering a Zen retreat, where she lived for two years, undergoing strict training in Zazen meditation. While living there, Kaye meditated at least four hours daily. At this same time she was forbidden to speak with anyone about the strong emotions that surfaced during her meditation. She was observing a partial vow of silence which prevented her from discussing topics other than superficial household tasks.

Despite the rigor of this routine, Kaye initially benefited from being at the retreat. An ulcerative colitis which she had previously suffered from disappeared entirely. She seemed relieved at being in a quiet, protective place where she did not have to face humiliating rejections from the outside world, and her tension level reduced accordingly.

Eventually, however, an emotional 'bottleneck' began to develop. Intense feelings and stressful memories were rapidly surfacing during Kaye's long hours of meditation, which she could not discuss with anyone. Because of her enforced silence she was unable to receive social support for these painful emotions and became increasingly threatened by them as time went on. Finally she found herself with a cauldron of explosive conflicts which she could no longer handle. Meditation was continually bringing up new emotionally charged material which she could not deal with fast enough.

At this point, Kaye fled from the Zen center and began to travel from city to city, temporarily living with room-mates who were also Zen meditators. Each time when she inevitably failed to get along with her new room-mates, she became more troubled. She continued to meditate many hours a day, but without the support of the Zen center, where she had felt cared for and protected, her defenses gradually broke down and serious psychiatric symptoms emerged. At this point her meditation was no longer calming her; it was *causing* anxiety. When in desperation she finally abandoned meditation, it was too late. The rapidly developing emotional breakdown continued.

Eventually Kaye admitted herself to a psychiatric hospital. She was experiencing racing thoughts which she could not control and was suffering from intense anxiety attacks. Following a brief hospitalization, she made an appointment to see me. I saw Kaye for a few sessions before referring her for more extensive treatment than I was able to offer. During these sessions she obtained relief from outbursts of emotion which were so intense that she would tremble violently, almost convulsively, while experiencing them.

Without talking it over with me (I would have advised against it), Kaye later decided to try meditation again. She had only been meditating forty-five minutes, however, when she found herself once more becoming disoriented in her thinking and experienced rising panic. On the basis of this brief attempt, we were both able to agree that she was not yet ready to return to the practice. I recommended that if she should ever resume meditating, it would be wise to do so only in a very gradual fashion, probably meditating for no more than five or ten minutes a day, until she found herself fully able to tolerate a slightly longer time than this. This advice seemed to relieve her of conflict over whether or not to recommence meditation. From that point on she was able to plan for herself and was ready to enter into a constructive treatment program.

Although traditional Zazen practices such as those Kaye followed are more rigorous than the simpler centering techniques, it is unlikely that it was the Zazen teaching, *per se*, which caused Kaye's difficulty. Many people can use this method of meditation very beneficially. Her problem seemed to have arisen from an unfortunate combination of circumstances. This emotionally disturbed, intensely withdrawn young woman had been over-meditating in a setting which did not permit her any relief from the accumulated tensions which almost inevitably surface from such long hours of meditation. She was forbidden to talk about her feelings and could achieve no understanding of them.

A person with a healthier personality than Kaye's might have meditated constructively even under such a strict regime, arriving at a socially withdrawn but adaptive mode of life. No doubt this often occurs in monasteries, retreats and other similar settings. Even Kaye might have withstood this excessive meditation if she had had a chance to talk over her feelings regularly so that she could assimilate them. Or, on the other hand, if she had been exposed to meditation only in small daily doses she might have been able to adjust to it without becoming imbalanced.

Another instance of over-meditation occurred in a TM meditator who had been carefully instructed not to meditate more than twenty minutes twice a day. When Dudley contacted me for advice he reported a list of symptoms sufficiently distressing to cause almost anyone to panic. While physical and neurological examinations had shown that he had no identifiable diseases, he complained of dizziness, pressure in his head, physical 'rushes' that would 'go to his eyes, ears, nose, and throat', and an inability to tolerate bright lights. More distressing to him, however, was his feeling that people seemed 'unreal' and only a reflection of his own consciousness. He had an intense feeling of alienation and experienced a 'tremendous gulf' between himself and others. He also could experience only what was in his immediate visual field; the back of a house did not 'exist' for him unless he walked around to the other side and actually saw it. If a person left the room where he was, that person ceased to 'exist' until he or she reappeared. The present felt eternal. When he went to sleep he felt he was 'leaving' his body; and one night when he saw a horror movie on TV he vividly imagined, in fact was convinced, that, like the figure on the screen, he was carrying ice picks in his hand. He was terrified of what he might do with them.

The more Dudley meditated, the worse these symptoms became. When he contacted me he reported that he was regularly meditating three hours a day, *plus* repeating his mantra to himself throughout the day. What was particularly significant was that Dudley claimed he had not realized that he should not meditate this much. Since TM teachers and checkers repeatedly stress the proper amount of time for meditation, this young man clearly had chosen to 'selectively inattend' to what they were saying. For reasons of his own, he had apparently needed to escape into an oblivion created through over-meditating.

Some of Dudley's symptoms superficially resemble some of the experiences reported by mystics: the disappearance of time, the eternal moment, the sense of leaving the body, the reflection of one's own consciousness in the universe, for example. When these experiences are under the control of the person having them and are *intentional*, they can be an important part of a person's spiritual development. In Dudley's case, however, no amount of guidance from meditation teachers had been able to change his chaotic experience into a constructive, positive one. He was reporting *compulsive* symptoms, perhaps unconsciously borrowed from the reports of spiritually inclined people, but used for his own maladaptive purposes. They were out of his control and consistently negative.

Dudley's background emerged during the diagnostic interview. He was an only child still living at home with his parents at age twenty-seven and closely tied to his mother. Because of this, he was presently unable to leave home to go to a professional school of his choice. For many years numerous personality problems had prevented him from growing up emotionally. Treatment with such therapies as behavior modification and hypnosis had been to no avail. While the specific symptoms that Dudley was now experiencing were apparently released by over-meditation, their basic cause seems to have been the disturbed adjustment which he had had all his life. Dudley and his mother had carried on continuous psychological warfare against his father, who appeared to be the scapegoat in a family triangle. The more symptoms Dudley developed, the greater his emotional stranglehold on his mother, and the greater his guilt toward his father, who was supposed to be 'unsympathetic' to Dudley's many ills and to his 'lack of initiative' at age twenty-seven. At night Dudley would often experience such rage against his sleeping father that he feared he might harm him.

To cope with his growing rage, frustration and shame, Dudley had begun to bury himself in meditation as one might lose oneself in a drug. An intelligent man, he must have known that he should not over-meditate in that fashion, but had chosen to do this until he was literally flooded by unpleasant symptoms. When he consulted me he had recently stopped meditating entirely (a decision which I advised him to stick to) but his symptoms continued to worsen as the time to leave home and enroll in a professional school in a distant city rapidly approached. Dudley's main problem at this point appeared to be the separation anxiety which he was experiencing – he knew he would soon have to leave his mother. Coupled with this was his deep guilt at his childlike dependency on his mother and his intense hostility toward his father.

Dudley is typical of those who consistently over-meditate. His symptoms seemed to stem not so much from meditation in and of itself as from the neurotic misuse of meditation. When he was challenged in a single diagnostic interview to face some of the basic issues which were underlying his problem, his symptoms temporarily became much less intense. His sense of time returned and his orientation in space and sense of reality were almost entirely reinstated by the end of two hours of conversation with the therapist.

While over-meditation seems to have paved the way for Dudley's emotional disturbance, it cannot be said to have actually caused it, considering the ease with which, temporarily at least, his symptoms cleared up with insight. What his case teaches us is the necessity for probing deeply into the causes of excessive over-meditation. The chances are that over-meditation will be found to reflect deep emotional problems. These problems must be treated in order to effect a permanent cure for whatever symptoms arise.

This is an important point to bear in mind, because some of the so-called super-cults require that their followers meditate for many hours each day. At one time the members of the International Society for Krishna Consciousness spent two to three hours chanting the 'Hare Krishna' when awakening in the morning and followed this by additional sessions of chanting at various points throughout the day. Other groups such as the Unification Church of Sun Myung Moon, which flourished in the 1970s, encouraged similar intensive meditation in their followers. The control of such super-cults over their followers raises a number of questions about possible exploitation of followers who have been confused and rendered highly suggestible by over-meditation.

Obviously over-meditation on a wide scale could have serious consequences. In this book, however, we are discussing the practical forms of meditation which, when properly followed, are always used in moderation. While moderation is insisted upon for ordinary practitioners, teachers of some forms of practical meditation, on the other hand, may be required to meditate continually for long periods of time every day as part of their training. TM teachers, for example, are periodically required to attend residence courses where intensive regimes of meditation (up to several hours a day) are required for periods of six or more weeks at a time. Not surprisingly, an occasional TM teacher has been known to develop serious emotional problems either during or shortly after such training, and several such cases have been called to my professional attention. In light of the heavy meditational requirement for TM *teacher* trainees, therefore, it would seem that a decision to become a TM teacher should be weighed just as carefully as a decision to undertake any other regime requiring extensive meditation would be.

In light of the temptation to over-meditate that is seen in certain susceptible individuals and the potential risk involved for their mental health if such a person were to do so, it is essential for anyone thinking of joining a movement which includes meditation as part of its program to inquire about the amount of time they will be asked to spend daily in this practice. Prospective meditators may also want to look carefully at other aspects of any movement they are thinking of joining to make certain their own personal liberty and freedom of thought will be preserved. Responsible training programs offering intensive meditation should supply low pressure, non-coercive and supportive retreats where every participant is free to remain fully in command of her own life, to make her own decisions, and to come and go as she wishes. To make certain of the non-coercive atmosphere of any large-scale 'spiritual' training program may take careful investigation since a number of the more notorious organizations now recruit through 'front' organizations with names that are unknown and seemingly innocuous. A wise procedure for anyone who is considering attending a preliminary meeting of such an organization is first to read about the organization and its strategies from a viewpoint different from that advanced by the organization itself. Almost any library contains non-fiction books about super-cults which are a reliable source of information. Even if the specific names and details in these books are not always up to date (the scene changes rapidly, with previously highly active cults fading away as the public becomes suspicious of them, and new ones appearing seemingly overnight) such books often accurately describe the highly questionable *tactics* of many of the super-cults with respect to the civil liberties and mental and physical health of their practitioners. The newspapers and magazines found in libraries are another good source of information which any research librarian can guide you to. A preliminary investigation of any cult's background is crucial if one's personal safety and mental health are to be safeguarded.

Even in the most unpressured and genuinely supportive retreat, however, as with Kaye described above, catastrophes sometimes arise, and the addition of an adequate clinical staff of trained mental health professionals appears essential for such programs. If professionally trained assistance does not exist in an intensive meditation-based program, the decision to enter a group requiring large amounts of meditation every day requires careful thought. Small, decentralized meditation settings, where considerable personal guidance is afforded each trainee by a highly qualified teacher, or else responsible home instruction, are usually preferable to the mass organizations.

These special precautions do not ordinarily apply to the practical forms of meditation undertaken by the average person, however. Practical meditation may add an important dimension to our lives, but it does not become a way of life. For this reason it seems to be the only type of meditation appropriate for use along with formal psychotherapy as this is practiced in the West. Whether it can be considered a form of therapy *in its own right* is the question we will look at next.

Chapter 17

A THERAPIST'S
VIEW

'Psychotherapy', in some form or another, has been universally
employed by human beings throughout the ages. Every person
who tries to console a despairing friend or help a panicky child
calm down is, in a sense, practicing psychotherapy – they are
using psychological means to restore the emotional balance of
another person. These common, everyday methods are based
on some attempt to understand the problem, at least on an
intuitive level, even though the reasoning involved may lack
scientific sophistication. Psychotherapy, as a formal discipline,
is different only in that it is systematic and practiced according
to established principles which are based on our present knowledge of human nature. Psychotherapy is the formalization of
the 'helping hand'.

There are a number of different forms of psychotherapy but
in general they all have certain goals in common. Psychotherapy
seeks to help the person become more mature, competent, effective and able to enjoy life more. These goals are not necessarily
easy to achieve. Individuals' confused views about themselves
in relation to the world or their unhealthy ways of looking at
themselves are often the end-product of painfully disturbed
parent–child relationships, reinforced later by years of unsatisfactory life experiences. We cannot expect a psychotherapist to
step in and in a short period of time undo the entire past history
of the patient. Psychotherapy is, however, often effective, particularly if patients are anxious to cooperate in a program for
their own improvement.

The goals for psychotherapy may differ according to the
person, their needs, and which forms of psychotherapy they
choose. 'Psychodynamic' psychotherapy seeks to resolve the

fundamental inner conflicts which are often unconscious, and to help the patient change on a deep level. Behavior modification therapy, as its name implies, often seeks to change only specific behaviors, with the remainder of the personality left unaltered. Both approaches have distinct value and the two may be used in a supplementary fashion. There are other forms of psychotherapy, but the most frequently used are the 'dynamic' and 'behavioral' approaches just described.

To understand where and how meditation can contribute to any of these therapies two questions come to mind: How 'deep' are the changes brought about by meditation, and is meditation *itself* a form of psychotherapy?

How Deep Does Meditation Go?

A study conducted at Princeton University by Christopher Ross and Hilary Brown investigated a group of TM meditators and a group of students who regularly practiced Progressive Relaxation.[1] They compared these 'regular practicers' with a group of students who rarely or never practiced these same techniques. The question they sought to answer was whether regular meditation and/or relaxation leads to changes in the content of people's dreams. Dreams were chosen because they tend to be a very stable measure of personality; that is, they reflect basic conflicts and coping mechanisms which remain the same over long periods of time. In a study conducted by psychologist Calvin Hall, for example, one man's dreams collected over a fifty-year period, from early adulthood to death, were studied to see how consistent his dream content was over the years. Hall found that each dream category which he studied had remained essentially unchanged for fifty years![2] In studying the dreams of other individuals, Hall also found that whenever a significant change in dream content was apparent, this generally represented a similarly profound change in the individual's behavior and personality. In other words, dream life does not easily change.

Ross and Brown decided that meditators' dreams might be a good way to find out if meditation can change a person's underlying personality. As we have seen, many kinds of changes have been reported in meditators over periods of only three months. These researchers set out to study changes over this same time period, but this time on a deeper level. They began by collecting a two-week daily dream diary from these subjects before they had learned their techniques of TM meditation or progressive relaxation, and another such diary after they had been practicing their respective techniques for three months. The subjects also kept daily mood checklists during the study.

The researchers then scored the dreams for forty-eight different aspects, or 'variables', which ranged from such simple characteristics as the number of characters in the dream or amount of verbal or physical aggression, to the presence of anxiety, self-reflection, bizarre imagery, or 'environmental threat' – among others.

What Ross and Brown found was that the overwhelming majority of these dream scores showed no change whatever, either in the regular meditators and regular progressive relaxers or in the group that did not practice their techniques regularly at all. This occurred even though a number of the subjects reported *feeling* much better on follow-up questionnaires. The regular practicers scored as considerably 'less anxious' on a written test which measured their level of anxiety, and their daily mood checklists showed that they were 'happy' much more often than they used to be before practicing meditation.

What does this mean? Did nothing happen to these subjects after they commenced to meditate or relax regularly? Does the lack of change in their dreams mean that those dramatic improvements in the lives of meditators which are so often reported to use may just be 'all in the imagination'?

Decidedly not. Something *had* happened to those subjects who had practiced their techniques regularly; they were less anxious and happier. Despite these changes, however, regular meditation and relaxation left untouched other *deeper* levels of their personalities. Their dreams and a test which reflects underlying personality dynamics by asking subjects to make up stories about pictures (the TAT) showed no changes at all over the three months. A test measuring changes in self-image – the way people tend to view themselves – also remained unchanged over the course of the study.[3]

As indicated previously, other studies *have* shown changes with meditation on tests measuring self-actualization, field independence and other aspects of personality. None of these studies, however, employed the 'projective techniques' which measure deeper layers of the personality, or dreams. The work of Ross and Brown and of Zevin (using the TAT)[4] suggests that it is these deeper levels of personality which often resist change through meditation.

My late husband and I noticed in our meditating patients the same kind of limitations seen in the Princeton study. After we began publishing articles on meditation, patients who were long-term meditators frequently came to us seeking therapists familiar with meditation. Some of these people had had years of intensive practice in one or another of the commonly used meditation techniques and some were even teachers of meditation.

We found that often these long-term meditators reported that they had become more emotionally responsive, tranquil, insightful and energetic after commencing meditation. Despite these gains, however, they came to us because of unresolved emotional conflicts revolving around such problems as personal relationships, marriage and career, and because of various disturbing symptoms. In other words, although they had changed through intensive practice of meditation in *certain* important respects, they had not changed in others.

Some other experimental evidence bears on this question. Its results are in agreement with Ross and Brown and our clinical observations. When Dr Leon Otis of the Stanford Research Institute administered personality tests to TM meditators and to a control group of non-meditators who were signed up to learn the technique, he discovered that TM had no discernible effects on self-image over the year's test period for those people who continued to practice it in his experiment.[5] Otis concluded that the data 'supports the notion that TM does not alter *basic personality characteristics*', a conclusion quite in line with that of the Princeton study.

Just as the latter found that *certain* behavior and moods did change with meditation, however, so in his study Otis also found that the TM group ranked significantly higher in enjoyment of life, restfulness of sleep, happiness, energy level, sexual adjustment and creativity than did the control group. These changes occurred despite the fact that *deeper* personality characteristics seemed to show no difference.

Taken together, the research studies and clinical observations suggest that while the effects of meditation can be impressive, it is doubtful whether meditation can change personality in any basic sense. To effect truly deep change meditation may need to become part of a more general change in the way one lives one's life. However, practical meditation does reduce tension and improve functioning on a number of levels. This may lead to some startling changes in behavior and the way the meditator views himself even if deep-seated emotional problems remain untouched. A patient with whom I worked at a guidance clinic illustrates this dual action of meditation. She was immensely helped by meditation, which seemed to supplement her psychotherapy, but at the same time remained unchanged in at least one basic aspect of her personality.

When Elvira came to the clinic she was in her mid-thirties. At that time, she was both depressed and highly anxious. She had had the sole responsibility of raising five children because her divorced husband had defaulted in child support. She was receiving welfare and three of the children were already showing severe emotional problems – her oldest son refused outright to attend school.

Almost from the first Elvira responded well to psychotherapy. Once she knew she could count on the assistance of an interested therapist she was able to use her intelligence and basic strength to begin to cope. Eventually she returned successfully to work, voluntarily removing herself from the welfare roles with a sense of pride. She was not only able to support her children and deal with them with less stress and anxiety, but her depression had lifted entirely.

One troublesome problem did remain, however. Elvira had been unable to resolve a generally destructive relationship with an emotionally disturbed lover. This unstable man was extremely possessive of her and acted more like another child in the household than an additional adult. He was intensely jealous of any attention she gave to her own children, drank heavily, and on several occasions had threatened her and her family with violence. At one point he was admitted to a psychiatric hospital, where he remained for several weeks.

For some time Elvira had felt she must end this relationship for her own safety and that of the children, but she was unable to think seriously about doing this without starting to weep uncontrollably. She experienced intense guilt when she thought of 'throwing him out'.

As her therapy proceeded, she became much less willing to

tolerate her lover's bullying behavior and experienced a growing conflict between her newfound personal dignity and her continuing dependence on his presence. At this point, she became unusually tense and on several occasions alarmed herself by drinking so heavily that she blacked out and later could not remember what had happened during the time she was drinking, something that had never happened to her before. I felt it important to arrest further development of the drinking and suggested to her that she learn meditation as a possible means of reducing the tension that was building up. Elvira was enthusiastic about the idea. She also hoped it would help her with her severe insomnia. She was now getting only three to four hours of fitful sleep per night.

Meditation was almost immediately effective. She looked peaceful, almost glowing, when she came to her first therapy session after learning it and within a few days of commencing meditation she slept restfully for a whole night. Since that time, her sleep remained extremely restful even during periods when she had to face high stress.

Her sporadic drinking stopped immediately following commencement of meditation and was never again a problem. Unexpectedly she also lost any sense of urgency about smoking marijuana, which she had formerly used daily. She also found herself forgetting to buy regular cigarettes for herself or to smoke them when they were present in her home. In addition, she had more composure and calmness at work and was experiencing a generally quieter, more understanding relationship with her children. Her most notable change, however, was a marked growth in independence. After her first three weeks of meditation, she firmly ordered her lover out of the house, despite his protests and threats, and arranged for police assistance in the event of his becoming violent. She followed through with her plan to make him leave without her accustomed guilt and self-recrimination. She felt appropriate grief after he left – this had been a long-lasting and close relationship – but despite this, she slept peacefully throughout the night, and attributed her ability to carry through with this decision directly to meditation.

Although some months later Elvira was reunited with her lover, this time their relationship was on a different footing. She was now more independent, having in the interim built up a number of outside activities, interests and relationships which she would not give up and she now insisted upon her rights and those of her children. Despite this fact, however, it was clear from her subsequent behavior that meditation was unable to change the underlying personality dynamics which had led Elvira to select such a disturbed individual to begin with. Meditation had both 'succeeded' and 'failed'. It had changed Elvira importantly in some respects and left her the same in others.

Is Meditation Psychotherapy?

Psychiatrist Harold Bloomfield has quoted TM's founder, Maharishi Mahesh Yogi, as saying that with psychiatric patients who regularly meditate, the role of the psychotherapist becomes one of 'holding the patient's hand while TM does the healing'.[6] Dr Bloomfield himself has, in his well-known book on meditation, subscribed to this point of view, although he sees dispensing drugs as an additional means for controlling more serious forms of psychiatric illness, and the occasional use of behavioral techniques and some short-term marriage counseling (along with TM) as useful.[7] Bloomfield summarizes his position by saying that essentially what a psychiatric patient needs from a psychotherapist is 'only encouragement to meditate regularly and to engage in dynamic activity'.[8]

The picture Bloomfield paints of meditation and its effectiveness as a psychotherapy in its own right is a glowing one. Unfortunately, however, it does not agree with the experience of a number of mental health professionals. Since my articles on the use of meditation in psychotherapy have appeared in professional journals, psychotherapists from many different disciplines and parts of the world have contacted me, volunteering information about their experiences with meditating patients. I have observed a consistency in their accounts. Almost all these people were very encouraging about the possibilities of using meditation along with psychotherapy and have recommended it to their patients. None felt, however, that meditation was a substitute for psychotherapy; that it was effective for every patient; or that its use was invariably without problems; and none of these therapists was as impressed by its 'cure-all' properties as the psychiatrists who had worked closely with the TM organization such as Dr Bloomfield. With rare exceptions, they did not find that all that was necessary was to sit by and 'hold the patient's hand' or dispense supplementary drugs, while meditation did the work.

Although, combined with psychotherapy, meditation can be an excellent means of helping a patient, I do not recommend it for any seriously disturbed person who is not simultaneously undergoing psychotherapy. While it *may* be effective as a sole treatment, in some instances it creates difficulties for emotionally disturbed people because of the unusually intense stress-release that such an individual may undergo. It is therefore desirable for such a person to be under the care of a trained psychotherapist while adjusting to meditation.

By this I do not mean that people who are tense or anxious or who suffer from a stress-related illness such as hypertension may not get relief from meditation without simultaneously being in psychotherapy, or that they should not necessarily try it, provided of course they remain under medical care for their physical ailment. I am speaking, rather, of people who suffer from serious psychiatric symptoms: depressions, phobias, addictions to drugs or alcohol, and other emotional disorders which require professional help. It is such people who may be a high-risk group with respect to meditation and who should approach learning it with caution and common sense. They should be under the care of a qualified psychotherapist with whom they should discuss their decision to learn meditation, and should *under-meditate* until they and their therapist are certain the experience is benefiting them. If necessary they should also have the wisdom to stop meditating altogether if it appears that this practice is not beneficial. With such precautions, they should run little risk from trying meditation and stand to gain considerable relief if it turns out to be effective for them.

My clinical observations in this respect are instructive. Over the past several years I have been consulted by a number of patients with a previous history of severe psychiatric disturbance who had happened to learn TM at a time when they were not in psychotherapy. By 'severe' I mean that these people had a past history of such disturbed behavior as being a recluse for many years, living in a fantasy world where 'evil forces' were feared, or had shown other evidence of serious emotional disturbance. By no means all of them had had psychiatric breakdowns requiring hospitalization, however, and many of them had never before sought psychotherapy for their problems.

These patients reported to me that disturbing psychiatric symptoms had appeared soon after they had commenced meditation, or that previous symptoms were reactivated by meditation. Three of them suffered complete mental breakdowns for which they had to be hospitalized within a matter of weeks of commencing the practice of meditation. Each attributed the breakdown to meditation, and as far as I could discern, none of them had been *over-meditating* at that time. They reported that they had not meditated more than the prescribed twenty minutes twice daily and their TM teachers later confirmed these observations. Even this moderate meditation time had apparently been too much for them. They seemed to be abnormally sensitive to meditation, and unable to take it even in average doses.

It is of course possible that immediate reduction in the amount of time they were asked to meditate per day, together with simultaneous psychotherapy, might have enabled these people to cope with their meditation without developing a severe psychiatric condition. On the other hand, it may be that a psychotherapist who had experience with meditation would have advised them to stop meditating entirely at this point in their lives and been correct in doing so. In any event, meditation by itself certainly did not serve as a therapy in these instances.

Our present clinical experience suggests therefore that while the changes brought about by meditation are often genuinely therapeutic, they are also incomplete, and because of the occasional undesirable side-effects, meditation used *by itself* as a form of treatment for psychiatric disorders is undesirable. Conventional psychotherapy can, of course, at times be incomplete too and it may be that the combination of psychotherapy *plus* meditation will be found to be more effective in many instances than either technique used alone. A study by psychologists Leah Dell Dick and Robert Ragland at the University of Oklahoma showed that people who obtained counseling from a student mental health center responded better to a *combination* of meditation and psychological counseling than they did either to meditation alone or to counseling alone.[9]

The Meditating Therapist

Quite apart from any effects that meditation may have on patients, several of my meditating psychotherapist colleagues and I have noticed changes in our work with patients after we commenced meditation, and this value to the therapist has been confirmed by research as well.[10]

We have experienced personal benefits from practicing meditation which have no doubt contributed indirectly to our professional skills, but our methods of dealing with patients have changed too. Several of us have noticed that our ability to sense patients' moods sharpened since we commenced meditating. We became more effortlessly aware of their deeper struggles and unconscious conflicts. My late husband, Dr Ephron, had the experience of watching his meditation sessions actually assist him directly in his work. On a number of occasions when he had been particularly puzzled about a certain patient's problem, he found that during his next meditative session after seeing the patient, he experienced vivid mental imagery. When studied later on, these imagined scenes turned out to contain new and accurate insights into the patient's difficulties. Often they contained an answer to a problem which had been baffling him.

One young woman was unable to work out a deep-seated problem relating to her fiancé. She left my husband's office on a particular day frustrated because she could not understand her compulsion to attack her lover, whom in many ways she loved and whom she felt she genuinely wanted to marry. During his own meditation session later that afternoon, though not consciously thinking about this patient and her problem, Harmon visualized King Lear with two of his daughters; in the scene the daughters were being destructive and exploitive toward their father. As in Shakespeare's play, they had reduced him to rags and to madness. While still meditating, the name of this patient flashed into his mind and the scene seemed to be a symbolic statement of her problem. Perhaps, he thought, this young woman, together with her divorced mother, had deliberately tried to exploit the girl's wealthy father and use his riches for their own needs. Could the fact that she had never faced her own guilt at her destructive exploitation of her father be one of the causes of this young woman's present discomfort in the presence of men, and of her defensive need to attack them as though *they* were the monsters?

During the patient's next psychotherapy session, Harmon explored this by asking her whether she and her mother had ever treated her father as though he were, in effect, like King Lear. The patient was startled at the wording of the question, and replied that her father had often complained to her mother and to herself by saying, 'I feel like King Lear in this house.' This information led to a productive session in which the patient could, for the first time, examine the validity of her father's complaints that he was being treated badly in his own home. By doing this, she was able to explore the manner in which she had developed her own exploitive patterns and how they were still contaminating her relationships – both toward her father and toward other men in her life, including her fiancé, a young man of great wealth.

On the occasions when meditation brings about this kind of insight into a patient's problems, the free-floating attention of the meditative state makes it possible for the therapist to combine his previous observations of the patient in such a way that a creative insight emerges. This is much like other creative syntheses in the meditative state which lead to artistic achievement or scientific discovery.

Several of us in psychotherapeutic work have also noticed that our ability to understand the symbols in a patient's dreams and to help the patient deal constructively with these symbols has increased since we have been meditating. It is as though we ourselves were now more comfortable with this 'primary process' material since it is often the type of material that the meditative state brings about. Another difference is our increased 'staying power'. When patients' appointments follow one another in a long succession over the course of the day, we now have less of a tendency to become fatigued or drowsy from work stress, an occupational hazard in the 'sitting professions'.

Psychotherapists are at times called upon to face severe bursts of hostility from patients. Expression of such hostility can be a useful, even necessary part of the treatment for the patient, but may be stressful for the therapist, particularly if the patient's angry outburst is unexpected. I found that after I had commenced meditating regularly, my ability to cope with such negative reactions on the part of patients improved. I no longer felt threatened by a patient's sudden outburst; it was as though I were now 'cushioned' from it. I therefore had a more balanced and constructive attitude toward what the patient was doing. This seems to be an extension of my generally greater tolerance of irritating or potentially upsetting situations which developed since commencing meditation.

Meditation may also foster the kind of 'evenly suspended attention' when listening to patients in psychotherapy that Freud considered essential to psychotherapists. Freud pointed out that too deliberate an attention to what patients are saying during treatment may actually prevent a deeper understanding of the real meaning of their comments.[11] Instead of actively listening, he therefore advised the psychotherapist to 'turn his own unconscious like a receptive organ toward the transmitting unconscious of the patient'. As we have seen, the non-directed goal-less state achieved during meditation brings about a greater than usual openness to inner and outer impressions and an increased awareness of emotional reactions. Perhaps meditation might be considered an exercise designed to strengthen the very 'psychic muscles' necessary to achieve Freud's ideal state of evenly suspended attention.

This aspect of meditation seems to be related to what psychologist Terry Lesh discovered when she studied the effects of meditation on clinical psychology students studying to be psychological counselors. Empathy (that is, the ability to 'feel with' another person as though her feelings were your own) cannot really be taught, yet it is essential for good psychotherapy. Lesh wondered whether meditation might improve the capacity of future psychologists to empathize with their patients.

She chose to study the effects of Zazen meditation on the development of empathy. What she found was that empathetic ability significantly improved in those counselors who regularly practiced meditation during the course of the study, and either did not improve or got worse in the two groups of psychological counselor trainees who did *not* practice meditation.[12] Lesh's study and our own observations have led myself and my meditating colleagues to think that learning meditation might be a valuable addition to standard training for students entering the mental health professions.[13]

With respect to the relationship between meditation and

psychotherapy, I would suggest that meditation can be a most useful partner to psychotherapy, but that this alliance seems to work best when it is a partnership in the true sense of the word, each discipline supplementing the other.

Chapter 18

MEDITATION IN THE WORKPLACE

Deep within the labyrinthian corridors of the New York Telephone Company building at 375 Pearl Street in New York City, a group of employees were seated around a long table in a windowless seventh-floor conference room. They were waiting for a reporter sent by the prestigious Wharton School of Business, one of the top business schools in the United States. Word had spread in the business community that the meditation program at New York Telephone was relieving stress for its workers. Since the method being used was both cost-effective and exportable to other organizations, the Wharton's magazine thought information about it might interest its readers.

The reporter interviewed Mary Knoble first, an administrative clerk just a few years away from retirement. She described herself as having been 'so sweet and so quiet' before learning meditation that she would rarely speak unless spoken to. 'I hated that inferiority complex,' she said. Now, since she had been meditating, she had begun to speak up. 'I have more respect for myself now and can look people in the eye,' she said.

A company business executive in his thirties by the name of Erenesto Roque was next to express himself. He explained that he was continually dealing with customers and that before meditation, when he got a complaint, he would often become angry at the company. 'Now I don't have as many of those temper tantrums,' he told the reporter. He said he found himself trying to look at the whole situation with a sense of perspective instead. 'Shouting isn't going to get it done,' he explained.

A middle-aged woman named Lillian who worked as a drafter in the engineering department told the reporter that before meditating she had been a 'very uptight' person whose doctor had called her 'the best customer he ever had'. She had suffered from constant headaches, asthma and very high blood pressure. Now she almost never had a headache, her symptoms of asthma had greatly lessened, and her blood pressure was considerably improved.

New York Telephone Adopts CSM

These employees of the phone company were talking about their experiences before and after learning CSM. At the time of the Wharton interview, 300 workers had already learned to meditate and over the next few years the company was to teach close to 5,000 employees CSM. This was to become one of the most successful stress management programs ever instituted in a major corporation.

Unlike typical stress management programs elsewhere, the meditation program at New York Telephone was not just aimed at a small group of executives. Any employee judged to be suffering from stress was eligible, and workers from company offices around the state participated, most of them after having the meditation training recommended to them by a doctor or nurse in the medical department.

The company was not trying to promote the program. The idea was to focus on those most likely to need it and thus most likely to persevere. Word had spread, however, that the program was beneficial, and now there was a sizable waiting list.

Luis Mejia, an assistant engineer, described how the meditation program had affected him. He admitted that he was 'a bit leery about it at first' because he had associated meditation with 'incense, the Lotus Position and so forth'. But at the recommendation of a company nurse he had finally tried CSM, partly out of curiosity and partly in the hope that it would alleviate his insomnia, stomach cramps and tingling hands. For the first few months he noticed little change – perhaps, he thought, because he was in the midst of serious personal problems at that time. But as he kept on with his meditation program he began to see a difference. His friends told him that he seemed 'a lot more relaxed and a lot less quiet', and he found that he no longer had so much bottled-up tension. His physical symptoms also began to improve markedly at this time and were still getting better. He was very pleased.

Minnie, a clerk in the engineering department and mother of five children, told the reporter that she now had far fewer headaches, more energy at work, and was 'not nearly so tired when I come home'. She had already introduced one of her daughters to meditation through the recordings and was planning to try it out with her other children as well.

Like Mary and, to some extent Luis, Minnie found that meditating was making her more assertive, but in a constructive way. She was now less willing to 'do someone else's work' while at the same time she was finding that she was more tactful in dealing with people. She was also turning up at work more often. Reduced absenteeism was reported by a number of those interviewed and some of these people had even won attendance awards. All the employees with whom the reporter spoke felt that meditation had helped them deal better with stress in their daily lives.[1]

The somewhat revolutionary idea of introducing a meditation program at the New York Telephone Company was the idea of Dr Gilbeart H. Collings, Jr, the company's forward-looking medical director. When asked about this Dr Collings admitted that the meditation program had initially met with 'the usual and normal amount of healthy skepticism from executives and others', but that many of the skeptics were converted when they saw the impact it had on someone they knew.

As medical director of a company with some 80,000 employees spread around the state of New York, Dr Collings found that logistics were at the heart of most programs that he faced. It was relatively simple to devise a program for fifteen, twenty or 100 people, but he was constantly looking for ways to take things that were easy to do on a one-to-one basis and convert them to something practicable for thousands.

It was while he was trying to figure out ways to help employees suffering from stress that Dr Collings contacted me because he had read my book and articles on meditation. He wanted to know if I could work with their medical department to study the effectiveness of meditation for reducing stress among company employees. I was immediately interested, accepted the invitation, and, working with the medical department, began recruiting participants for the upcoming study at the company. We admitted employees at all managerial levels, from telephone repair people to top management executives.

The study which emerged continued for five and a half months and ended up with strong positive results. A total of 160 employees were assigned to four groups of forty people each. Each of three groups was trained in a specific form of meditation – relaxation: either progressive muscle relaxation, Benson's Respiratory One Method (ROM), or the CSM technique. The fourth group did not learn any technique but was studied 'before' and 'after' – they were the 'control group' in the experiment. Participants in the meditation–relaxation groups learned their required techniques in their own homes, making uses of tape cassettes and supplementary reading material. They were asked to practice their method twice a day in sessions of fifteen to twenty minutes each. A trainer then contacted them after the first week to be certain that they understood what to do, and there were group meetings after two weeks to deal with any questions they might have and discuss how the method could be adjusted to fit each individual's needs.

To evaluate the whole program, we administered tests at various points. Most notably, meditators and members of the control group took a psychological evaluation questionnaire before the study got underway, after six weeks into the program, and again at the end of the five and a half months that the study lasted. On this self-report inventory, known as the SCL-90-R,[2] the subject is asked to indicate, on a scale of zero to four, how much he or she is 'bothered' by problems that range from 'feeling inferior to others' and 'feeling pushed to get ahead', to 'felt terror or panic' and 'having the urge to break or smash things'. The SCL-90-R also covers many areas of physical symptoms such as headaches, stomach problems, dizziness, nausea, etc. In scoring, these items are divided into various categories to evaluate different types of distress such as anxiety, hostility, depression and stress-related physical disorders, among others. Since the SCL-90-R had previously been given to large numbers of so-called 'normal' people in the general population as well as to psychiatric patients, reliable norms were available, and it was possible to compare distress levels of subjects at New York Telephone with members of these larger groups as well.

The results were striking. At the outset of the study, the

participants (including members of the control group) had test profiles that were considerably higher (that is, showed more distress) than those of the general population. In fact, these employees' profiles hovered right at the edge of the 'clinical range', the point at which treatment of some sort often becomes mandatory. By the end of the study, however, the average stress scores of the meditators had come down so much that they now fell well within the normal range for the general population – and in one key category, stress-related physical symptoms, the meditators were now considerably 'healthier' than the normal population.

The study also used another measure – a questionnaire designed to discover such things as participants' attitudes toward meditation and their perception of its shortcomings or benefits as the case might be. On this questionnaire the employees were also given an opportunity to make spontaneous comments about the impact of meditation on their lives and many of them did so. They noted such changes as improved ability to think clearly and to organize their work, improved social skills, and more control over negative emotions, among others.

We had obtained valuable information from the formal study at New York Telephone. The study was subsequently published in the *Journal of Occupational Medicine*,[3] but the companywide meditation program that followed the formal study gave us a chance to interview thousands of meditators who provided us with additional information of great value. The company had chosen CSM for its companywide program since the research study had shown it to be the most popular and frequently practiced of the techniques, and so it was CSM meditators who reported to us in this larger program.

When Jean Cole, the able administrator of the meditation program at New York Telephone, talked with meditators who were participating in the numerous company discussion groups, she discovered that aside from the marked reduction in tension which so many people reported, one of the most appreciated benefits was the lowering of irritability and aggression which these people had noticed in themselves after learning to meditate. Not only had their hostility scores on the SCL-90-R reduced significantly after several months of meditating, but participants told of other ways that meditation had changed their relationships as well. These people described themselves as now having more tolerance and being more patient with themselves and others, and as less likely to get angry when other people did not do what they wanted.

Ed (not his real name which he requested be withheld) is an example of the lowering of irritability. A company repairman, in his discussion group he told how before he had learned meditation his job had been very difficult for him. The people whose phones he was servicing often seemed to blame *him* for 'all the problems they had ever had with their phone service, including billing mistakes and the current cost of service – I was a dumping ground'. Because the customer was 'always right', Ed didn't argue back at them but when he got home he would lose his temper. If, for example, his wife met him at the door and told him that the children had been fighting, he would 'blow up'. 'I have wonderful kids and I love them,' he told us, 'but my boiling point was so low that I'd explode.'

After he had been practicing meditation for close to a month, Ed discovered that he had changed. Now when he went into customers' homes he felt as though there were a 'buffer zone' surrounding him. This mental barrier didn't let the customers' complaints 'get to him'. 'I hear the same old accusations,' he told us, 'but they don't get under my skin anymore.' Now he would look his customers in the eye and say quietly, 'That must be tough ' To his surprise they were often satisfied with this comment and usually stopped complaining.

To make his point about the change in himself he told us about a recent experience on coming home from work. His wife had once again told him that the children were fighting, but this time he said, 'Okay, I'll talk with them,' and sat down and meditated – his new pattern upon arriving home. When he finished he said to the children, 'I know you've been fighting, but right now we're all going to sit at the table and spend the only time that we'll have together today peacefully. I want you to call a truce during dinner – just *cool* it. Then you can finish fighting later on – if you have to.'

Ed thinks his calmness must have been catching because the children stopped fighting, sat down at the table, and soon began to talk and laugh together – and they didn't go back to fighting when the meal was over. He was very grateful for these changes in himself, saying that they were allowing him to be the kind of father he really wanted to be.

His comments were typical of the meditators in the program. Many of them were reporting improved family relationships. One woman described the change she observed in herself this way: 'My daughter says I'm less grouchy, and my mother says I don't act as though I "know everything" now. I guess I used to act as though nobody was right but *me*.'

Another employee was finding herself much more receptive to other people's opinions and ideas since she had been meditating. This allowed her to absorb anything she might be reading or hearing better and to listen to other people's points of view, including her children's, in a way she had never done before. Because of this new openness, she was getting along much better with people.

A woman who worked as a telephone operator said she had first realized that meditation was making a difference when, on coming home, she found that even though her daughter's room was 'all messed up, *I didn't yell at her!*'

A salesman reported that the greatest benefit he had realized from meditation was that he was now getting along with his mother-in-law. She had lived in the house with his family for twelve years and during that time she and he had 'fought continuously. But now we're getting along beautifully. I think it's probably the change in me.'

The manner in which the meditation program was impacting employees' performance at work was of particular interest to the telephone company, and Jean Cole kept careful notes on this. Here are some typical comments she collected:

- A secretary in the comptroller's office insisted that her practice of CSM had improved her tardiness '100 percent'. Before, she had been late to work almost every single day. Two months after she commenced meditating she was now consistently arriving at work on time. Her boss, jokingly commenting on this, had said, 'I've been noticing you haven't been late for a month. Apparently you have a new clock and they put an extra hour on it to get you to work on time!' When she explained the change was because of meditation she discovered that her boss was in the company program too and that meditation had helped him stop smoking. He strongly approved of her continuing in the practice.

- Another employee reported that his time for meditation was during his morning commute. The first week or so after he learned to meditate, on coming out of his meditation session his mind had been 'as clear as a bell'. As the months went by, however, meditation became more of a peaceful, relaxing type of experience for him. Now he would come out of it ready to face the rest of his journey to work and a day in the office with quiet confidence. As a result he was was finding that he could handle situations in the office that 'all people have – tough deadlines and tension' much better.
- A manager in the accounting department reported that he was now so calm that he no longer noticed the pressure at work in the same way, although there was, he said, a lot of it because the company was changing to a new system. While there were many things left over to be done at the end of each day, somehow these no longer bothered him the way they used to and he said he was dealing with them just as well *without* the worrying.
- Another employee reported that he was not feeling the same urgency to get things done at work since he had been meditating, but that to his surprise he was getting these things done even more effectively. 'I don't seem to be working any harder,' he told us, 'but I have so much more energy that I have a lot left over at the end of the day. I'm not just dead tired and sitting in front of the tube [TV] all evening. Now I go out shopping or bowling, or whatever I enjoy doing.'
- One man whose wife had started meditating at the same time as him reported that after the third week his wife suddenly found herself crying uncontrollably during her meditation sessions. This reaction lasted for three consecutive sessions until she felt she couldn't stand it and so took a 'vacation' from meditation which lasted about two months. After that she decided to start meditating again. This time her practice was going extremely smoothly, was very beneficial, and she had no further episodes of crying.
- A middle manager described how about one month after he started meditation he found that he now had a great deal of extra energy. He used to go home and start doing jobs but couldn't finish them – he'd run out of steam. Now he was

experiencing what he called an 'inner drive' to get things done, to realize his goals, and was able to do this.

• Another man reported that he was presently engaged in a project at the office that required him staying there until eight o'clock each night. Although he used to meditate only in the morning, he was now setting aside quiet time around five o'clock to take a meditation break at work and said this was helping a great deal. 'There are a lot of deadlines and problems with this project and doing the meditation has been a big asset,' he told us.

• An executive in the medical department who had entered the program because of high blood pressure had been recording his pressure meticulously (on both arms) ever since he started the program. He took a blood pressure reading as soon as he came home from work and another right after his meditation session. He reported that his pressure would regularly come down by about four to eight points after he had meditated. Before he learned meditation, his blood pressure had been consistently elevated.

Management Takes Note

These are only a few of the reports obtained from the New York Telephone Company employees which served to confirm previous research findings. These reports also pointed to some areas of concern to business and industry which had not been systematically studied before but which may well be helped by meditation. It is extremely difficult to conduct research on the effect of meditation on absenteeism, for example, because so many factors can operate together to cause it. Similarly, it's not easy to trace the effects of meditation on tardiness because this too can can be influenced by many factors.

One area in which meditation may affect large organizations *has* been studied carefully, however. A common management concern is how to improve group problem-solving effectiveness. Groups engaged in problem-solving play a major role in establishing the plans, policies and procedures that guide large-scale organizations. Any factor that can improve the effectiveness of these groups in terms of the quality and speed of their performance, or in terms of participant commitment, could be economically and socially significant.

With these considerations in mind, Dr Herbert Kindler of the UCLA Graduate School of Management in California decided to test the possibility that the CSM method of meditation might be suitable for introduction by organizational managers as an aid to improving group problem-solving effectiveness.[4]

Kindler's study was unusual. He used 230 management graduate students randomly assigned to five person teams; this created forty-six teams. Each team was assigned two group problem-solving tasks (puzzles to piece together), one of which was performed at the commencement of the study, and the other after an interval during which half of the subjects (the 'experimental' group) learned CSM, and the other half (the 'control' group) listened to a lecture on problem-solving.

Each team had to assemble various geometric shapes into squares, and only one arrangement could succeed. If a 'bad' square was formed, it blocked that team from achieving the correct solution and the game is so constructed that these 'bad' squares appear with regularity. The point of the experiment is to assess what happens once these deceptive 'failures' occur – will the team be insightful and flexible enough to switch gears and proceed to find the correct solution? The requisite attribute for moving ahead to obtain the correct solution is the *ability to cooperate in restructuring a problem.*

During this puzzle-solving task, the participants were forbidden to speak to each other or to solicit a portion of a puzzle from a team-mate (although they could receive unsolicited pieces of the puzzle). To make matters worse for those participating, elapsed time was announced loudly every five minutes during the puzzle experiment to create time pressure and increase the competition between teams.

Each team was measured before and after the experimental condition (either meditation training or the lecture on problem-solving) in a number of ways. Student observers in the room recorded the amount of time individual teams required to solve each problem, the number of transactions they required to reach the solution, and the team's number of laughter occurrences (which were considered a measure of tension-release). Afterwards participants filled out self-report questionnaires describing their experience.

The results were enlightening. In terms of time elapsed to solve the problem, the teams consisting of those who had learned meditation achieved significantly better scores than did the control-group teams who had *not* learned to meditate. In terms of number of transactions used to arrive at a correct solution, the meditating teams again achieved significantly better scores than the controls. With respect to the participants' self-reports, more members of the meditation teams than of the control teams reported that during the testing they felt calm and at ease. With respect to the number of laughter occurrences, the meditation teams had significantly 'better' scores (that is, less 'nervous laughter') than did the control teams. Also, significantly more members of the meditation group reported that their team had worked 'very well' or 'fairly well' together, while significantly more members of the control group reported that their team had worked 'so-so' or 'poorly' together.

What the study showed, then, was that those participants who had practiced meditation before they worked together to solve a common problem, completed tasks more quickly and with fewer transactions needed than those who had *not* practiced meditation. Based upon this study and previous research on meditation, Kindler set forth the following conclusions with respect to the possible uses of meditation in organizations:

- The team rapport aspect of group meditation may help managers move into a cooperative mode in situations such as collaborative problem-solving.
- The education of managers, particularly in professional graduate schools, tends to emphasize the analytical and logical modes of reasoning. Meditation may unlock more of a manager's intuitive reasoning power, thereby leading to a greater flow of ideas.
- The quieting effects of meditation may help managers to avoid precipitous 'solutions' made before they gain an adequate appreciation of the underlying problems.
- A tendency in hierarchical organizations is to go along uncritically with suggestions of persons in higher echelons than one's self, thus frequently stifling creativity and innovation in an organization. The tendency of meditation to foster independent thinking may reinforce one's own convic-

tions and help overcome reluctance to contribute views different from those expressed by higher-ranking individuals.

• Many ambitious self-driving managers tend to develop illnesses related to tension. The calming effects of meditation may provide relief from dysfunctional levels of anxiety and may open avenues for heart attack-prone executives to relieve tension.

Kindler concluded that these potential benefits would more than likely offset the low cost involved in creating and conducting meditation programs in organizational settings.

It remains to be seen if the benefits of meditation will be widely utilized by business and industry, but given the interest in managing stress which is becoming more widespread, there is a possibility that meditation will increasingly be introduced into forward-looking companies. If meditation were to become an accepted part of corporate life, then we could expect to see some startling positive changes taking place in the lives of a huge number of people. It is impressive to think about the benefits to society which such deeply beneficial changes, in so many people, might bring about. Let us hope that we will soon be watching this happen.

Part 4

CONCLUSIONS

Chapter 19

WHY DOES MEDITATION WORK?

The evidence is impressive. Despite its seeming simplicity, meditation can bring about positive changes which may alter a person's life profoundly. It is a surprisingly powerful intervention. We now need to ask where this power comes from. What is meditation's 'secret'?

In trying to understand why meditation has the transforming effects it does, we might imagine watching many different streams flow into one river. The characteristics of the river can be explained only by its volume of water and the direction of the flow. Similarly, many factors converge in meditation, lending to it their combined power, something that is above and beyond the effects of any single component. While we may consider various explanations for its effectiveness, we must remember that the full experience of meditation is quite different from any of these and that our limited understanding can give only partial answers.

However, I do want to tell you about some interesting theories on why meditation works. Since I have written in detail about them elsewhere,[1] I will summarize them briefly here and offer some further ideas of my own on why meditation has the profound effect upon people that it does.

Taking the Charge Off Negative Emotions

Meditation may act much like an electrical demagnetizing circuit. When we demagnetize a tape, the electrical charge is removed from it and the tape is wiped clean or 'neutralized'. It is quite possible that the thoughts and feelings which trouble us are similarly neutralized by the process of meditating.

Psychologists know that if a person is asked to recall distressing thoughts, especially fears, while at the same time he is in a state of deep relaxation, the fears will lose their hold and thoughts about them will become converted into objective and relatively non-emotional concerns. It is not possible for a person to be acutely anxious and *at the same time* deeply relaxed. If we deliberately couple relaxation with distressing thoughts, therefore, this can bring about a sharp change in a person's reaction to those thoughts and this change may be more or less permanent in its effect. The process by which this is done is called 'systematic desensitization'. In this form of behavior therapy the person is deliberately presented with the distressing thoughts (and sometimes with the actual distressing situation) while he is in a state of deep muscle relaxation. This process is accomplished in small increments and may take many sessions to complete but it can overcome deep-seated fears and phobias in some people.

Psychologist Daniel Goleman has suggested that meditation may be a highly effective desensitization process which works much the same way as systematic desensitization except that it is much wider in its scope and under complete control of the meditator – no therapist is needed for it to work. He calls this process 'global desensitization' to indicate its all-inclusive nature.[2]

Dr Goleman has noted that when distressing thoughts and images float unbidden through the mind of a meditator, these typically occur in the deeply relaxed meditative state, and has suggested that this natural *linking* of distressing thoughts with deep physical calm makes the disturbing thoughts lose their emotional charge.

This concept feels very 'right' to those of us who work with meditation because it is supported by our observations. Meditators will often report that in a particular meditation session thoughts of a disturbing nature have passed through their minds, sometimes with great vividness, but that somehow they were able to remain calm despite the unpleasantness of these thoughts. After such a session the disturbing thoughts or fears seemed no longer to 'bother them' the same way. Something has happened. Meditation may well have acted to desensitize the individual who reports such experiences.

Breaking Up Old Patterns

Meditation can, it seems, also break up engrained patterns of thought and automatic ways of behaving – with very beneficial effect. Most of us are on 'automatic' pilot most of the time. By the time we are grown we are, as Emerson put it, a 'walking bundle of habits'. The mental reorganization provided by meditation, which researcher Arthur Deikman has called 'deautomatization', may therefore free us from our habitual ways of viewing things, bringing a freshness into our experiencing of life that many of us have not known since we were very young children.

Little children are not locked in to the mass of habits that consume the energy of adults. They are therefore more spontaneous, joyful and alive than most adults. Deikman believes that an unchanging or monotonously repeated stimulus (the object of focus in meditation), by preventing us from processing the world in the ways we are accustomed to, allows us to escape the stifling straitjacket of habitual behavior. This, he suggests, is the reason why so many people report an unusual sense of buoyancy and well-being when they practice meditation.

Balancing the Two Sides of the Brain

One of the most important characteristics of meditation is a change in cognitive (thinking) style. During meditation, the verbal, logical 'self' that reasons in orderly sequences and is highly aware of the passing of time seems to move into the background, and is replaced by a different 'self' – one that we usually encounter only under special circumstances such as the period just before we fall asleep, when our mind drifts among images and impressions whose content and meaning we feel or know only intuitively. The self we know during meditation operates in a dim but intimate world, removed from considerations of time and involvement with past or future. Our 'interior speech', that ever-present running stream of words that occupies our thinking during regular activity, is now either stilled or relegated to a background role. In the meditative sphere of our being, images and an awareness of space are often the most real aspects of our experience.

Research has shown that verbal, logical, time-linked thinking is usually processed through the *left* side of the brain in right-handed persons,[4] and that this 'left-hemispheric', more predominant type of thinking seems to be lessened during meditation.[5] Holistic, intuitive, wordless thinking, the kind that is usually processed through the *right* side of the brain, seems however to come to the fore when we meditate. The regular practice of meditation may therefore create a greater balance between the two sides of the brain by righting a skewed balance. In our fast-moving society the logical left hemisphere carries most of the workload – we are called upon to be very rational most of the time – while the use of intuition is generally down-graded. Meditation may correct this imbalance.

This effect of meditation can be significant because the highest achievements of human beings require the cooperation of *both* sides of our brain. Intuition and hunches must be shaped by logical, disciplined thinking to form a work of art. The most rigorous scientific and philosophical reasoning requires the rich leavening of hunch and inspiration to make it fruitful. We therefore need a harmony, a coming-together of our two 'selves' into one mind, one being, to be at our very best. Perhaps such a harmony, brought about by meditation, is the reason for the sense of wholeness experienced by so many meditators. In a literal sense, meditation may 'pull us together'.

Reducing Sensory Overload

It's obvious to anyone who meditates that the process of meditation reduces the intrusive effect of the external world. Sight, sound and touch become relatively unimportant as we focus on our chosen object of meditation, whether this be a mantra, a candle flame, the sensations of our own breathing, or some other repetitive or unchanging stimulus. As we engage with our chosen focus of meditation, our inner world comes to the fore as the outer world recedes. What effect does this have on us?

The answer may lie in what happens when human beings or lower animals are *bombarded* by stimuli. Too much stimulation can be annoying and, carried to an extreme, overstimulation can seriously break down the adequacy of our mental or physical functioning. The strategies of the 'third degree' and of 'brainwashing' are based on this principle. If a prisoner or someone else whose behavior is being manipulated is kept overstimulated by constant bombardment with intense lights, sounds or sense impressions for hours on end, day after day, the clarity of her thinking processes eventually deteriorates. At this point people often become susceptible to suggestions or willing to comply with demands which, in a more rational state, they would reject.

If animals are subjected to intense stimuli such as loud noises, bright flashing lights or impressions of rapid motion over long periods of time, a wide variety of serious symptoms occur. The heart rate and blood pressure of a group of rats subjected to these conditions, for example, changed in a manner indicating that the animals were undergoing severe stress – their adrenal hormone levels shot up, all manner of symptoms of anxiety were shown, and in a number of instances, death occurred.[6]

When animals are packed together in cages where they are subjected to constant inescapable stimulation from other animals, the consequences are serious. What happens has been described as the 'behavioral sink'. By this is meant that the behavior of these animals deteriorates until there is an extreme breakdown in social behavior; normally cooperative animals become hostile and destructive to each other. There is also a sharp increase in the death rate of the animals, with many early deaths that would not normally have been expected. The effects of overcrowding on animals has been studied because of the possible implications this may have for human beings. If overcrowding breaks down the inner controls of animals to such a radical degree that it makes them seriously destructive and anti-social, what happens to human beings confined in the constant overstimulation of ghettos in large cities?

These are important questions for us to ask in an age where sensory overload seems to be the order of the day. Without realizing it, the average person faces an increasing amount of sensory bombardment in her daily life. An obvious example of this are certain discotheques where intense lights, sounds and colors are flashed in rapid succession so that the mind cannot adapt and an altered state of consciousness is created. Over-amplified rock music is also a sensory overload with which we are all becoming familiar today. The music may stimulate the nervous system to eventual exhaustion, at which point perceptions and thoughts become altered and the listener may feel temporarily 'high'. The long-term effects of such massive overstimulation on the nervous system is unknown; although we do know that sounds greater than seventy-five decibels (typically rock music is amplified to at least 108 decibels) increase the pulse and respiration and that very loud noises leave us shaky. Increasing numbers of people, particularly young people, are exposed to such noise, and tests have shown that by the time they have reached college age, 61 percent of the youth of today (a generation exposed to unusual amounts of high noise) show some loss of hearing acuity.

Such activities as listening to a hi-fi turned up to the maximum volume or going to loud concerts are voluntarily sought out. Hopefully not *all* of us are exposed to conditions of sensory overload unless we want to be – or are we? The unfortunate fact is that we may no longer realize when we are experiencing sensory overload because this condition has become so much a part of modern life. High-pressure advertising and dramatically presented newscasts are flashed to us constantly over the mass media. Billboards and supermarket shelves compete for our attention with vividly colored displays. The noise of cars, motorcycles and planes intrudes into even the quietest country resort. And these are only some of the ways that high levels of stimulation invade our lives today.

What makes matters even more difficult is that with overstimulation, our normal tendency to withdraw from intense stimuli seems to be dulled. At this point instead of withdrawing from excitement, we may actually reach for more. An example familiar to most people is the young child who stays up for a special occasion and becomes overstimulated and refuses to go to bed although what he now needs most is quiet. If left to his own resources, such a child may drive himself to an even higher pitch of excitement until he 'goes to pieces'. Perhaps this tendency to drive ourselves to more and more exhausting levels of stimulation is one reason why meditation is beginning to be looked upon favorably by so many people in the modern world. We may sense that we are being caught in a trend which, unless we stop it, may continue until we drop in our tracks.

Human beings, interestingly, are the only animals that observe a seventeen hour period of continuous wakefulness. Lower animals periodically nap throughout the day. Awakening for an hour or so and then going back to sleep, they take 'cat-naps' throughout their active hours. Only humans force themselves to remain almost constantly awake, a feat for which we must be trained. Infants and young children who are not yet trained in this manner still require naps, while elderly people who can no longer conform as easily to this training tend to revert to this natural habit of napping during the day.

Because we humans do not generally punctuate our days with periodic sleep we may need other ways of limiting the quantity of input we are receiving. As suggested earlier, under natural conditions we all tend to lapse into a 'meditative mood' at certain times during the day. Perhaps these moods perform the same function for us as cat-naps do for animals. The research on ultradian rhythms which shows that reverie states occur in people at roughly one-and-a-half-hour intervals throughout the day, suggests that a tendency to retreat periodically from the stimuli which are pounding at us is still built into our nervous systems, even though we may refuse to allow ourselves to indulge in this to any degree. It seems that nature is not so ready to let us off the hook, however. We periodically take coffee breaks, eat, smoke cigarettes, or daydream even while we are at work. Perhaps we are not so different from the lower animals after all.

One of the most effective ways for us to re-establish a balance between too little and too great an amount of stimulation may be to meditate. If meditation restores us to a state of inner balance with respect to the adjustment of our stimulation level, its effects upon our health, both physical and mental, are highly beneficial.

Rediscovering Natural Rhythms

Although during meditation we withdraw from our awareness of external things, when we meditate we do not retreat into a mere absence of external stimulation, but into the *presence* of something else. When one level of stimulation is removed – that of the world which often acts on us in ways convenient to *it* rather than to *us* – we are released to sense more subtle forms of stimulation. In the quiet of the meditative state, we may become attuned to the voices of the body which are ordinarily obscured by waking activity.

Meditation seems to be the only natural state which is sufficiently still, and at the same time sufficiently *alert* so that when
we are in it we can clearly perceive our own inner rhythms.
People often report that during meditation they hear the beating
of their own hearts or sense their breathing as a compelling
occurrence, or sense other minute and delicate bodily processes
usually obscured by activity.

We might compare our insensitivity to bodily processes when
active to our inability in the daytime to perceive stars in the
sky. Although they are present twenty-four hours a day, we
cannot see them when the sun is up because its brilliant light
obscures them. When the sun sets, however, the far more subtle
lights of the celestial bodies are readily seen and it is as though
a host of stars had 'appeared' in the sky. So it is with meditation,
which removes us from the bright light of activity to the softer
light of inner awareness – away from one level of perception
toward an entirely different one. When we cease to perceive
ourselves in active interaction with the world, we are set free
to see ourselves in our rhythmic livingness.

It seems no coincidence, therefore, that established meditative
systems so often make use of components which reflect natural
bodily rhythms. Our positive response and sense of peacefulness with respect to the rhythms of heartbeat, breathing and
other bodily processes may go back as far as human memory
extends. Regularly repeated sounds or rhythmic movements are
widely recognized as soothing. Parents from all cultures and
eras have rocked agitated infants to quiet them, or have repeated
affectionate sounds in a lilting manner, or have bounced their
babies on their laps with an intuitive awareness of the soothing
effects that these rhythmic activities have on them.

Dr Reginald Lourie of the George Washington University
School of Medicine has studied the role of such rhythmic patterns in the development of children.[7] He reports that as they
grow, a certain number of healthy children supply their own
rhythmic patterns. At two to three months of age, a few of them
are rocking or moving their heads, the only part of their bodies
over which they have some control. At six to ten months of age,
even more are rocking their heads while others have now taken
up increasingly dramatic forms of rhythmic activities such as
banging their heads against the crib or getting up on hands and
knees to rock vigorously back and forth.

In some of these children, these rhythmic movements are transitory, lasting only until age two or three. But in others such movements remain much longer. Tracing these rhythmic activities through various stages of development, Dr Lourie has found that while at first rhythmic activities seem to be done predominantly for pleasure – a number of children will rock when they have had a particularly satisfying meal, or when they are praised, or are successful in accomplishing a simple task – by the end of the first year these rhythmic patterns seem to have changed in purpose. Now they have become a means of relieving *tension* and are used when the child is angry, frustrated, tired, bored or hungry. This tension-relieving aspect of rhythm continues throughout life and is useful for all of us, the basis, it seems, of many habits which serve to release tension.

Sooner or later, of course, these rhythmic activities meet with interference from adults who are annoyed or even alarmed by the disturbance they create, and pressure is put on children to stop them. No matter what ingenious devices are employed, however, they do not stop these activities. The children may seem to conform to the wishes of the adults around them but they do not actually give up the rhythmic patterns – they simply substitute others. Tooth-grinding, ear-pulling, finger-tapping, nose rubbing and other forms of repetitive activity now evolve and may continue for a long time. The reach toward the comforts that rhythm brings seems too deeply entrenched to be easily abandoned.

This profound effect of rhythm on human beings has been studied in the laboratory. To find out whether the sound of the human adult heartbeat, similar to the sound of the mother's heartbeat which the child has become accustomed to before birth, might have a particularly soothing effect on newborn infants, psychologist Lee Salk of the Rockefeller Institute in New York City studied a large group of newborns in a hospital nursery. He observed them from immediately following their birth until the time they were four days old.[8] All these infants were treated according to the ordinary routine of the nursery except for one thing – they were continuously played a tape-recording of a normal adult heartbeat sound (seventy-two beats per minute) over an intercom without interruption day and night, for the first four days of their lives.

Salk had originally intended to have another group of infants hear the heartbeat speeded up to an abnormally fast rate (128 beats per minute) but he quickly discontinued this part of the experiment. This speeded-up heartbeat turned out to be so upsetting to the infants that their crying increased dramatically and they showed other agitated behavior. The fast heartbeat sound had to be discontinued for the well-being of the children, another example of the disturbing effects of overstimulation. For the sake of comparison, therefore, Salk selected a group of newborns for whom no tapes at all were played during the first four days in the nursery. These infants were just treated according to regular hospital routine.

The results of the experiment were striking. Seventy percent of the infants who heard the heartbeat rhythm increased in body weight over the first four days, as against only 33 percent of the infants who did not hear the heartbeat rhythm – a highly significant difference. Crying was heard in the nursery only 38 percent of the time among those children who were listening to the heartbeat rhythm as against 60 percent of the time among those children who did not hear the heartbeat played. Since there was no difference at all between the two groups in the amount of food they consumed, why did the experimental group gain more weight? Salk suggested that since the more contented group had less exercise from crying, this might have accounted for their weight gain. He expressed the theory that the mother's heartbeat is one of the major sounds heard by the fetus before birth and that the unborn infant may have learned to associate these rhythmical heartbeat sounds with the relatively tension-free state in the womb. After birth, the mother's heartbeat (or other similar rhythms) may be soothing because of this early conditioning.

Perhaps nowhere do we get so profound a statement about the deep rhythms of the intrauterine state as in the writings of Dr Frederick Leboyer, the French obstetrician whose pioneer work in obstetrical methods has changed delivery room procedures in many parts of the world. Leboyer indicates that before birth the infant is in 'perpetual motion'. Even when his mother is asleep, there is always the great rhythm of her breathing, of her diaphragm, and of course there is the steady sound of her pulsebeat. Then, about a month before delivery, uterine contractions (far less intense than those of labor) begin, lasting a whole month – the ninth. Leboyer emphasizes the infinitely slow rhythm of these contractions and advises the hands holding the newborn infant to 'remember the slowness, the continuous movement of the uterine contraction, the "peristaltic wave" the child grew to know so well during the final month before its birth. . . .'[9]

Psychoanalyst Joost Meerloo has suggested that the unborn child's early experiences with heartbeat rhythms may be the basis for the profoundly soothing effects of poetry, music, and dance. Perhaps, he says, these rhythmic experiences are all grounded in 'various reminiscent feelings of a lost long ago and far away happiness'.[10]

Aside from the fact that we may have *learned* to connect natural rhythms with soothing experiences before birth, it is also possible that we may instinctively find those regular rhythms that approximate the normal rhythms of our own bodies to be deeply comforting because physiologically they signify that 'all is well', that nature is running smoothly. A study we conducted at Princeton set out to investigate this possibility by looking at the ways in which undergraduate college students responded to various types of syncopated (two-beat) rhythms sounded on a drum.[11] These drumbeats were first carefully regulated as to speed and then recorded on tape so that we were able to obtain five different speeds.

We wanted to find out what effects various rhythms might have on the mood of the listener – whether people responded differently to rhythms that were closer to the speed of the normal heartbeat than they did to those which were farther from it. Our results strongly supported the notion that adults are more comfortable with rhythms within the normal adult heartbeat range. The subjects rated rhythms in this range (the recorded speeds of sixty and seventy-two beats per minute) as making them feel 'relaxed', whereas they rated rhythms which were either much faster or much slower than the normal heartbeat as making them feel 'tense' and 'anxious'.

These soothing effects of bodily rhythms may help explain some of the deeply calming effects of meditation. Repetition of the mantra is a consistent rhythmic activity, as is one's own breathing. Even as the meditator is paying attention to his particular meditational focus, other rhythms such as heartbeat and respiration often come sharply into awareness during meditation. We may be more aware of these natural rhythms in meditation than at any other waking moment. In the previously mentioned questionnaire distributed to CSM and TM meditators, 74 percent of those who responded reported being more aware of bodily processes such as breathing and heartbeat during meditation than they were ordinarily, with 43 percent of the meditators saying they were *far more* aware of such processes during meditation than normally.

Even when attention is not consciously directed to our bodily rhythms, there seems to be a natural tendency to focus upon them. During regular mantra meditation, although the people we questioned had never been instructed to link their mantra with their breathing (in fact they had been told *not* to make any effort to do this), 76 percent of the meditators who filled out the questionnaire reported that their mantra spontaneously linked itself up with the rhythm of their breathing either sometimes or often, and 6 percent said it was always linked to their breathing.

Not surprisingly, a number of meditation techniques have made natural bodily rhythms their object of focus. As we have seen, Zazen meditation demands careful attention to one's breathing and the techniques of Hatha Yoga (the Yoga of physical exercises or 'postures') is based on a subtle coordination between the exercises and one's breathing – a coordination that we tend to lose sight of at most other times. When we synchronize action with breath, as is done in Yoga, our breathing becomes a regulating rhythm which gives a feeling of centeredness and calm.

The regularly repeated mantra, attention given to the natural rise and fall of the breath, or other repetitive meditational device, can create a deep sense of calm. An entry in my own meditation journal describes this:

> ... The waves of the mantra wash over me repeatedly. I feel them physically, slowly pulsing through me ... At various times the mantra is a soft spread of light; a cushion caressing my face; a cloud of mist rhythmically dispersing; the echoing toll of a distant bell; a faint sensation over and around my eyes; or just quiet beats. Sometimes I have no imagery. At such times it is as though the mantra was some deep biological presence existing amidst profound silence.

By giving attention to natural rhythms during meditation, or by creating rhythms to suit the need of the moment, we may be applying an ancient, intuitive knowledge of the calming effects of rhythms which are appropriate for adults as well as children. Meditation may be one of the most comforting rhythmical activities available to us after childhood ends, restoring through its lulling repetitions a natural balance between tension and repose.

The Lessons of Meditation

Because meditation gives us time off from our normal activities to discover depths within ourselves which are not usually accessible, in meditation we come to know, in a profound sense, who we *really* are, and this awareness may affect our lives outside of meditation in an important manner. As one meditator wrote:

> As I sit here quietly in my meditation, I am suddenly aware that I exist ... I am a being unto myself ... I am separate from lover, friend, mother, father, therapist, whomever ... but in my meditation I do not sense this aloneness as loneliness, I know it as closeness to myself and to life.

Meditation is a complete experience in and of itself. When in this state the outer world may threaten us, sights and sounds may pound at us for attention, but we recognize that none of this fundamentally changes who we are. Through it all, the quiet intake and outflow of breath goes on, the gentle rhythms of our pulse coordinate with the soundless beat of our mantra or with the motion of our breathing, and we know that whatever else may or may not happen, *life goes on*, and that this life extends beyond our individual life, it is fundamental, and – it is part of us.

This sense of sureness about our own existence tends to linger with us after meditation and it changes things. Matters which formerly distressed us often shrink to relative unimportance alongside this immediate experience of livingness. This new sense of self may lay the base for a new awareness of our inner resources and the rights of all human beings including ourselves – attitudes which, as we have seen, are often reported by meditators.

During meditation we also learn not to force our minds or bodies to do what we want them to do or what we believe they should do, but rather to follow gently where they lead. This experience of trusting the wisdom of our own inner selves makes meditation an unusual experience for most of us in today's world. Our society encourages us to manage ourselves as though we were objects, to *force* ourselves to do things (or not to do them). This attitude is the byproduct of a culture that measures work efficiency in terms of speed of production – the more we force, the greater the profits, or so the thinking goes. Many of our personal problems may, in fact, be the products of our excessively time-oriented culture. In an agricultural society people learn to have infinite patience with the slow and compelling rhythms of nature and so may develop a somewhat different attitude – a greater appreciation for the value of waiting and watching, of flowing with the stream of life rather than fighting it. Meditation may lead us to such a receptive attitude as well, for we cannot meditate if we *try* to meditate, only if we *permit* meditation to occur.

The Lesson of Self-Acceptance

Self-blame may be reduced through another of meditation's lessons. Children are often effectively shamed by the looks and gestures coming from others around them even before they can understand language. They are also scolded through *words*. In this way a child's upbringing can create mental messages such as 'I am a bad child'; 'I am sloppy'; 'dirty'; 'dumb'; 'selfish'; or whatever other disapproving terms they have learned to direct at themselves. Unfortunately these negative messages continue to repeat themselves long after parents, teachers and friends have ceased to criticize them in this manner. The phrase 'a still small voice' to describe the conscience was therefore well chosen; our conscience is in many respects a 'voice'. If we tune down the language centers of the brain during meditation and allow the wordless aspects of experience to come into the forefront of our consciousness, we tend to take the sting out of much of our self-blame.

In meditation, self-criticism seems to recede along with other abstract concepts which rely on words, until it remains only a distant whisper. Simultaneously there seems to be a desensitization during meditation of the *wordless* experiences of shame from very early childhood. This two-pronged attack on self-blame ... the reduction of our self-criticizing statements to ourselves about ourselves, and the removal of the negative charge on early wordless shame experiences – is a powerful one. As a result, when meditating, we are often able to experience even the least desirable aspects of ourselves without anxiety. We readmit them to awareness, make friends with them, as it were, and in this way can begin at last to come to terms with these parts of ourselves which had long ago become buried by a sea of negative and painful emotions.

These and other aspects of meditation constitute a profound self-education. Repeated daily over a period of time, these lessons form a conglomerate of experiences and attitudes which can affect our outlook on daily life in fundamental ways. One of the most profound lessons of meditation comes from temporarily experiencing the totality of ourselves, a totality which is unknowable through the limited concepts of our rational mind alone. In this sense, meditation opens up fresh vistas, unexplored territories. Where this new 'meditative' awareness is likely to lead us, as a society, is the final question we will consider.

Chapter 20

THE PROMISE OF
THE FUTURE

No technique works for everyone, people are far too individual in their responses. But meditation has some striking advantages that make it a preferred method for relieving stress and coping with an increasingly demanding world. The practical forms of meditation are so easy to teach that almost anyone can learn them in just a few properly conducted instruction sessions. Even more important, meditation constitutes *its own reward*. People look forward to meditating and because of this they are more likely to remain meditating over a period of time, while many of the other methods for relieving stress, although valuable in the short term, can become tedious and be soon discarded.[1] These advantages make meditation probably the most effective of all known relaxation techniques for assisting large groups of people to increase their mental and physical health. This is a high qualification for usefulness in our society.

For those who are accustomed to link advances in the human condition with technological innovation in areas such as medicine or electronics, the promise of meditation may be difficult to understand. Can the carefully studied and controlled use of a natural practice be more efficient in bringing about effective results than manufactured devices such as pharmaceuticals or biofeedback machines?

As we progress in scientific knowledge, we find that answers crucial to our survival are often found by working closely with the processes of nature and respecting their wisdom. In the long run this is a far more productive approach than trying to control the natural world. Meditation fits into a general trend which seeks to work in harmony with the natural processes. It is simple. It relies on no gadgetry. It is available to all. In tune with our present-day outlook it is therefore likely to play an increasingly important role in contemporary life.

In Medicine

In the future, the meditative techniques may be used extensively, along with conventional medical treatments, for relieving many stress-related illnesses. I was recently asked by a major teaching hospital in the United States to form an advisory committee with a distinguished colleague of mine, Dr Paul Lehrer, who is prominent in the field of behavioral medicine. Our task was to suggest criteria to be used by that hospital's new Department of Alternative Medicine for selecting teachers of meditation to whom the department could refer patients. What is enlightening about the hospital's request is that such an action on the part of a major medical center would not have occurred even two years ago. The climate is rapidly changing and I believe we can look forward to an increasing acceptance of the value of meditation by the medical world.

What is more, this growing acceptance is by no means confined to any particular country. Richard Berg, a BAC accredited counselor, reports similar developments in England. Richard is particularly involved in helping people to manage stress, and when he first held his stress management clinics he was often asked to advise on ways to learn meditation. Group participants were looking for a simple and affordable method of instruction, and expressed concern about the risk of falling in with a practice or organization with a 'hidden agenda'. As a long-term meditator, he was immediately responsive to their requests and made enquiries which led him to the head of the local psychology service who had been recommending CSM to his own patients. CSM seemed a very satisfactory answer for people seeking a medically approved, easily learned meditation method. Since that time, Richard and his wife Jacquie (also a meditator) have been distributing the CSM recorded course throughout the United Kingdom and to various parts of the world. They find that many of those who send for the course heard about it through medical sources.

CSM is presently being recommended in the United Kingdom for sufferers of the chronic fatigue syndromes, and there is increasing use of this method along with medical treatment for illnesses which have a stress-related factor, including cancer. Richard spent over twenty years in practice as a chartered accountant before training to become a counselor and firmly believes the use of meditation can be an important factor in resolving the problem of spiraling medical costs worldwide. He points out that there is now ample research evidence which shows that people who meditate will remain more healthy and so will be less of a burden on the community's medical resources.

The use of meditation with pre-surgical patients has been shown to be valuable,[2] and an additional use of meditation might be as an analgesic or pain-reducer. The technique of meditating upon one's pain in order to reduce it can be very effective. Related to the area of pain control is the use of meditation in *thanatology*, that branch of the behavioral sciences which deals with helping the dying person come to terms with his experience in a more peaceful and meaningful manner.

At the Maryland Psychiatric Research Center, a group of psychiatrists headed by Dr Stanislov Grof achieved remarkable results with terminal cancer patients using meditative states assisted by the administration of LSD under carefully standardized conditions.[2] After taking this medication, the patients were gently guided to the depth of consciousness which they personally could best tolerate. The resulting transformation in their view of themselves often brought about a difference in their entire medical and psychological condition. Although this did not necessarily prolong their lives, it did radically change the quality of their final days and months. In a controlled study with these procedures, the researchers found a marked lessening of depression, anxiety and pain in most of the patients who had received this treatment. These people also tended to be less afraid of dying, to feel less isolated, and to be more accepting of the care offered by hospital staff. While it might be argued that these results were due to the use of a chemical agent (LSD) and had nothing to do with the induction of the meditative mood, this seems extremely unlikely. LSD is known to be dependent for its effects upon the setting in which it is taken. A sensitive guided experience by expert therapists was an essential part of the Maryland study. The therapists actively helped the patients to achieve states of consciousness which were strikingly similar to some of the more profound meditative states.

It is also possible that meditation will be found to speed up the healing process. This idea is supported by a number of informal clinical reports as well as by research such as that at the University of Pennsylvania Hospital which suggests that gum infections may heal more rapidly in patients practicing meditation.[3] More research is likely to appear in this area in the future, and regular use of meditation in rehabilitation programs could become the norm.

Doctors may also prescribe the use of practical forms of meditation on a continuing basis for some categories of patient. For example, a hypertensive (or Type A Behavior*) person who is advised by her physician to 'slow down', 'enjoy' herself more or to 'stop worrying' is being asked to change her whole way of life. The injunction to change some deeply entrenched habits could even challenge her conception of what life is all about, and such a perceived threat to the patient's understanding of her world might even cause her to cling more steadfastly to her problematic life-style. Although meditation can often bypass this emotional inclination to 'stick with the devil you know', habits are powerful, and variations of meditation may be needed to support the person threatened by such change. For example, learning to meditate while walking, jogging, swimming, bicycling, or during any other form of repetitive exercise, or through the use of mini-meditations sprinkled throughout the day, may be best for an extremely active individual.

Although such changes in routine may not at first glance appear to fit in with the demands of a technological society which measures performance in terms of speed of output and volume of goods produced, rather than in terms of human resources conserved, they can be extremely valuable to the casualties of our society – those people who suffer physical and emotional damage because they are overcome by our rapid pace of life and cannot 'get off the merry-go-round'. Special techniques designed to provide these people with the regenerative qualities of the meditative mood have much to offer. The benefits of meditation will be life-enhancing to the individuals concerned and can clearly benefit society as a whole.

---

* Type A Behavior is a form of compulsive behavior characterized by more or less continuous self-driving activity. It has been shown to be prevalent in heart attack-prone individuals.[4]

In Psychotherapy

In the future meditation may be employed more widely by mental health practitioners as part of their treatment programs for the relief of anxiety, and for all types of stress-related disorders. It may also be used as an adjunct to psychotherapy in the treatment of addictions and the milder forms of depression.

Besides these more specific applications, the current use of meditation in psychotherapy as a general 'facilitator' of adjustment is likely to receive wider acceptance. Meditation can help to ameliorate troublesome emotions and behaviors such as irritability, low frustration tolerance and uncontrollable tempers. Conversely, patients who have tended to suppress their feelings to an unhealthy extent may be helped to be more emotionally 'alive' as a result of meditation. The balancing, normalizing effects of meditation will also be helpful to patients who suffer from a poor sense of identity and find it difficult to assert themselves.

Psychotherapists will probably want to supervise their own patients' meditation practices, and may be able to assign an appropriate mantra for each patient's condition based on future research on the effects of sound on personality. Some psychotherapists may meditate with their patients on occasions when this seems indicated for therapy; and in group therapy, meditating together may be found useful for increasing rapport between participating group members.

In Education

Use of meditation in the school systems is likely to encounter resistance from those who confuse it with prayer. Prayer in public (state-funded) schools is banned in America by the constitutional guarantee of separation of Church and State. To get around this, an occasional religious organization in the United States has attempted to introduce prayer into public schools by disguising it as 'meditation', thereby confusing the issue in the minds of both teachers and the public. When educators finally come to realize, however, that strictly secular forms of meditation are available which can be taught by regular school personnel at minimal cost and with no inconvenience to the school system, their negative attitudes toward meditation may begin to change. Only at that point are American school systems likely to become receptive to meditation. The place of prayer in schools differs from country to country, however. In the United Kingdom, for example, communal prayer is first in the daily routine in most schools. The delayed acceptance of meditation by schools in the United States may therefore not become a problem elsewhere.

There are many benefits potentially available to those schools which *will* make use of meditation. Meditating before commencing the day's work could become an effective means of enhancing the creative flow of ideas and diminishing excessive self-criticism on the part of students. Used intermittently to break up long hours of concentration, mini-meditations may be adopted as a way of 'recharging the battery' – a replacement for the daydreaming which pupils naturally fall into to refresh their flagging concentration (often to the exasperation of their teachers). People who meditate together also report a greater sense of harmony with those around them, an effect which is likely to increase the energy and enthusiasm of students and their teachers.

In Business and Industry

As to the future of meditation in the workplace, it seems likely that corporations will take to using meditation only when they are convinced that it will increase productivity and enhance profits. Whether workers on a production line will actually *produce* more if they meditate is uncertain, but relaxed people usually handle jobs more easily, efficiently and accurately than tense ones, which should make meditation a decided asset for business and industry. The health of meditating workers will also tend to be better (fewer stress-related illnesses), which is likely to lead to a reduction in absenteeism. Certain forms of addiction can be helped by meditation as well – a fact which should appeal to the corporate world where this can present a serious problem. Meditation 'breaks' during the day may also improve job satisfaction and make for greater alertness and fewer mistakes, thus cutting down on work accidents. Because of its potential benefits in these areas, meditation is likely to be adopted by companies with the foresight to see that such improvements in the quality of the work, health and job satisfaction of employees could turn out to be extremely profit-able in the long run.

On the executive level, since it fosters initiative, imagination and independence, traits which are highly desirable in manage-ment, meditation could prove particularly valuable. Since executives are also prone to be 'Type A Behavior' people, execu-tive mini-meditation programs are not difficult to envision becoming a company policy. In the same way, the use of group meditation before brainstorming sessions could create a greater flow of ideas; meditation before board meetings lead to more harmonious teamwork among participants; and periodic medi-tation breaks during day-long conferences can be extremely relieving to people forced to concentrate for many hours on the presentation of detailed information.

Meditation in the Future

Used widely, meditation may bring about some interesting inno-vations in our lives, the most prominent of which may be the meditation break and the meditation room.

If meditation is embraced by large organizations, a meditation room will be a necessity. Since this need only be a simple place, partially soundproofed and with a few comfortable straight-backed chairs, low lighting, a carpet and perhaps a green plant or two, the modest cost of establishing such a room could be a good investment in terms of the relief it would bring to people who needed it during a high-pressure working day. When we set up such a meditation room in the psychology building at Princeton, students expressed a strong sense of loss when it had to be dismantled at the end of the semester.

Religious institutions have traditionally supplied sanctuaries in places of worship where people could be alone and turn inward. The tranquility of a religious sanctuary strongly encour-ages prayer and contemplation, and it strongly evokes the meditative mood. The decline of participation in organized religion in recent years, coupled with the frequent need today for churches and temples to remain closed to the public when services are not in progress, for fear of vandalism, make this manner of evoking the meditative mood relatively inaccessible for many people today – an additional reason why modern men and women may be in need of a new socially sanctioned retreat – a meditation break or a meditation room respected by others.

Not only may institutions find it to their advantage to schedule meditation breaks in a systematic manner, but this practice may become accepted for social gatherings as well. My meditating friends and I have found that when we have guests who are meditators, they are usually delighted with the suggestion that we all meditate together before dinner. After we have done so, we feel closer to one another, and the usual social role-playing is gratefully set aside. Similarly, those of us who serve on the Board of Directors of the Holistic Health Association of the Princeton Area will often meditate together before our board meetings. This creates an atmosphere of exceptional ease and comfort and an enhanced sense of unity with regard to our common purpose.

It seems likely that in today's world meditation will continue to be used primarily as an emergency measure for some time to come – put to work to patch up imbalances, counteract some of society's excesses, and perhaps make the 'system' work better. Companies may use it so that workers will complain less; the military so that soldiers can tolerate battle stress better; and, if they consent to use it at all, schools may at first adopt meditation in order to ensure that children are less trouble to their teachers. But will meditation remain only a palliative? While some of the larger institutions may initially view it as strictly functional, it is doubtful if meditation will become simply a means of oiling the machinery of production. Meditation, even in its practical forms, has an impact on values, and changes brought about by its wide-scale use could conceivably alter some of our basic values as a society.

Toward a New Perspective

If large groups of people begin to practice meditation, we may see a number of unexpected shifts occur. One of these may be a new way of viewing our pace of life. Meditation widely practiced could lead to a collective easing of life-pace and a new attitude toward time in a society that faces continuous time-related stress. Not only would meditation be an anti-stress measure, but it could be of considerable help to people who have unwittingly been brought up to be compulsive 'work-horses'. Today many people on the work treadmill find themselves at a loss when they have to slow their hectic pace even momentarily to spend time with themselves. They may plunge into escapist activities to obliterate the necessity of doing so. Meditation can make a major contribution toward a more effective use of time because it teaches us to spend a greater portion of it simply 'living' and less in compulsive accomplishing. Widely practiced, meditation may result in a gradual lessening of our present day over emphasis on *extrinsic* rewards (those rewards derived from advantages outside of the experience itself, such as money, power or prestige) and an increased emphasis on *intrinsic* rewards (the rewarding aspects of experience valued for *its own sake*).

A society influenced by the perspective which meditation offers will also be likely to develop a respect for the human body different from that which has prevailed in the past century. One of the fundamental lessons of meditation is that we exist as *living beings*. This realization may lead to renewed interest in that which is healthy and an aversion to that which is unhealthy, for ourselves and our environment. A society with a meditative outlook may avoid foodstuffs, environments or activities which run counter to natural rhythms, just as individual meditators now tend to shy away from the abuse of addictive substances. If this happens, a new kind of ecological awareness may flow from a deep inner sense of our own interrelatedness with all that surrounds us – our fellow human beings, animals, plants and the resources of this earth.

If society absorbs the lessons of meditation we may be less likely to view science as a tool in an inevitable battle between humans and natural forces, less eager to define scientific achievement as the winning of yet another round in our fight to subdue the earth and make her bend to our wishes. Instead, we may begin to heed the gentle voices of order and balance that come to us from the natural world. This should result in our supporting a science and technology that work hand in hand with nature.

The widespread use of meditation will undoubtedly bring about a greater sensitivity to spiritual values. We will come to accept some intangible aspects of life more readily. This change will stem from the meditative experience itself, an experience that reflects the flow of life with all its inevitability and unknowable essence. Because of their contact with that which is natural and essential, a population of meditators might come to feel, at last, a unity with the universe. This in turn could conceivably help change our basic way of viewing our own role in the destiny of this planet.

I believe that the most telling aspect of studies such as the one at the New York Telephone Company, where large numbers of meditators reported their reactions, is the overwhelming evidence they present that human beings *want to be good people*. The participants' gratitude at the positive changes that meditation brought about in them shows that people long to love their families and friends and to work with others in harmony, respect and helpfulness. It is only when they are not able to do this that they become aggressive, bitter, impatient and destructive.

Meditation is, in a sense, a grace that releases people from negative behaviors such as these. The responses that we as researchers have received from thousands of people who meditate show that when they have had an opportunity to tune into their true selves through meditation, an overwhelming majority of these people have become more patient, compassionate, and cooperative human beings.

Meditation – this simple, gentle method – has a profound gift for humanity. If we recognize this gift and use it wisely the result could be a new flowering of the human spirit.

NOTES

CHAPTER 1 The Start of the Journey

1 A. Watts, 'The Art of Meditation', in *What Is Meditation?* ed. John White (Garden City: Anchor Press/Doubleday, 1974), p. 34.
2 TM instructors, as quoted in P. D. Hemingway, *The Transcendental Meditation Primer* (New York: McKay, 1975).
3 J. H. Schultz and W. Luthe, *Autogenic Therapy*, 6 vols (New York: Grune, 1969), vol. I, p. 7.
4 TM instructors, as quoted in Hemingway, op. cit., pp. 17 and 29.
5 H. Johari, *Dhanwantari* (San Francisco: Ram's Head, 1974), p. 76.
6 M. Sadhu, *Meditation* (London: George Allen, 1967) p. 72.
7 TM instructors, giving International Meditation Society standard lectures on Transcendental Meditation, Edison, N. J., 15 January 1973.
8 H. H. Bloomfield, M. Cain, D. T. Jaffe and A. Rubottom, 'What is Transcendental Meditation?' in White (ed.) op. cit., p. 88.
9 S. N. C. Yati, 'Entering the World of Meditation,' in ibid., p. 42.
10 B. R. Dass, *The Only Dance There Is* (Garden City: Anchor Press/ Doubleday, 1974), p. 50.
11 TM instructors, as quoted in Hemingway, op. cit., p. 17.

CHAPTER 2 The Ageless Practice

1 A. J. Maslow, *Toward a Psychology of Being*, (rev. edn, 1968) (Princeton, N.J.: Van Nostrand, 1962).
2 J. Leserman, E. M. Stuart, M. E. Mamish and H. Benson, 'The Efficacy of the Relaxation Response in Preparing for Cardiac Surgery', *Behavioral Medicine*, 15 (1989), pp. 111–17.
3 Meditation journal of George Edington (personal communication).
4 E. Conze, *Buddhist Meditation* (New York: Harper, 1969), p. 83.
5 B. S. Rajneesh, *Dynamics of Meditation* (Bombay: A Life Awakening Movement Publication, 1972), p. 130.

6 M. Mahesh Yogi, *Transcendental Meditation* (New York: New Am. Lib. (Signet), 1963).

7 R. K. Wallace and H. Benson, 'The Physiology of Meditation', *Scientific American* (February 1972), pp. 84–90; R. K. Wallace, H. Benson and A. F. Wilson, 'A Wakeful Hypometabolic Physiologic State,' *American Journal of Physiology*, 221 (1971), pp. 795–9; R. K. Wallace, H. Benson, A. F. Wilson and M. D. Garret, 'Decreased Blood Lactate During Transcendental Meditation,' *Federation Proceedings*, 30 (1971), p. 376.

8 H. Benson, *The Relaxation Response* (New York: Morrow, 1975.

9 Ibid., p. 114.

10 J. Kabat-Zinn, 'An Out-Patient Program in Behavioral Medicine for Chronic Pain Patients Based on the Practice of Mindfulness Meditation: Theoretical Considerations and Preliminary Results', *General Hospital Psychiatry*, 4 (1982), pp. 33–47.

11 J. Kabat-Zinn, A. O. Massion, J. Kristeller et al., 'Effectiveness of a Meditation-Based Stress Reduction Program in the Treatment of Anxiety Disorders', *American Journal of Psychiatry*, 149 (1992), pp. 936–43.

12 J. Kabat-Zinn, *Wherever You Go, There You Are* (New York: Hyperion Books, 1994).

CHAPTER 3 Is Meditation Unique?

1 E. W. Maupin, 'Meditation', in *Ways of Growth*, ed. H. A. Otto and J. Mann (New York: Viking, 1968), pp. 189–98.

2 R. E. Shor, 'Hypnosis and the Concept of the Generalized Reality Orientation', in *Altered States of Consciousness*, ed. C. T. Tart (New York: Wiley, 1969), pp. 233–50.

3 Ibid., p. 241.

4 R. White, 'A Preface to a Theory of Hypnotism', *Journal of Abnormal and Social Psychology*, 36 (1941), pp. 477–506.

5 N. Kleitman, *Sleep and Wakefulness* (Chicago: University of Chicago Press, 1963), pp. 329–38.

6 L. Cheitok and P. Kramarz, 'Hypnosis, Sleep and Electroencephalography', *Journal of Nervous and Mental Disease*, 128 (1959), pp. 227–38; A. L. Loomis, E. N. Harvey and C. A. Hobart, 'Electrical Potentials of the Human Brain', *Journal of Experimental Physiology*, 19 (1936), pp. 249–79; J. B. Dynes, 'Objective Method for Distinguishing Sleep from the Hypnotic Trance', *Archives of Neurology and Psychiatry*, 57 (1947), pp. 84–93; A. Kasamatsu and T. Hirai, 'An Electroencephalographic Study on the Zen Meditation (Zazen)', in Tart (ed.), op. cit., pp. 489–501.

7 Kasamatsu and Hirai, op. cit.

8 A. Maslow, as quoted in Shor, op. cit., p. 249.

9 J. H. Schultz and W. Luthe, *Autogenic Therapy*, 6 vols (New York: Grune, 1969).

10 J. Breuer and S. Freud (1893), 'Studies of Hysteria', in *Standard Edition of the Complete Psychological Works of Sigmund Freud*, ed J. Strachey, vol. 11 (London: Hogarth, 1955).

11 S. Freud (1895), 'The Psychotherapy of Hysteria' in ibid., pp. 255–305.

12 E. Jacobson, *You Must Relax* (New York: McGraw, 1934).

13 E. Jacobson, *Progressive Relaxation* (Chicago: University of Chicago Press, 1938); *Modern Treatment of Tense Patients* (Springfield, Ill.: C. C. Thomas, 1970); *Biology of Emotions* (Springfield, IU.: C. C. Thomas, 1967); *Tension in Medicine* (Springfield, Ill.: C. C. Thomas, 1967).

14 J. Wolpe, *Psychotherapy by Reciprocal Inhibition* (Stanford: Stanford University Press, 1958).

15 D. A. Bernstein and T. D. Borkovec, excerpt from *Progressive Relaxation Training Record* (Champaign, Ill.: Research Press, 1973).

16 B. B. Brown, *New Mind, New Body* (New York: Harper, 1974).

17 E. E. Green, A. M. Green and E. D. Walters, 'Voluntary Control of Internal States', *Journal of Transpersonal Psychology*, 2 (1970), pp. 1–25.

18 Kasamatsu and Hirai op. cit.

19 G. Schwartz, 'Biofeedback, Self-Regulation and the Patterning of Physiological Processes', *American Scientist*, 63 (1975), pp. 314–24.

CHAPTER 4 The Scientist Takes Note

1 E. Green and A. Green, 'The Ins and Outs of Mind-Body Energy', *Science Year* (1974), Field Enterprises, Chicago, Ill.

2 For a description of 1970s' experimentation with psychedelic drugs see R. Ashley, 'The Other Side of LSD', *New York Times Magazine*, 19 October, 1975.

3 P. K. Bagchi and M. A. Wenger, 'Simultaneous EEG and Other Recordings During Some Yogic Practices', *Journal of Electroencephalography and Clinical Neurophysiology*, 10 (1958), p. 193.

4 B. K. Anand, G. S. Chhina and B. Singh, 'Studies on Sri Ramanand Yogi During His Stay in an Air-Tight Box', *Indian Journal of Medical Research*, 49 (1961), pp. 82–9.

5 K. P. K. Bagchi and M. A. Wenger, 'Electrophysiological Correlates of Some Yogi Exercises', *Journal of Electroencephalography and Clinical Neurophysiology*, 7 (1957), pp. 132–49.

6 B. K. Anand, G. S. Chhina and B. Singh, 'Some Aspects of Electroen-

cephalographic Studies of Yogis', *Journal of Electroencephalography and Clinical Neurophysiology*, 13 (1961), pp. 452–6.

7 A. Kasamatsu and T. Hirai, 'An Electroencephalographic Study on the Zen Meditation (Zazen)', in *Altered States of Consciousness*, ed. C. T. Tart (New York: Wiley, 1969), pp. 489–501.

8 R. K. Wallace, 'Physiological Effects of Transcendental Meditation', *Science* (27 March, 1970), pp. 1751–4; R. K. Wallace, H. Benson and A. F. Wilson, 'A Wakeful Hypometabolic Physiologic State', *American Journal of Physiology*, 221 (1971), pp. 795–9.

9 P. C. Fenwick, 'Metabolic and EEG Changes during Transcendental Meditation' (paper read at conference on 'TM: Research and Application', Institute of Science and Technology, University of Wales, Cardiff, 1974).

10 Wallace, op. cit.

11 J. Allison, 'Respiratory Changes During the Practice of the Technique of Transcendental Meditation', *Lancet* (18 April, 1970), pp. 833–4.

12 Ibid.

13 N. N. Das and H. Gastaut, 'Variations de l'Activité Electrique du Cerveau, du Coeur, et des Muscles Séquellétiques au Cours de la Méditation et de l'Extase Yogiqiue', *Journal of Electroencephalography and Clinical Neurophysiology*, Supp. 6 (1957), pp. 211–19; Wallace, op. cit.; Wallace et al., op. cit.; J. P. Banquet, 'EEG and Meditation', *Journal of Electroencephalography and Clinical Neurophysiology*, 33 (1972) pp. 449–58.

14 Banquet, op. cit.

15 L. S. Otis, 'TM and Sleep' (paper presented before the Annual Meeting of the American Psychological Association, New Orleans, 1974); J. Younger, W. Adriane and R. Berger, 'Sleep during Transcendental Meditation', *Perceptual and Motor Skills*, 40 (1975), pp. 953–4; R. R. Pagano, et al., 'Sleep During Transcendental Meditation', *Science* (23 January, 1976), pp. 308–10.

16 Otis, op. cit.

17 Banquet, op. cit.

18 B. C. Glueck and C. F. Stroebel, 'Biofeedback and Meditation in the Treatment of Psychiatric Illness', *Comprehensive Psychiatry*, 16 (1975), pp. 303–21.

19 L. Goldstein, personal communication to the author, March 1976, New Jersey College of Medicine and Dentistry, Piscataway, N.J.

20 Wallace, op. cit.

21 G. E. Schwartz, 'Pros and Cons of Meditation: Current Findings on Physiology and Anxiety, Self-Control, Drug Abuse and Creativity' (paper delivered before the 81st Annual Convention of the

American Psychological Association, Montreal, 1973); Glueck and Stroebel, op. cit.

22 D. Orme-Johnson, 'Autonomic Stability and Transcendental Meditation', *Psychosomatic Medicine*, 35 (1973), pp. 341–9.

23 Ibid.

24 D. J. Goleman and G. E. Schwartz, 'Meditation as an Intervention in Stress Reactivity', *Journal of Consulting and Clinical Psychology*, 44 (1976), pp. 456–66.

25 Wallace et al., op. cit.

26 M. Jones and V. Mellersh, 'Comparison of Exercise Response in Anxiety States and Normal Controls', *Psychosomatic Medicine*, 8 (1946), pp. 180–87; F. Pitts, 'The Biochemistry of Anxiety', *Scientific American* (February 1969), pp. 69–75.

27 H. Ritterstaedt and H. Schenkluhn, 'Measuring Changes of the Skin Temperature During the Practice of Transcendental Meditation' (unpublished paper, Max Planck Institute, Germany, 1972); R. R. Wallace and H. Benson, 'The Physiology of Meditation', *Scientific American* (February 1972), pp. 84–90.

28 H. Benson, B. R. Marzetta and B. A. Rosner, 'Decreased Systolic Blood Pressure in Hypertensive Subjects Who Practiced Meditation', *Journal of Clinical Investigation*, 52 (1973), p. 8a.

29 H. Benson, *The Relaxation Response* (New York: Morrow, 1975).

30 K. S. Blasdell, 'The Effects of Transcendental Meditation Technique upon a Complex Perceptual-Motor Task', in *Scientific Research on the Transcendental Meditation Program: Collected Papers*, ed. D. W. Orme-Johnson and J. T. Farrow (Livingston Manor, NY: Maharishi European Research University Press, 1978, pp. 322–5. A. G. P. Rimol, 'The Transcendental Meditation Technique and its Effects on Sensory and Motor Perception' (Livingston Manor, NY: Maharishi European Research University Press, 1978), pp. 326–30.

31 M. Pirot, 'The Effects of the Transcendental Meditation Technique Upon Auditory Discrimination', in Orme-Johnson and Farrow, (ed.), op. cit., pp. 331–4.

32 F. M. Brown, W. S. Stewart and J. I. Blodgett, 'EEG Kappa Rhythms During Transcendental Meditation and Possible Perceptual Threshold Changes Following' (paper delivered to the Kentucky Academy of Sciences, 13 November, 1971).

33 E. Braütigam, 'The Effect of Transcendental Meditation on Drug Abusers' Research report, City Hospital at Malmö, Sweden, December 1971); S. Nidich, W. Seeman and T. Dreskin, 'Influence of Transcendental Meditation: A Replication', *Journal of Counseling Psychology*, 20 (1973), pp. 565–6; P. D. Ferguson and J. Gowan, 'Psychological Findings on Transcendental Meditation', in Farrow, (ed.), op. cit., pp. 484–8; L. A. Hjelle, 'Transcendental Meditation

and Psychological Health', *Perceptual and Motor Skills*, 39 (1974) pp. 623–8; S. Shackman, 'Effect of Two Relaxation Techniques on Anxiety, Self-Concept and Personality Growth' (senior thesis, Princeton University, 1974); D. Ballou, 'The Transcendental Meditation Program at Stillwater Prison', in Orme-Johnson and Farrow (ed.), op. cit., vol. I, pp. 569–76.

34 Shackman, op. cit.; Glueck and Stroebel, op. cit.

35 A. I. Abrams, 'Paired-Associate Learning and Recall: A Pilot Study of the Transcendental Meditation Program', in Orme-Johnson and Farrow (ed.), op. cit., vol. I, pp. 337–81.

36 D. E. Miskiman, 'The Effect of Transcendental Meditation on the Organization of Thinking and Recall (Secondary Organization)', in ibid., pp. 385–92.

37 M. J. MacCullum, 'Transcendental Meditation and Creativity', in ibid., pp. 410–14.

38 R. W., Collier, 'The Effect of Transcendental Meditation upon University Academic Attainment', in ibid., pp. 393–5.

39 D. R. Frew, 'Transcendental Meditation and Productivity', *Academy of Management Journal*, 17, no. 2. (1974), pp. 362–8.

40 Hjelle, op. cit.

41 W. Seeman, S. Nidich and T. Banta, 'Influence of Transcendental Meditation on a Measure of Self-Actualization', *Journal of Counseling Psychology* (1972), pp. 184–7; Ferguson and Gowan, op. cit.

42 Ballou, op. cit.; M. Cunningham and W. Koch, 'The Transcendental Meditation Program and Rehabilitation: A Pilot Project at the Federal Correctional Institute at Lompoc, California', in Orme-Johnson and Farrow, (ed.), op. cit., vol. 1, pp. 562–8.

43 M. Shafii, R. Lavely and R. Jaffe, 'Meditation and the Prevention of Drug Abuse', *American Journal of Psychiatry*, 132 (1975), pp. 942–5; T. J. Murphy, R. R. Pagano and G. A. Marlatti, 'Life-style modification with Heavy Alcohol Drinkers: Effects of Aerobic Exercise and Meditation', *Addictive Behaviors*, 11 (2) (1986), pp. 175–86.

44 A. P. Shapiro, 'Behavioral Methods in the Treatment of Hypertension', *Annals of Internal Medicine*, 86 (1977), pp. 626–36.; H. Benson, 'Systemic Hypertension and the Relaxation Response', *New England Journal of Medicine*, 296 (1977), pp. 1152–6.; R. H. Schneider, F. Staggers, C. N. Alexander et al., 'A Randomized Controlled Trial of Stress Reduction for Hypertension in Older African Americans', *Hypertension*, 26 (5) (1995), pp. 820–27.

45 H. Benson, S. Alexander and C. L. Feldman, 'Decreased Premature Ventricular Contractions Through the Use of the Relaxation Response in Patients with Stable Ischaemic Heart Disease', *Lancet*, 2 (1975), p. 380.

46 J. W. Zamarra, R. H. Schneider, I. Sesseghini et al., 'Usefulness of

the Transcendental Meditation Program in the Treatment of Patients with Coronary Artery Disease', *American Journal of Cardiology*, 77 (10) (1996), pp. 867–70.

47 J. W. Zamarra, I. Besseghini and S. Wittenberg, 'The Effects of the Transcendental Meditation Program on the Exercise Performance of Patients with Angina Pectoris', in Orme-Johnson and Farrow, (ed.), op. cit., vol. 1, pp. 331–4.

48 C. Heriberto, 'The Effects of Clinically Standardized Meditation (CSM) on Type 11 Diabetes', (unpublished doctoral dissertation), Adelphi University, Institute of Advanced Studies, 1988.

49 M. J. Cooper and M. M. Aygen, 'A Relaxation Technique in the Management of Hypercholesterolemia', *Journal of Human Stress*, 5 (1979), pp. 24–7.

50 K. K. Deepak, S. K. Manchananda and M. C. Maheshwari, 'Meditation Improves Clinicoelectroencephalographic Measures in Drug-Resistant Epileptics', *Biofeedback and Self-Regulation*, 19 (1) (1994), pp. 25–40.

51 V. Kumaraiah, H. Mishra et al., 'Therapeutic Effects of Vipassana Meditation in Tension Headache', *Journal of Personality and Clinical Studies*, 6 (2) (1990), pp. 201–6; A. Vasudevan, V. Kumaraiah, H. Mishra et al., 'Yogic Meditation in Tension Headache', *NIMANS Journal*, 12 (1) (1994), pp. 69–73.

52 I. Gaston, 'Efficacy of Imagery and Meditation Techniques in Treating Psoriasis', *Imagination, Cognition and Personality*, 8 (1) (1988), pp. 25–38.

53 K. H. Kaplan, D. I. Goldenberg and M. Galvin-Nadeau, 'The Impact of a Meditation-Based Stress Reduction Program in Fibromyalgia', *General Hospital Psychiatry*, 15 (5) (1993), pp. 284–9.

54 R. Honsberger and A. F. Wilson, 'Transcendental Meditation in Treating Asthma', *Respiratory Therapy – The Journal of Inhalation Technology*, 3 (1973), pp. 48–81.

55 R. L. Woolfolk, K. Carr-Kaffashan, P. M. Lehrer et al., 'Meditation Training as a Treatment for Insomnia', *Behavior Therapy*, 7 (1976), pp. 359–65.

56 N. Muskatel, R. L. Woolfolk, P. Carrington et al., 'Effect of CSM Meditation Training on Aspects of Coronary-Prone Behavior', *Perceptual and Motor Skills*, 58 (1984), 515–18.

57 Glueck and Stroebel, op. cit.; P. Carrington and H. S. Ephron, 'Meditation as an Adjunct to Psychotherapy', in *New Dimensions in Psychiatry – A World View*, ed. S. Arieti and G. Chrzanowski (New York: Wiley, 1975), pp. 262–91.

58 D. R. Morse, 'The Effect of Stress and Meditation on Salivary Protein and Bacteria: A Review and Pilot Study', *Journal of Human Stress*, 8 (4) (1982), pp. 31–9.

59 I. M. Klemons, 'Changes in Inflammation in Persons Practicing the Transcendental Meditation Technique', in Orme-Johnson and Farrow (ed.), op. cit., vol. 1, pp. 287–91.

CHAPTER 5 The Other Side of Research

1 P. B. C. Fenwick, 'Metabolic and EEG Changes during Transcendental Meditation' (paper read at conference on 'TM: Research and Application', Institute of Science and Technology, University of Wales, Cardiff, 1974).
2 R. K. Wallace, 'Physiological Effects of Transcendental Meditation', *Science* (27 March 1970), pp. 1751–4.
3 M. Shafii, R. Lavely and R. Jaffe, 'Meditation and Marijuana', *American Journal of Psychiatry,* 131 (1974), pp. 60–63.
4 S. Shackman, 'The Effect of Two Relaxation Techniques on Anxiety, Self-Concept end Personality Growth' (senior thesis, Princeton University, 1974).
5 J. C. Smith, 'The Therapeutic Effects of Transcendental Meditation with Controls for Expectation of Relief and Daily Sitting', *Journal of Consulting and Clinical Psychology,* 44 (1976), pp. 630–37.
6 M. Shelly, personal communication to the author, Kansas University, Lawrence, Kans., February 1976; P. Davies, personal communication to the author, Kansas University, Lawrence, Kans., February 1976; L. S. Otis, 'TM and Sleep' (paper presented before the Annual Meeting of the American Psychological Association, New Orleans, 1974).

CHAPTER 6 Learning How to Meditate

1 J. C. Smith, 'Transcendental Meditation and Anxiety' (dissertation proposal, Michigan State University, 1973), p. 29.

CHAPTER 7 The Challenge of Tension-Release

1 J. H. Schultz and W. Luthe, *Autogenic Therapy,* 6 vols (New York: Grune, 1969), vol. 1.
2 Ibid., p. 29.
3 Ibid., vol. II, p. 12.
4 Ibid., vol. V, pp. 180–81.
5 Ibid., vol. IV, pp. 119–123.
6 Ibid., vol. V.
7 Ibid., vol. VI.
8 S. Otis, 'The Psychobiology of Meditation: Some Psychological

Changes' (paper presented before the Annual Meeting of the American Psychological Association, Montreal, 1973).

9 A. A. Lazarus, 'Psychiatric Problems Precipitated by Transcendental Meditation (TM)', *Psychological Reports*, 39 (1976), pp. 601–2.

10 R. Woolfolk, quoted in ibid.

CHAPTER 8 How to Use Meditation Under Stress

1 J. H. Schultz and W. Luthe, *Autogenic Therapy*, 6 vols (New York: Grune, 1969), vol. III, p. 154.

2 Ibid., p. 158.

3 Ibid., p. 172.

4 J. Leserman, E. M. Stuart, M. E. Mamish and H. Benson, 'The Efficacy of the Relaxation Response in Preparing for Cardiac Surgery', *Behavioral Medicine*, 15 (3) (1989), pp. 111–17.

5 A. D. Domar, J. M. Noe and H. Benson, 'The Preoperative Use of the Relaxation Response with Ambulatory Surgery Patients', *Journal of Human Stress*, 13 (3) (1987), pp. 101–7.

6 L. Boudreau, 'Transcendental Meditation and Yoga as Reciprocal Inhibitors', *Journal of Behavior Therapy and Experimental Psychiatry*, 3 (1972), pp. 97–8.

7 K. S. Blasdall, 'The Effects of the Transcendental Meditation Technique upon a Complex Perceptual-Motor Task', in *Scientific Research on the Transcendental Meditation Program: Collected Papers*, ed. D. W. Orme-Johnson and J. T. Farrow (Livingston Manor, NY: Maharishi European Research University Press, 1978) vol. I, pp. 322–5.

8 A. G. P. Rimol, 'Transcendental Meditation and its Effects on Sensory and Motor Perception' (senior thesis, Princeton University, 1974).

9 E. E. Solberg, K. A. Berglund, O. Engen et al., 'The Effect of Meditation on Shooting Performance', *British Journal of Sports Medicine*, 30 (4) (1996), pp. 342–6.

10 D. Goleman and G. E. Schwartz, 'Meditation as an Intervention in Stress Reactivity', *Journal of Consulting and Clinical Psychology*, 44 (1976), pp. 456–66.

11 Schultz and Luthe, op. cit., p. 183.

12 Ibid., p. 184.

CHAPTER 9 Some Intriguing Rhythms

1 N. Kleitman, *Sleep and Wakefulness* (Chicago: University of Chicago Press, 1963), pp. 145–7.

2 G. G. Luce, *Body Time* (New York: Bantam Books, 1973), p. 45.

3 H. Johari, *Dhanwantari* (San Francisco: Ram's Head, 1974).

4 Kleitman, op. cit., pp. 363–70.

5 H. S. Ephron and P. Carrington, 'Rapid Eye Movement Sleep and Cortical Homeostasis', *Psychological Review*, 73 (1966), pp. 500–26.

6 T. Wada, 'Experimental Study of Hunger in its Relation to Activity', *Archives of Psychology*, 8 (1922), pp. 1–65.

7 S. Friedman and C. Fisher, 'On the Presence of a Rhythmic Diurnal, Oral Instinctual Drive Cycle in Man: a Preliminary Report', *Journal of the American Psychoanalytic Association*, 15 (1967), pp. 317–43.

8 M. B. Sterman and D. McGinty, as quoted in C. G. Luce, *Biological Rhythms In Psychiatry and Medicine* (Chevy Chase, Md.: National Institute of Mental Health, 1970), p. 26.

9 D. F. Kripke, F. Hallberg, T. Crowley, et al., in Luce, op. cit., p. 26.

10 D. F. Kripke and D. Sonnenschein, 'A 90 Minute Daydream Cycle', *Sleep Research*, 2 (1973), p. 187.

11 M. Gauquelin, *The Cosmic Clocks* (Chicago, Regnery, 1967).

12 Luce, op. cit.

13 M. Takata, 'Blood Serum and the Sunrise', *Symposium Internationale sur les Relations Phénoménales Solaires et Terrestriales* (Brussels: Presses Académiques Européenes, 1960), p. 172.

14 C. F. Stroebel as quoted in Luce, op. cit., pp. 104–7.

15 E. D. Weitzman, H. Schaumberg and W. Fishbein, 'Plasma 17 – Hydroxycorticosteroid Levels During Sleep in Man', *Journal of Clinical Endocrinology and Metabolism*, 26 (1966), pp. 121–7.

16 Johari, op. cit., p. 76.

17 R. Hittelman, *Guide to Yoga Meditation* (New York: Bantam Books, 1969), p. 180.

CHAPTER 10 The Mystery of the Mantra

1 R. E. Ornstein, *The Psychology of Consciousness* (New York: Viking, 1972) p. 122.

2 D. Retallack, *The Sound of Music and Plants* (Santa Monica, Calif.: De Vorss, 1973); P. Weinberger and M. Measures, as quoted in P. Tomkins and C. Bird, *The Secret Life of Plants* (New York: Avon, 1974), p. 167.

3 H. Roffwarg, J. Herman and S. Lamstein, 'The Middle Ear Muscles: Predictability of Their Phasic Activity in REM Sleep from Dream Materials' (paper presented before the Association for the Psychophysiological Study of Sleep, Edinburgh, 1975).

4 D. Moltz, 'Effects of Internally Generated Sounds on Mood' (senior thesis, Princeton University, 1976).

5 A. Daniélou, *Hindu Polytheism*, Bolligen Series (New York: Pantheon Books, 1964), p. 335.
6 S. Bhatnagar, personal communication to the author, September 1975.
7 *The Religion of the Hindus*, ed. K. W. Morgan (New York: Ronald, 1953), p. 168.

CHAPTER 11 A Few Nagging Questions

1 P. Wienphal, *The Matter of Zen* (New York: New York University Press, 1946), p. 22.
2 M. Sadhu, *Meditation* (Hollywood: Wilshire Books, 1973), p. 97.
3 B. R., Dass, *Be Here Now* (New York: Crown, 1971), p. 83.

CHAPTER 12 A New Partnership

1 B. C. Glueck and C. P. Stroebel, 'Biofeedback and Meditation in the Treatment of Psychiatric Illness', *Comprehensive Psychiatry*, 16 (1975), pp. 303–21.
2 H. Benson and R. K. Wallace, 'Decreased Drug Abuse with Transcendental Meditation: A Study of 1862 Subjects', *Congressional Record*, 92nd Congress, 1st session, June 1971, Serial #92–1.
3 M. Shafii, 'Smoking Following Meditation' (unpublished paper, University of Michigan Medical Center, Ann Arbor, Mich., 1973); M. Shafii, R. Lavely and R. Jaffe, 'Meditation and Marijuana', *American Journal of Psychiatry*, 131 (1974), pp. 60–63; M. Shafil, R. Lavely and R. Jaffe, 'Meditation and the Prevention of Drug Abuse', *American Journal of Psychiatry*, 132 (1975), pp. 942–5.
4 A. Royer, 'The Role of Transcendental Meditation Technique in Promoting Smoking Cessation: A Longitudinal Study', *Alcoholism Treatment Quarterly*, 11 (1994), pp. 221–39.
5 P. Gelderloos, K. G. Walton, D. W. Orme-Johnson et al., 'Effectiveness of the Transcendental Meditation Program in Preventing and Treating Substance Misuse: A Review', *International Journal of the Addictions*, 26 (3) (1991), pp. 293–325.; C. N. Alexander, P. Robison and M. Rainforth, 'Treating and Preventing Alcohol, Nicotine, and Drug Abuse Through Transcendental Meditation: A Review and Statistical Meta-Analysis.', *Alcoholism Treatment Quarterly*, 11 (1–2) (1994), pp. 13–87.
6 L. S. Otis, 'The Psychobiology of Meditation: Some Psychological Changes' (paper presented at the Annual Meeting of the American Psychological Association, Montreal, 1973).
7 A. Weil, *The Natural Mind* (Boston: Houghton, 1972).

8 Ibid., p. 68.

9 H. Benson, *The Relaxation Response* (New York, Morrow, 1975).

10 R. H. Schneider, F. Staggers, C. N. Alexander et al., 'A Randomized Controlled Trial of Stress Reduction for Hypertension in Older African Americans', *Hypertension*, 26 (1995), pp. 820–27; C. N. Alexander, R. H. Schneider, F. Staggers et al., 'Trial of Stress Reduction for Hypertension in Older African Americans. II. Sex and Risk Subgroup Analysis', *Hypertension*, 28 (1996), pp. 228–37.

11 R. Honsberger and A. F. Wilson, 'Transcendental Meditation in Treating Asthma', *Respiratory Therapy: The Journal of Inhalation Technology*, 3 (1973), pp. 79–81.

12 M. P. Sharma, V. Kumaraiah, H. Mishra et al., 'Therapeutic Effects of Vipassana Meditation in Tension Headaches', *Journal of Personality and Clinical Studies*, 6 (1990), pp. 210–16; A. Vasudevan, V. Kumaraiah, H. Mishra et al., 'Yogic Meditation in Tension Headache', *NIMHANS Journal*, 12 (1994), pp. 69–73.

13 Benson, op. cit., p. 109.

14 Glueck and Stroebel, op. cit.

15 M. H. Silverman and E. L. Hartmann, 'Transcendental Meditation and Sleep' (paper presented before the Association for the Psychophysiological Study of Sleep, Edinburgh, 1975).

16 D. E. Miskiman, 'The Treatment of Insomnia by the Transcendental Meditation Program', in *Scientific Research on the Transcendental Meditation Program: Collected Papers*, ed. D. W. Orme-Johnsonn and J. T. Farrow (Livingston Manor, NY: Maharishi European Research University Press, 1978) vol. I, pp. 296–300.

17 R. L. Woolfolk, L. Carr-Kaffashan, P. M. Lehrer and T. F. McNulty, 'Meditation Training as a Treatment for Insomnia', *Behavior Therapy*, 7 (1976), pp. 359–65.

CHAPTER 13 More Open to Life

1 Meditation journal of Harmon S. Ephron (personal communication).

2 B. C. Gluek and C. F. Stroebel, 'Biofeedback and Meditation in the Treatment of Psychiatric Illness', *Comprehensive Psychiatry*, 16 (1975), pp. 303–21.

3 Meditation journal of George Edington (personal communication).

4 M. Hines, 'Meditation and Creativity: A Pilot Study' (senior Thesis, Princeton University, 1970).

5 W. Linden, 'Practicing of Meditation by School Children and Their Levels of Field Dependence-Independence, Test Anxiety, and Reading Achievement', *Journal of Consulting and Clinical Psychology*, 41 (1973), pp. 139–43.

6 K. R. Pelletier, 'The Effects of the Transcendental Meditation Program on Perceptual Style: Increased Field Independence', in Orme-Johnson and Farrow, (ed.), op. cit., vol. I, pp. 337–45.

7 D. James, 'The Short-Term Effects of Transcendental Meditation on Field Independence: A Pilot Study' (unpublished paper, Princeton University, 1976).

8 L. C. Fergusson, 'Field Independence and Art Achievement in Meditating and Nonmeditating College Students', *Perceptual and Motor Skills*, 75 (1992), pp. 1171–5.

9 E. Fromm, *Man for Himself* (New York: Rinehart, 1947).

10 Ibid.; K. Horney, *The Neurotic Personality of Our Time* (New York: Norton, 1937); H. S. Sullivan, *The Interpersonal Theory of Psychiatry* (New York: Norton, 1953); C. R. Rogers, *On Becoming a Person* (Boston: Houghton, 1961).

11 H. Shecter, 'The Transcendental Meditation Program in the Classroom: A Psychological Evaluation of the Science of Creative Intelligence', in Orme-Johnson and Farrow, (ed.), op. cit., vol. I, pp. 403–9.

12 D. Ballou, 'The Transcendental Meditation Program at Stillwater Prison', in ibid., pp. 569–76.

13 M. Cunningham and W. Koch, 'The Transcendental Meditation Program and Rehabilitation: A Pilot Project at the Federal Correction Institute at Lompoc, California', in ibid., pp. 562–8.

CHAPTER 14 The Creative Meditator

1 M. Dellas and E. L. Gaier, 'Identification of Creativity: The Individual', *Psychological Bulletin*, 73 (1970), pp. 55–73.

2 T. V. Lesh, 'Zen Meditation and the Development of Empathy in Counselors', *Journal of Humanistic Psychology*, 10 (1970), pp. 39–74.

3 E. W. Maupin, 'Individual Differences in Response to a Zen Meditation Exercise', *Journal of Consulting Psychology*, 29 (1965), pp. 139–45.

4 S. Suzuki, *Zen Mind, Beginner's Mind* (New York: Walker/Weathethill, 1970).

5 R. May, *The Courage to Create* (New York: Norton, 1975), p. 67.

6 M. Hines, 'Meditation and Creativity: A Pilot Study' (senior thesis, Princeton University, 1970), p. 11.

7 M. J. MacCullum, 'Transcendental Meditation and Creativity', in *Research on the Transcendental Meditation Program: Collected Papers*, ed. D. W. Orme-Johnson and J. T. Farrow, (Livingston Manor, NY: Maharishi European Research University Press, 1978) vol. I, pp. 410–14.

CHAPTER 15 Some Problems Arise

1 M. Csikszentmihalyi, *Flow: The Psychology of Optimal Experience* (New York: HarperCollins, 1991).

2 M. Csikszentmihalyi, *Beyond Boredom and Anxiety* (San Francisco: Jossey-Bass, 1975).

3 Ibid., p. 39.

4 Ibid., p. 40.

5 Ibid., p. 44.

6 Ibid.

7 Ibid.

8 Ibid., p. 47.

9 B. C. Glueck, personal communication to the author, July 1976.

10 B. S. Rajneesh, *Dynamics of Meditation* (Bombay: A Life Awakening Movement Publication, 1972), pp. 60–62.

11 B. C. Glueck, 'Current Research on Transcendental Meditation' (paper delivered at Rensselaer Polytechnic Institute, Hartford Graduate Center, Hartford, Connecticut, March 1973)

12 Meditation Journal of Sarah Eaton (personal communication).

13 L. S. Otis, 'The Psychobiology of Meditation: Some Psychological Changes' (paper presented before the Annual Meeting of the American Psychological Association, Montreal, 1973).

CHAPTER 17 A Therapist's View

1 C. A. Ross, 'The Effect of Two Relaxation Techniques on Mood, Sleep and Dreams' (senior thesis, Princeton University, 1974).

2 C. Hall, 'Frequencies in Certain Categories of Manifest Content and Their Stability in a Long Dream Series', *American Psychologist*, 3 (1948), p. 274.

3 S. Shackman, 'The Effect Of Two Relaxation Techniques on Anxiety, Self-Concept and Personality Growth' (senior thesis, Princeton University, 1974).

4 W. A. Zevin, 'Effects of Transcendental Meditation on Loneliness Anxiety as Measured by the TAT' (unpublished paper, Department of Psychology, Princeton University, 1974).

5 L. S. Otis, 'The Psychobiology of Meditation: Some Psychological Changes' (paper presented before the Annual Meeting of the American Psychological Association, Montreal, 1973).

6 H. H. Bloomfield, M. Cain and D. Jaffe, *TM: Discovering Inner Energy and Overcoming Stress* (New York: Delacorte Press, 1975), p. 127.

7 H. H. Bloomfield and R. B. Kory, *Happiness: The TM Program, Psychiatry and Enlightenment* (New York: Simon & Schuster, 1976).

8 Ibid., p. 143.
9 L. D. Dick and R. E. Ragland, 'A Study of Meditation in the Service of Counseling', *Journal of Humanistic Psychology* (in press).
10 T. V. Lesh, 'Zen Meditation and the Development of Empathy in Counselors', *Journal of Humanistic Psychology,* 10 (1970), pp. 39–74.
11 S. Freud (1912), 'Recommendations to Physicians Practicing Psychoanalysis', in *Standard Edition of the Complete Psychological Works of Sigmund Freud,* ed. J. Strachey (London: Hogarth, 1958), vol. XII, p. 112.
12 T. V. Lesh, op. cit.
13 P. Carrington and H. S. Ephron, 'Meditation and Psychoanalysis', *Journal of the American Academy of Psychoanalysis,* 5 (1975), pp. 43–57.

CHAPTER 18 Meditation in the Workplace

1 W. A. McGeveran, Jr, 'Meditation at the Telephone Company', *The Wharton Magazine,* Fall 1981, pp. 29–32.
2 L. R. Derogatis, K. Rickels and A. F. Rock, 'The SCL-90 and The MMPi: A Step in the Validation of a New Self-Respect Scale', *British Journal of Psychiatry,* 128 (1976), pp. 280–90.
3 P. Carrington, G. H. Collings, H. Benson et al., 'The Use of Meditation-Relaxation Techniques for the Management of Stress in a Working Population', *Journal of Occupational Medicine,* 22 (4) (1980), pp. 221–31.
4 H. S. Kindler, 'The Influence of a Meditation-Relaxation Technique on Group Problem-Solving Effectiveness' (doctoral dissertation, UCLA Graduate School of Management, 1978).

CHAPTER 19 Why Does Meditation Work?

1 P. Carrington, *Theoretical Underpinnings of the Meditation Techniques* (Kendall Park, N. J,: Pace Educational Systems, 1998).
2 D. Goleman, 'Meditation as Meta-Therapy: Hypothesis Toward a Proposed Fifth State of Consciousness', *Journal of Transpersonal Psychology,* 3 (1971) pp. 1–25.
3 A. J. Deikman, 'Experimental Meditation', in *Altered States of Consciousness,* ed. C. T. Tart (New York: Wiley, 1969) pp. 199–218.
4 R. W. Sperry, 'The Great Cerebral Commisure', *Scientific American* (January 1964), pp. 42–52; M. S. Gazzaniga, 'The Split Brain in Man', in *The Nature of Human Consciousness,* ed. R. E. Ornstein (San Francisco: Freeman, 1973), pp. 87–100.
5 Earle, J. B., 'Cerebral Laterality and Meditation: A Review of the Literature', *Journal of Transpersonal Psychology,* 13 (1981), pp. 155–73;

S. Warrenburg, and R. R. Pagano, 'Meditation and Hemispheric Specialization: Absorbed Attention in Long-Term Adherents', *Imagination, Cognition, and Personality* (1982–3), pp. 211–29.

6 A. M. Ludwig, 'Sensory Overload and Psychopathology', *Diseases of the Nervous System*, 36 (1975), pp. 357–60.

7 R. S. Lourie, 'The Role of Rhythmic Patterns', in *The Five-Minute Hour* (Ardsley, N. Y.: Geigy Pharmaceuticals, January 1976).

8 L. Salk, 'The Role of the Heartbeat in the Relations Between Mother and Infant', *Scientific American*, (March 1973), pp. 24–9.

9 F. Leboyer, *Birth Without Violence* (New York: Knopf, 1975), p. 60.

10 J. A. Meerloo, 'The Universal Language of Rhythm', in *Poetry Therapy*, ed. J. J. Leedy (Philadelphia: Lippincott, 1969), pp. 52–66.

11 J. Markowitz, 'The Effects of an Externally Generated Rhythm on Mood' (senior thesis, Princeton University, 1974).

CHAPTER 20 The Promise of the Future

1 P. Carrington, G. H. Collings, H. Benson et al., 'The Use of Meditation-Relaxation Techniques for the Management of Stress in a Working Population', *Journal of Occupational Medicine*, 22 (4) (1980), pp. 222–31.

2 S. Grof, *Realms of the Human Unconscious* (New York: Viking, 1975).

3 I. M. Klemons, 'Changes in Inflammation Which Occur in Persons Practicing Transcendental Meditation', in *Scientific Research on the Transcendental Meditation Program: Collected Papers*, ed. D. W. Orme-Johnson and J. T. Farrow (Livingston Manor, NY: Maharishi European Research University Press, 1978) vol. 1, pp. 287–91.

4 M. Friedman and R. H. Rosenman, *Type A Behavior and Your Heart* (New York: Knopf, 1974).

OTHER AUDIO-TAPES AND BOOKS BY DR CARRINGTON

Health care providers who wish to use CSM as a clinical or research tool can obtain a CSM Instructors Kit which will enable them to supervise the use of this method for their patients or trainees. The kit contains clinical lectures on the use of CSM with varied personality and health problems (on three audio-tapes) and an Instructor's Manual. To obtain information, contact the following centers in the United Kingdom or the United States.

UNITED KINGDOM: Learning for Life, Ltd. The Coach House, Chinewood Manor, 32 Manor Road, Bournemouth, BH1 3EZ. Phone/Fax: 01202 390008 (International + 22 1202 390008).

UNITED STATES: Pace Educational Systems, Inc., 61 Kingsley Road, Kendall Park, NJ 08824. Toll-free phone # 1–800–297–9897 Fax#: 732–297–0778.

Information on other tapes and books by Dr Carrington is also available from the above sources.

CSM has considerable value when used within organizational settings.
For information about introducing CSM into:

- Commercial organizations
- Public authorities
- Stress and life-style management courses

Contact: Learning for Life Ltd (see above address).

Learn to Meditate Kit

THE COMPLETE COURSE IN MODERN MEDITATION

Patricia Carrington PhD

Includes four 60-minute audio tapes and step-by-step instruction manual

I cannot imagine a more ideal way to learn meditation. The recordings beautifully convey the deeper mood and spirit of the practice.

ALFRED J. CANTOR MD
past President, Academy of Psychosomatic Medicine

In her own voice Dr Carrington leads you through instruction in the acclaimed CSM method of meditation, in the manner which she has found particularly effective when giving personal instruction in the technique. The audio tapes:

- help you prepare to learn meditation
- sensitively guide you through your initial experience in it
- give complete post-instruction guidance
- teach you how to use 'mini-meditations' in daily life
- provide a special tape which automatically times your meditation practice

The accompanying workbook contains on-the-spot questionnaires which help you customize your meditation practice so that it suits your own personality and life-style.

The best recorded training method I have ever encountered.
MARTIN R. SCHACHED DC
Founding Member, Holistic Health Association of the Princeton Area

Dr Carrington's voice on the tapes is a unique blend of authority, soothingness and genuine caring.
RHONDA E. GREENBERG PsyD
Director of Psychology Program in Preventive Cardiology
University of Medicine & Density of New Jersey

ELEMENT

ISBN 1 86204 191 1

INDEX